transitions

General Editor: Julian Wolfreys

(continued overleaf)

Transitions
Series Standing Order
ISBN 0–333–73634–6
(*outside North America only*)

You can receive future titles in this series as they are published. To place a standing order please contact your bookseller or, in the case of difficulty, write to us at the address below with your name and address, the title of the series and the ISBN quoted above.

Customer Services Department, Macmillan Distribution Ltd
Houndmills, Basingstoke, Hampshire RG21 6XS, England

---

transitions

Literary
Feminisms

Ruth Robbins

palgrave

Published by
PALGRAVE
Houndmills, Basingstoke, Hampshire RG21 6XS and
175 Fifth Avenue, New York, N. Y. 10010
Companies and representatives throughout the world

PALGRAVE is the new global academic imprint of
St. Martin's Press LLC Scholarly and Reference Division and
Palgrave Publishers Ltd (formerly Macmillan Press Ltd).

Outside North America
ISBN 0–333–68919–4 hardcover
ISBN 0–333–68920–8 paperback

Inside North America
ISBN 0–312–22807–4 cloth
ISBN 0–312–22808–2 paper

This book is printed on paper suitable for recycling and
made from fully managed and sustained forest sources.

A catalogue record for this book is available
from the British Library.

A catalogue record for this book is available
from the Library of Congress

Transferred to digital printing 2003

Printed and bound in Great Britain by
Antony Rowe Ltd, Chippenham and Eastbourne

Contents

General Editor's Preface

Transitions: *transition-*, n. of action. 1. A passing or passage from one condition, action or (rarely) place, to another. 2. Passage in thought, speech, or writing, from one subject to another. 3. **a**. The passing from one note to another **b**. The passing from one key to another, modulation. 4. The passage from an earlier to a later stage of development or formation ... change from an earlier style to a later; a style of intermediate or mixed character ... the historical passage of language from one well-defined stage to another.

The aim of *Transitions* is to explore passages and movements in critical thought, and in the development of literary and cultural interpretation. This series also seeks to examine the possibilities for reading, analysis and other critical engagements which the very idea of transition makes possible. The writers in this series unfold the movements and modulations of critical thinking over the last generation, from the first emergences of what is now recognised as literary theory. They examine as well how the transitional nature of theoretical and critical thinking is still very much in operation, guaranteed by the hybridity and heterogeneity of the field of literary studies. The authors in the series share the common understanding that, now more than ever, critical thought is both in a state of transition and can best be defined by developing for the student reader an understanding of this protean quality.

This series desires, then, to enable the reader to transform her/his own reading and writing transactions by comprehending past developments. Each book in the series offers a guide to the poetics and politics of interpretative paradigms, schools and bodies of thought, while transforming these, if not into tools or methodologies, then into conduits for directing and channelling thought. As well as transforming the critical past by interpreting it from the perspective of the present day, each study enacts transitional readings of a number of well-known literary texts, all of which are themselves conceivable as having been transitional texts at the moments of their first appearance. The readings offered in these books seek, through close critical reading and theoretical engagement, to demonstrate certain possibilities in critical thinking to the student reader.

It is hoped that the student will find this series liberating because rigid methodologies are not being put into place. As all the dictionary definitions of the idea of transition above suggest, what is important is the action, the passage: of thought, of analysis, of critical response. Rather than seeking to help you locate yourself in relation to any particular school or discipline, this series aims to put you into action, as readers and writers, travellers between positions, where the movement between poles comes to be seen as of more importance than the locations themselves.

Julian Wolfreys

Acknowledgements

To all my colleagues in Literary Studies and Comparative Literature at the University of Luton, my thanks. To Jill Barker, Claire Jones and Karen Sayer, thank you for loan of books, for tolerating frantic conversation about strange things, and for all-round general kindness. To Moyra Haslett and John Brannigan, thanks for those things too, but also thank you for sharing your ideas as well as your time. To the students who have taken modules in Literary Theory and Women's Writing over the past couple of years: you have helped immeasurably by reminding me of what can be difficult about theory, and still having the courage to try it out. Thank you all. My gratitude also to the various library staff at Luton and the University of Warwick who have helped out in lots of different ways.

To Julian Wolfreys, for all his kindesses and for all his faith, thank you.

To my parents, who have always encouraged my intellectual pretensions, and always bought me books, thank you.

And by no means least, thanks to Richard Andrews: for light, warmth, tolerance, good humour and love. Just what the doctor ordered.

Elizabeth Barrett-Browning wrote that the fate of the woman poet was to be bereft of a tradition: she searched everywhere for grandmothers and found none. I was lucky in that my grandmothers were always there when I wanted them. Now they are both gone; this book is affectionately dedicated to the memories of Elizabeth Robbins (née French) and Frances Parkin (née Green).

RUTH ROBBINS

A Note on Editions Used

This book is aimed at student readers. For that reason, as far as possible, textual references are to readily available, modern paperback editions. This can have the effect of making references look rather odd: Mary Wollstonecraft was not still publishing in 1992 – that is just the date of the edition used. The Bibliography contains original publication dates for your reference.

Introduction: Gestures towards Definitions

W is certainly for Woman and Witch. She picked up a nineteenth-century reprint of an old herbal in a bookshop once, cheap because second-hand and slightly damaged, the thick laid paper spotted and foxed, the headband rubbed. She cradled it between her hands, and then opened it, leafing idly through the index. The male author's entries for W rivet her: warts; weevils; whites, women's whites, how to control; witches, how to guard against; wolfbane; womb: women's weeping therefrom; women in childbed; women's complaints, how to soothe; women's courses, how to stop, how to bring on; women's diseases, women's longings; women's pains; worms in the ears. When she turns the leaves of the index back to M, she finds no corresponding entry for Man.

Michèle Roberts, *The Visitation*

... the greatest thing a human soul ever does in this world is to *see* something, and tell what it *saw* in a plain way.

John Ruskin, *Modern Painters*

The word, defining, muzzles; the drawn line
Ousts mistier peers and thrives, murderous,
In establishments which imagined lines

Can only haunt.

Sylvia Plath, 'Poems, Potatoes'

This is a book about feminist literary theory, though the phrase itself is contested and cannot be taken for granted. Maybe the place to begin is with some definitions of the terms I need to use to talk about that phrase, feminist literary theory. What happens when these three words – feminist, literary, theory – come together?

First of all, though, a word of warning about definitions. By definition, definitions are exclusive. They operate as much by what they leave out as by what they include. The word 'define' comes from the Latin verb *definire*, derived from the noun *finis*, meaning a limit. A definition literally sets limits on meaning. Ideally it does so with the intention of producing clarity, of outlining those sharp edges which, in both visual and written fields, are supposed to make things easily seen and understood. The limit, to paraphrase Ruskin's remark, permits the reader/viewer to see clearly, and to speak/write clearly of what she has seen. Definition gives you something firm to focus on; something solid to look at; firm ground from which to speak. The ideal, however, by definition, is not always what 'really' happens.

As the passage from Roberts's novel suggests, there are power relationships in definitions. In the old herbal to which Helen, the novel's heroine, refers, it is assumed that Man needs no definition; he is the norm against which Woman is defined as an aberration, a pathological condition, associated with 'complaints' and 'weeping' and 'pains'. There is no corresponding entry for Man, no symmetry between the terms Man and Woman: Man is somehow separated from the pains associated with the body to the extent that one might wonder if men have bodies at all. In this set of definitions, Woman *is* body; Man is infinite possibility since that which is not definite (defined) is infinite (without limits). Or, as Simone de Beauvoir puts it in *The Second Sex*:

> woman is defined exclusively in her relation to man. The asymmetry of the categories – male and female – is made manifest in the unilateral form of sexual myths. We sometimes say 'the sex' to designate woman; she is the flesh, its delights and dangers. The truth that for woman man is sex and carnality has never been proclaimed because there is no one to proclaim it. Representation of the world, like the world itself, is the work of men; they describe it from their own point of view, which they confuse with absolute truth. (de Beauvoir 1997, 174–5)

De Beauvoir's text insists throughout on what she calls the 'otherness' of women in relation to the self-declared 'norm' of men. The proclamations of female flesh versus male mind are important. They silence women who are disabled from proclaiming the sexedness (and sexiness) of men; representation repeatedly replicates women's status as other; representation becomes reality, confused with absolute truth. These are important insights for thinking about literary texts and the realities which they supposedly reflect and sometimes create. Representations, in the word, of the world are confused and confusing.

The definitions I want to produce and reproduce here should all therefore be thought of as provisional, contingent, not that firm in fact, because I don't want to harm or limit anyone with my definitions. It's not that meaning doesn't matter. Of course it does: feminism and its derivations are not mere words without any status or power in reality. Rather, it's that my understanding of the word 'feminism', one of the words most at stake in this book, is that it is anti-totalising: it is not confused with absolute truth. It does not have one catch-all, all-or-nothing meaning, but many meanings which depend on contexts, subject positions, languages, the material worlds we inhabit, and our own psychic spaces, all mixed up together. And one of feminism's meanings has precisely to do with overstepping boundaries, defying limits and refusing to be contained in or by ready-made systems of signification. It is about *making* meanings as well as referring to the old ones.

The title of this book, with its insistence on feminisms as a plural noun, is a case in point. The spell-checker on my computer does not recognise this particular plural, and asks me: 'are you sure?' What a question. I am sure that the plural was deliberate, that I really meant to write feminisms, not feminism. But I'm not sure why the computer dislikes it, as it dislikes many of the plural abstract nouns I type in. Probably the word is rejected because the dictionary from which the spell-checker was compiled did not contain feminism as a plural form. There's nothing especially sinister in that. Dictionaries often don't contain plurals. But just maybe the dictionary is a political tool which reflects and reproduces power relations: if the word 'feminisms' does not exist, then I should not use it because it is a neologism (a new word) and therefore a solecism (a breach in language, linguistic bad manners). It is an improper word, and that sense of its impropriety is a way of policing and limiting my conceptual framework for the world.

The plural form feminisms is political because it disrupts the notion that 'feminism' is a single category, with clear limits, fixed in a single semantic space. The plural form rewrites the category as something potentially transgressive or subversive. If there's more than one feminism, feminisms might be anywhere, might do anything, might spread out like virulently contagious diseases, might be uncontainable. This is, of course, the point. Feminisms are multiple. And while this book might have its own views, don't be fooled into thinking that it's the last word.

If you spend time with dictionaries (there's more than one, of course, more than one set of meanings, more than one set of limits on any given word, itself a potentially subversive fact), there are bound to be differences in emphasis in how words are defined, not least the differences that come through time. The three words in the phrase 'feminist literary theory', have to be looked up separately in most dictionaries and in this context they have what appear to be quite incompatible sets of definitions. Read those disparate definitions together though, and some interesting ideas might be thrown up.

The word 'feminist' for example, is a relatively recent word, if the *Oxford English Dictionary* is to be believed. It appears first in the Supplement to the dictionary (1933, reprinted and revised in 1972), with two meanings: as an adjective it signals 'pertaining to feminism, or to women'; as a noun, a feminist (since 1895, when the first usage is recorded) is 'an advocate of feminism'. The entries for 'feminist' refer us back to the earlier word 'feminism' (which has no plural form in the *OED*). In the early editions of the dictionary feminism appeared, marked 'rare', as meaning alternatively 'the state of being feminine' or 'a feminine, or woman's, expression', neither of which appears to be what feminism means to us. The Supplement deletes 'rare', gives a derivation for the word from the French *féminisme*, and adds two further possibilities: feminism is the 'advocacy of the rights of woman (based on the theory of the equality of the sexes)'; it is also a pathological description of 'the development of female secondary characteristics in a male'. The latter definition may not appear to have that much to do with this book and its concerns, except that feminism has often been viewed with hostility: a biological pathology in which men might turn into women is possibly one reason for the hostilities – men fear becoming women, becoming feminised. And by extension, they perhaps also fear women becoming men.[1]

In their turn, the definitions of 'feminism' send us further back into the dictionary to consider the word 'feminine'. For this word there is a long entry, with six distinct meanings in the original dictionary, and a further two in the Supplement. Whatever 'feminine' is, it's clearly not quite secure or fixed. It means first: 'Of persons or animals, belonging to the female sex, female. Now rare' (the word or the concept, I wonder?); second: 'In same sense, of objects to which sex is attributed, or which have feminine names *esp.* one of the heavenly bodies'

– a metaphorical usage which describes stars amongst other things, and seems to have relatively little to do with biological sex or with real women. Thirdly, feminine means 'of or pertaining to a woman, or to women; consisting of women; carried on by women'. Fourthly: 'Characteristic of, peculiar or proper to women; womanlike, womanly'. Fifthly, a depreciative usage or insult: 'Womanish, effeminate'. Lastly, the grammar usages of the word, as in the feminine genders of nouns which describe objects or concepts that are not inherently female. The Supplement adds to the grammar usages the phrase 'feminine ending', meaning weak rhyme; and 'Eternal Feminine' as a translation of Goethe's concept of *das ewig-Weibliche*, an interesting addition, since it implies that the Eternal Feminine has not been around all that long.

I could go on, and look up 'woman', and its offshoots, but I don't want to reproduce the dictionary so much as to comment on it. The point of this semantic excursion is that the word feminism does not have a single secure meaning – as, indeed, no word ever does. The earliest meanings of feminism recorded in English see it as 'the state of being feminine' and 'a feminine or woman's word or expression'. What for later generations has become a term involved in issues of political advocacy and agency, referred first of all to biology and to language, terms which might be rewritten as 'nature' and 'culture', or, indeed as 'bodies' and 'language'. Feminism has to do with bodies (women's bodies, mostly, I suppose) and with how those bodies speak in such a way that their sex is registered in their language.

Similarly, the word feminine starts with biology, originally signalling female sex, though the dictionary regards that usage as rare. It does not however take long for this word, too, to move from nature to culture, from bodies to codes of behaviour, including linguistic behaviour. The metaphorical usage which associates femininity with stars is one example. But it is the third, fourth and fifth definitions that interest me most here. In the third definition, biology returns: here femininity appears as a natural and defining (limiting?) characteristic of women. In the fourth, culture returns. The feminine is what is 'proper' to women where proper means both what 'belongs to women', but also what is *expected* of women, what is womanlike or womanly. In amongst the illustrative quotations for the word under its fourth heading, however, we find a quotation from Bulwer Lytton's 1835 novel *Rienzi* which separates femininity from the female sex: 'There was something almost feminine in the tender deference with which *he* appeared to listen' (my emphasis). So the feminine is not the exclusive preserve of women; men can have feminine characteristics if Lytton's novel is to be believed. What does the dictionary think of men who have such characteristics? The question is answered indirectly by the fifth 'depreciative' definition: 'womanish, effeminate', both words used about men rather than about women, and which imply a derogation of masculinity, of proper maleness in male behaviour. A man with feminine characteristics is not a proper man, whereas a woman who is womanish or effeminate is merely fulfilling her biological and cultural destinies.

None of which fixes the meaning of the word feminism or defines feminisms. The dictionary's confusions over female, feminine, feminist signals nonetheless something important for the project of this book. These three words for contemporary feminist writers in the Humanities and the Social Sciences describe slightly different things. Female is a biological category which defines the sexual characteristics of a body: female describes biological sex. Feminine is a sociological category which defines the behavioural characteristics associated in different contexts and at different times with female biology: feminine describes gender, and tends to suggest that gender is not the natural attribute of sex. Feminist refers to a political category which suggests that the confusion of biology with culture (sexual characteristics with socially acceptable behaviour on the grounds of sex) can and should be questioned: feminist describes politics (see Moi in Jefferson and Robey 1986, 204–21, for the full working out of these definitions).

That initial confusion, though, remains important. Even as I try to separate out the strands of these three words, I have to remember that sex and gender are slippery terms. In the attempt to disentangle them I don't want to forget that it is precisely the confusions of real bodies with social possibilities, the confusions of nature and culture that these words articulate, that are the subject of this discussion, not already foreclosed by neat definition. There's a leakage between female, feminine and feminism. If the politics of feminisms have anything in common in all their varieties, they start in some sense from bodies: the bodies of real women. Feminisms are concerned with how bodies and the material world, bodies and work, bodies and reproduction, bodies and culture, bodies and sexualities, bodies and class, bodies and race, bodies and minds, bodies and representations, bodies and behaviour, bodies and the law, intersect. Feminisms put real bodies into question in the metaphorical realm of the body politic.

It is not, however, just a question of looking at things, noting them, and then passing on. If feminisms are political then presumably the point is to change things. What happens when feminisms look is that they often don't like what they see, and they tell of their dislike. All kinds of bodies have suffered oppression, torture, imprisonment, enslavement and rape through history. Women's bodies – and the minds inhabiting those bodies – have often suffered more, continue now to suffer more. So while feminisms are concerned to define distinctions between sex and gender, between femaleness and femininity, they do not, on the whole, want to forget biology completely. There are strategic reasons for remembering bodies. There is a necessary activism in feminisms, an activism that wants to change what happens to biological women because of the social structures of gender. Sex and gender are not, however, the only sites of women's oppression – one can be oppressed because one is poor, Black, undereducated, lesbian, enslaved, imprisoned. But where entire groups are oppressed, women often get it worse. Feminisms are therefore politicised discourses which uncover the symptoms of oppression, whatever their grounds, diagnose the problem, and offer alternative versions of liveable realities. But their primary focus is on the female *bodies* which have been oppressed perhaps most forcefully because they are *female* bodies.

Literature, especially in its more traditional formulations, might seem light years away from such concerns. Early attempts to define it, by critics like Matthew Arnold who sought in literature 'the best that has been thought and said', or William Empson who saw a poem as a 'well-wrought urn', an artefact without political meaning, are wishy-washy. The question of defining literature is a notoriously difficult one as the first chapter of Terry Eagleton's *Literary Theory: An Introduction* amply demonstrates in its suggestion that we should think of literature 'less as some inherent quality or set of qualities displayed by certain kinds of writing ... than as a number of ways in which people *relate themselves* to writing' (Eagleton 1996, 8). The consequence of this insight is that the nature of 'the best that has been thought and said', the qualities of the 'well-wrought urn' are relative, historically and culturally specific, not absolute, neither transcendent nor transhistorical. Without a working definition of what literature is, it is presumably also impossible to say what the 'literary' is either. The *OED* tells us of literature that it is one of several possibilities:

1. Acquaintance with letters or books; polite or humane learning; literary culture. Now *rare* and *obs*. ...
2. Literary work or production; the activity or profession of a **man** of letters; the realm of letters ...
3. (a) Literary production as a whole; the body of writings produced in a particular country or period, or in the world in general. Now also in a more restricted sense, applied to writing which has claim to consideration on the ground of beauty of form or emotional effect. (This sense is of very recent emergence in England and France.)

   (b) The body of books and writings that treat of a particular subject.

   (c) *colloq* Printed matter of any kind. (My emphasis)

To have literature is to have a particular kind of education – 'polite or humane learning' – but that's rare and obsolete (I wonder if that's the education in question, or the meaning invoked by the definition). Literature is also just about anything produced by a man [*sic*] of letters. A woman of letters does not exist in this dictionary. But literature is also writing which is *valued* because of its 'beauty of form and emotional effect'. Who decides what beauty is, or whether a given piece is emotionally effective is not made clear. The dictionary at once disguises the power relations of definitions even as it also articulates them. When one looks at the definition of 'literary', however, it seems unlikely that such judgements might be made by women. The literary pertains to 'letters or polite learning', 'to books and written compositions'; it refers to texts that have 'value on account of [their] qualities of form.' Someone who *is* literary is one who is 'engaged with literature as a profession, occupied in writing books. Of a society, etc.: consisting of literary *men*' (my italics).

What seems to come from these definitions is an emphasis on education and on the value that accrues to certain written forms, and, by extension, in the gaps of the definitions, an assumption that education and value accrue to men not women. The two terms, education and value, are connected. Only those who have an acquaintance with 'letters or books, polite or humane learning, literary culture' are fitted to pronounce on the value of the letters, books, learning or culture. This is an important issue for feminist theory, for, throughout much of history, it is precisely education that has been denied to women. The denial has, of course, occurred in different degrees for different classes. Aristocratic or upper-class women have often been taught to read, though they were denied university education in Britain and the United States until the end of the last century. Working men and women seldom had even limited educational opportunities until the end of the nineteenth century. Nonetheless, a very large majority of Western populations, and particularly women, has traditionally been excluded from achieving the means by which they might comment on 'value'.

Thus, while the definitions of 'literature' and the 'literary' appear to be radically separate from the category of politics, there is a political dimension buried under the apparently objective voice of the dictionary. Who tells us what is valuable, what is *in* or *out* in literary culture? Who decides on the qualities of form that produce and reproduce literary value? What I want to suggest here is that literature must be understood as a powerful political term. Indeed, the major feminist theorist, Julia Kristeva, as Leon S. Roudiez notes in his introduction to her *Desire in Language,* goes so far as to refuse the term literature because of its abilities to exclude certain types of writing and to exalt other pieces into an untouchable category where criticism cannot reach them (Roudiez 1981, 5). Kristeva replaces 'literature' with 'poetic language' to signal any kind of writing in which form is more significant than transparent communication and to slip away from literature's constraining implications.

That is one kind of political gesture which has strategic importance for feminist theory. The other kind of gesture is to re-think the term 'literature' to make it inclusive and for readers to be more reflective about what is in or out of the category, and why. I have a marginal preference for the second route precisely because literature is a political and powerful term that I want to be able to use for political reasons. I want to push at the boundaries of its definition in order to make it include some of those 'other' things which have not traditionally been valued, or which have been displaced from representation as inappropriate, improper, obscene. The literary text at once reflects (often in a very indirect way) and creates the world in which it is written and read. The aesthetic is not therefore, as it is sometimes constructed, apolitical. The what and how of literature, the content and its formulations, matter. The forms writing takes, the events it expresses, the whole aesthetics of literature, are political. Political theories of literature – Marxisms, feminisms, post-colonialisms – enable me to say this and to claim some of the value as my own, and to take away from the notion of 'value' as self-evident and untouchable.

Literary studies has been a fruitful space in feminist theory. Although, as Miriam Brody says, no one went to the barricades for sexual equality after reading Mary Wollstonecraft's *Vindication of the Rights of Woman* (1792), because literature is an expressive mode which enables us to think that which has never happened yet, and indeed that which may not ever happen, the literary text can be a mind-expanding experience. As Rita Felski puts it: 'Literature does not merely constitute a self-referential and metalinguistic system ... but is also a medium which can profoundly influence individual and cultural self-understanding in the sphere of everyday life, charting the changing preoccupations of social groups through symbolic fictions by means of which they make sense of experience' (Felski 1989, 7). What appears to be impossible can be narrated as possible; if we can imagine something, then just maybe it might happen; and if we can express our imaginings in the value-rich category of literature, then the imaginings themselves partake of some of that value.

And what of theory? The *OED* has much to say, producing six separate meanings. The first two definitions derive from the word's etymology in the Greek word *thea*, which is the root word for looking at, viewing, contemplating. A theory is therefore 'a sight, a spectacle' (though the word in this meaning is both rare and obsolete); it is also a 'mental view, contemplation' (also obsolete). It is in definitions 3 to 6 that we come closer to the more common contemporary uses of the word:

3. A conception or mental scheme of something to be done, or of the method of doing it; a systematic statement of rules or principles to be followed ...

4. (a) A scheme or system of ideas or statements held as an explanation or account of a group of facts or phenomena; a hypothesis that has been confirmed or established by observation or experiment, and is propounded or accepted as accounting for the known facts; a statement of what are held to be general laws, principles, or causes of something known or observed ...

(b) That department of an art or technical subject which consists in the knowledge or statement of the facts on which it depends, or of its principles or methods, as distinguished from the *practice* of it ...

5. In the abstract: Systematic conception or statement of the principles of something; abstract knowledge or the formulation of it: often used as implying more or less unsupported hypothesis (cf. 6): distinguished from, or opposed to, practice (cf. 4 b): *In theory:* according to theory, theoretically (opposed to *in practice* or *in fact*) ...

6. In loose or general sense: A hypothesis proposed as an explanation, hence, a mere hypothesis, speculation, conjecture; an idea or set of ideas about something; an individual view or notion. (Emphases in original)

I've reproduced almost all of that definition because it shows clearly that the word theory is very slippery indeed. The original Greek word *thea*, from which theory derives, is a word that has to do with looking. The theorist might be thought of as being a kind of onlooker, one who looks but does not touch, one who is objective perhaps, has a proper perspective, one who sees only what is there to be seen, appearing to let the facts speak for themselves. This meaning comes back to haunt later parts of the definition, especially those which oppose theory and practice. In those definitions, theory doesn't get its hands dirty.

At the same time though, the middle definitions set up a relationship between theory and practice, in which practice depends on theory: theory is a statement of the facts on which practice depends. The word implies an interplay between distance and perspective on the one hand (the clean hand?), and proximity and praxis on the other (dirtier?) hand. Theory, in this formulation, is at once objective and subjective – what one sees when one looks is as much a matter of *how* one looks as of *what* is there to be seen. The ghost of subjective looking rather than an objective position based on 'fact' is traced in the gloss words 'speculation' and 'conjecture', and especially in the phrase 'an individual view or notion.' Speculation also has to do with looking. It comes from the Latin verb *specere*, to look at. But it contains the idea that seeing is not believing, since speculation often has to do with guesswork. Conjecture similarly has a Latin route and etymologically means 'throwing things together': a conjecture is a piece of guesswork whose results derive from putting disparate elements together. Hence the phrase 'individual view [another looking word] or notion' implies that theory might also have to do with the idiosyncrasies of the individual as much as with the institutional views of a given art or technical subject. Definitions 3 and 4 are the ones that make theory respectable. They limit it to what can be tested by practice, method, experiment or the close observation of the facts. They make theory objective, rigorous, scientific.

 In these terms, a feminist theory – of life, of art – under those rubrics might well appear a contradiction in terms, since in the phrase 'feminist theory' both politics and subjectivity come into play to disrupt the objectivity, rigour and science that theory claims for itself. And feminist literary theory produces all kinds of contaminations between the terms. The adjective feminist, with its implications of political action and political viewpoint is an attack on both the supposedly inherent apolitical value of literature and on the objectivity of theory. Feminist theory is a 'doing' as well as a way of seeing – practice impinges on the purity of theory. Literature is also modified by theory alone, since the will to theorise a thing implies that its value is not self-evident. And literature modifies feminism by putting the category of the aesthetic into a political sphere (politics resists aesthetics as often as aesthetics resists politics), and by providing an expressive forum for a politicised vision. The phrase feminist literary theory is quite a mixture, overspilling the old boundaries of definition: it makes quite a soup.

In her 1981 essay 'Feminist Criticism in the Wilderness', Elaine Showalter identified three common modes of feminist literary theory, and placed them as modes belonging to different national groups. She wrote: 'English feminist criticism, essentially Marxist, stresses oppression; French feminist criticism, essentially psychoanalytic, stresses repression; American feminist criticism, essentially textual, stresses expression. All, however, have become gynocentric. All are struggling to find a terminology that can rescue the feminine from its stereotypical associations with inferiority' (Showalter 1986, 249). Showalter was keen to emphasise the difference in method but the similarity of aim. British feminist criticism, described by Showalter by the terms Marxism and oppression, is a materialist approach. It is interested in the material conditions of real people's lives, how conditions such as poverty and undereducation produce different signifying systems than works produced and read in conditions of privilege and educational plenty, for example. This kind of approach is likely to be most interested in the content of a literary text as symptomatic of the conditions of its production. It is an overtly political approach. French feminist literary theory, defined here as psychoanalytic in approach and focusing on issues of repression is a psychological study. It focuses the text as a tangle of psychic symptoms to be unravelled and explained in relation to desires repressed to the unconscious, which surface to rupture the text's apparent seamless unity. It is political, though it is not necessarily associated with political activism. American feminist criticism is described as textual in focus and primarily interested in expression. Here, criticism has been institutionally based, and feminist criticism, in order to achieve for itself a measure of respect in the institutional context, has made use of traditional – often New Critical – methods, but with a different emphasis and for quietly subversive ends. Unlike British criticism, while it focuses on the 'how' and 'what' of literature (expression), it does not seek sociological explanations in the Marxist terms of class for what gets written, and often eschews the psychic consequences of material oppression.

These terms, oppression, repression, and expression map – with a little jiggling – onto the phrase feminist literary theory. If feminism is most commonly understood as meaning the 'advocacy of the rights of woman', then separate from both literature and theory, as well as in conjunction with them, feminism has to do with oppression. Feminist relationships with psychoanalysis have been both productive and fraught, as I shall show later. The theory of psychoanalysis nonetheless offers an alternative explanation for woman's oppression in terms of her repression: in the phrase feminist literary theory, some of the most powerful *theories* derive from psychoanalysis. The category of the literary is where Showalter's 'expression' takes place.

This book is about all of these terms and their interconnections. No single explanation is enough. Causes and effects are multiple. That's why we need more than one kind of explanation, more than one kind of feminism. It is also why in so much contemporary feminist writing the boundaries between categories of oppression, repression, expression, feminisms, theories and literatures are broken down. Showalter's separation of these categories was strategic rather than strictly accurate. She wanted to show the energy of feminist theory, and to demonstrate that, far from being in the wilderness in a starved and defeated state, feminist theory was actually at the frontier of thinking, and was coping rather well under difficult conditions. Feminist theories are pluralist. They borrow from wherever they find what is useful. A feminist literary theorist might well be a Marxist materialist with psychoanalytic leanings and fingers in several post-structuralist, post-colonialist and postmodernist pies, all of which help her to read texts closely, but also to read them against the grain. For if women have been oppressed by more than one set of structures, then they may need more than one set of explanations to describe their current conditions, and to prescribe for future improvements.

Where Showalter's description of feminist approaches was definitely right, though, was in the identification of feminism with gynocentrism – woman-centredness. *My* defining limitation on feminism is this: all literary feminisms worth the name share a double commitment to place women at the centre of their literary-critical discourses, and to do so as part of a wider political process. The sexual politics of the world outside the text, and the sexual politics of the world inside the text, however self-evident or disguised, are part of a continuum of political critique and action in feminist theories. The analysis of the text is linked to an analysis of the world as lived experience (whether the experiences are material or psychic). Literature is, after all, a social and economic product as well as a space for expression, for pleasure, for pain, for readers and writers. It provides us with ways of seeing ourselves and others. We might well act on what we see and on how we see it. It behoves us therefore to be aware of what we do when we read, when we write about what we read, and when we act on what we think.

What is shared by all feminist theories, then, whether literary theories or not, is a focus on women.[2] That bald statement conceals a multitude of possibilities and differences between women across history, class and geography. But whilst the plural nouns (women, feminisms) signal multiplicity and differences, they also 'semantically mark a collectivity' (Fuss 1989, 4). Women are not all the same, but they do share similarities in subject positions related to the cultures in which they live. The focus on women, however politically difficult the term's 'unity' may be, constitutes feminism's main impetus. If, for example, a Marxist critique tends to suggest that particular economic conditions are *formative* of the human psyche, a feminist critique might agree that this is the case, but then go on to suggest that women are troubled by other structures of oppression as well, structures that are dependent on their female bodies as well as on their economic situation. Amongst the social and psychic structures in which feminism is interested are: social deprivations which are not unique to women, but which in a space of disprivilege may impinge more on women than on men (poor access to education or well-paid work, poor access even to food); physiological oppressions which attack women by virtue of their bodies (childbearing and rearing defined as 'women's work', or the fact that women are physically less powerful than men, and can be subjected to violence and rape); cultural oppression (where women are viewed as objects rather than subjects); psychological oppression (where women internalise a view of themselves as inferior). The name given to the intersections of these structures is patriarchy, which means literally the 'rule of the father'. Feminist theories, in literature and beyond, identify patriarchy at work in the home, the state, religious institutions, the law, education systems, the work-place, in culture at large and even in women themselves, since women as well as men are formed under patriarchy and come to subjecthood under its aegis.

The reading of literary texts might well seem to be a long way from the kinds of overtly political actions which could lead to changes in the social systems to which all human beings are subjected. And yet, reading in its broadest sense (reading of not just texts, but behaviours, clothing, social situations) is what we do as part of the process of becoming who we are, so that there is always a sense in which reading is a kind of doing, a mode of political praxis. There is some kind of relationship between words and the world they describe. It is not a transparent relationship, nor even a coherent one, as the insights of structuralist critics have suggested, with their emphasis on Saussurean arbitrariness and structures of difference. But that does not mean that words are divorced from the real; merely that tracing the relationships between reality and language is difficult. For feminist literary theory, one of the key assumptions, therefore, is that reading is part of the process of learning to be, of writing the self, as it were, into its social roles. The move towards 'reading differently', then, which feminisms prescribe, offers the possibility of alternative modes of 'being'. Literature is not some transcendent space in which the contingencies of everyday life are elided or absent. In literate cultures, literature is *part* of reality. It reflects the real, though 'the mirror is doubtless defective' (Eliot 1985, 221); it creates the real, acting as a '*mediating*, moulding force in society rather than as an agency that merely reflects or records' (Hawkes 1977, 56); and it thereby *recreates* the real, offering both critiques of the present world and alternative ways of being in fantasies, utopias, dystopias or science fictions.

And if literature and the real are related, however tenuously that relationship may be articulated, reading is political, and has to do with power. Texts may seek to coerce their readers, representing and encoding 'proper' (limited?) forms of behaviour and belief. Texts may also be subversive, attacking dominant modes of understanding, and offering alternative ways of being and thinking. The force of the text, however, whatever its content and intentions, comes from the process of reading it. Reading is a political act that defines the reader's response to the text she is reading. She may read and be caught up in the text; she may read against the text – either position is politicised. As a feminist reader, however, she is determined to see the possibility of a better future in the real. Hence she diagnoses the symptoms of social and psychic sicknesses and meditates on appropriate prescriptions to alleviate the pain or to amputate the diseased parts of the body politic.

This might be seen as a slightly idiosyncratic book. It makes no claim to say everything there is to say on this subject, which is at least consistent with my view that feminisms are plural, and that they are also anti-totalising. The choices I've made about what to discuss are often pragmatic. This is, after all, an introductory book. A lot of French theory remains to be translated. And while I would wish to signal that a 'canon' of feminist theory is not entirely desirable, I have focused on materials that are easily available to student readers. Economic considerations always play their part in literary production and in literary theory. My aim is to show the relationships between theories and practices – to do feminist readings whilst elucidating feminist theories. A certain amount of familiarity in materials need not breed contempt, and helps to show how different approaches might work. I say again that this is not in any sense the last word; but I hope that for some readers it will act as first words on their way to speaking for themselves.

The organisation follows broadly chronological lines, though I would also wish to warn against *the* 'history' of feminist literature. The narratives of history, with their tendency to assume progress and teleology, are not an honest representation of feminist literary theory. It is not the case that the early feminist critics were well-intentioned but naive readers whilst contemporary writers are sophisticated and cunning ones. The various strands I draw out from the story of feminism supplement and complement each other, and no part of the story is over yet. Psychoanalytic readings make use of Marxism, post-structuralism depends, says Derrida, on structuralism, and Kristeva's subject in process rewrites but does not invalidate Mary Wollstonecraft's will to create human female selfhood. Critics, like writers, use the materials at their disposal. Thinking and the conditions in which thinking occurs change, which does not mean that the thinking of previous generations is invalid for our time, nor that we cannot borrow its models and reuse them in our own context. Rosi Braidotti (1994) speaks of the feminist reader as a nomadic subject, wandering to find sustenance. It is a useful metaphor for literary feminisms. Forage where ye may, use the useful, move on.

Notes

1. Rachel Bowlby makes similar points to these in her essay 'Still crazy after all these years' in Theresa Brennan (ed.), *Between Feminism and Psychoanalysis*, London: Routledge, 1990, 40–59.
2. The words woman and women require some complication. Athough we all 'know' what a woman is, there is a problem with a so-called 'common-sense' simple definition. Recently a number of critics, especially Judith Butler in *Gender Trouble* (1990) and *Bodies that Matter* (1993), have suggested that sexual identity is precisely what its at stake in feminism, and that the easy identification of women with biology is problematic. See below, Chapter 8, for the development of this point

Part I

Histories

1   Liberal, Materialist and Socialist Literary Feminisms

... unnatural generally means only uncustomary, and ... everything that is usual appears natural. The subjection of women to men being a universal custom, any departure from it quite naturally appears unnatural.

John Stuart Mill, 'The Subjection of Women'

Almost all the early forms of feminist political thinking based themselves firmly in the assumptions of liberal individualism and materialism. Broadly speaking, liberal individualism implies that the individual person, usually designated as male, is valued in his own right, and has certain rights (legal, social, economic, political, familial and rights of property) attached to his personhood. The individual is supposed to be understood as unique, and yet he is also part of a community of like-minded men who share most of the same views, privileges and rights. Raymond Williams, writing in his dictionary of culture and society, *Keywords*, traces the modern sense of individuality to the break-up of the medieval feudal system and the emergence of capitalism which stressed 'man's personal existence over and above his place or function in a rigid hierarchical society'. He aligns the development of the individual in Britain with the rise of Protestant Christianity, which stressed the personal relationship of the individual soul with God as opposed to Catholicism's relationships which were mediated through the priesthood. He also sees the move from living on the land to living from trade and manufacture as the defining economic mode of Western European life, with the emphasis shifting from community benefits to personal profits (Williams 1988, 161–5). In other words, the economic and spiritual organisation of societies profoundly affects the meaning of personhood within them.

An individualist definition of personhood tends therefore to be a materialist definition, since it focuses on the materials that the individual owns or has access to. 'A man's Self,' wrote William James in 1890, 'is the sum total of what he can call his; not only his body and his psychic powers, but his clothes and his house, his wife and his children, his ancestors and friends, his reputation and works, his lands and horses, and yacht and bank account' (quoted in Hobsbawm 1989, 165). The qualities of the individual's life can be measured in *material* terms: wealth and the status it brings, a privileged relationship with the law, education and even religious establishments, and power over others such as wives, children and employees. Material things have therefore both practical and psychic consequences; they bolster up the sense of valuable personhood for the individual who does the 'owning', producing and reinforcing a measurable estimate of his worth. Provided that the individual remains within certain limits of action – primarily that he does not infringe the rights/privileges of others who share his status – he is very free in the actions he is permitted. As Williams points out, liberal is a word which implies freedoms, but those freedoms take place within limits (Williams 1988, 179–83); for those with power, however, the limits were/are widely drawn.

One of the insights of early feminist writing was to notice that liberal individualism is an ideological formation that privileges male existence over female. The difficulties of the word 'ideology' are by now legendary, though it is an indispensable word for political and theoretical thinking.[1] It is used in two distinctly different ways. First, and this is the usage most common in everyday language, it describes a set of consciously held beliefs. One might describe oneself as Muslim or Catholic, for example, or as Socialist or Conservative. The description aligns the 'believer' to a set of transparently codified rules of conduct and faith. The rules are set down, and anyone can 'know' what they are. In this sense, ideology is often used as a term of insult to attack systems of belief with which one disagrees. Second, and for our purposes more importantly, however, ideology has also come to mean the unconscious beliefs of a given society or group, the structures in which we believe without being quite aware of where our belief comes from, the things we take, as it were, to be 'natural'. 'Ideology signifies the imaginary ways in which men [*sic*] experience the real world,' writes Terry Eagleton. Ideology tells us 'what it feels like to live in particular conditions, rather than [providing us with] a conceptual analysis of those conditions' (Eagleton 1976, 18). Liberal individualism is ideologically constructed since it is a social and historical formation (people have not always conceived themselves in this way) that presents itself as natural and immutable. It is very unwilling to examine the bases of its own formation.

Take, for example, the way in which George Eliot introduces the character of Dorothea Brooke in the opening paragraph of *Middlemarch*:

> Miss Brooke had that kind of beauty which seems to be thrown into relief by poor dress. Her hand and wrist were so finely formed that she could wear sleeves not less bare of style than those in which the Blessed Virgin appeared to Italian painters; and her profile, as well as her stature and bearing, seemed to gain the more dignity from her plain garments, which by the side of provincial fashion gave her the impressiveness of a fine quotation from the Bible, – or from one of our elder poets, – in a paragraph of today's newspaper. ... Miss Brooke's plain dressing was due to mixed conditions ... The pride of being [a lady] had something to do with it ... Young women of such birth, living in a quiet country house, and attending a village church hardly larger than a parlour, *naturally* regarded frippery as the ambition of a huckster's daughter. Then there was well-bred economy, which in those days made show in dress the first item to be deducted from, when any margin was required for expenses more distinctive of rank. Such reasons would have been enough to account for plain dress, quite apart from religious feeling; but in Miss Brooke's case, religion alone would have determined it. (Eliot 1965, 29–30, my emphasis)

Throughout this passage, and for much of the rest of the novel, Eliot's narrator pokes gentle fun at Dorothea Brooke, treating her with a certain irony.[2] The irony, however, is also tempered with admiration, for the novel is predicated on the fact that this individual woman's life and the narrative of her dilemmas are sufficiently interesting and important to keep us reading for around a thousand pages. Thus we are asked to consider in detail a figure who is presented to us as an aesthetic anomaly – she is beautiful *despite* the fact that she wears poor dress. She is remarkable in contrast to the workaday figures among whom she moves. She is a lady, with a lady's sensibility that prevents her dressing like a 'huckster's daughter'; and unusually, she has fine religious feelings which the novel establishes as the source of the split she feels so strongly between duty and desire.

What Eliot's apparently-knowing narrator disguises, however, is
that this individual, no matter how ironically presented, depends for
her existence on unseen networks of relations with other people and
with various economic systems. Dorothea's apparent poverty, for
example, is very relative. The hand and wrist that her plain sleeves
throw into relief are beautiful because they are not scarred with work;
Dorothea never has to bare her arms to the elbows and immerse them
in soapy water to do her laundry because someone else – we never see
who – does it for her. She can indulge in the 'strange whim' (31) of
staying up all night to read theological books, and can use her time to
learn passages from Pascal by heart because of the economic conditions she inhabits. At the most basic level, she is lucky enough to have
been taught to read when it seems unlikely that the maid who does
her laundry has such an accomplishment. Moreover, she has the
leisure to stay up all night – something that people who have to get up
in the morning to work do not have. And she lives in a house where
books are plentiful and she is allowed to read them, as presumably,
the servant-girl would not be, even had she the time, the inclination
and the education to do so.

Put like that, of course, Dorothea's aestheticised poverty looks rather
more like privilege. But the thrust of the novel, for all its interest in
networks of social relations, buries the economics of the situation
under the surface. The reader is not encouraged to think these things;
indeed, the reader is called into a position of admiration in relation to
Dorothea, who, for all her limitations, is presented as remarkable. The
point is that her particularity validates ours. The implied reader of
Eliot's novel lives in a world very much like the one that the novel
itself presents. As readers within liberal individualist societies, we too
are reliant on invisible networks of relations for our relatively
comfortable position. If we are reading *Middlemarch*, in some sense
we share Dorothea's privileged position; we have the means to read
(the education, the text itself, owned or borrowed as a material
commodity, the leisure). We are encouraged to buy her image. Not
only is *Middlemarch* a 'classic', so is its main protagonist, who
appears like a line from good poetry or the Bible, who looks like a
Renaissance Madonna. These are touchstones of value and beauty
that we are called to share as markers of our own decency and good
taste. We buy Dorothea's liberal individualist self because we are
supposed to recognise our own liberal individual selves in her. Like
Dorothea, and like Eliot's narrator, it does not do for us to delve too

deeply into the implications of our construction of identity. It is far less threatening to take our liberal individualist notion of ourselves as read, as natural and immutable, as merely a function of human nature.

The activist feminisms of the last two hundred years, in Western Europe and the United States, have taken place both within and against the ideological formation of the liberal individual. They have been against the traditional formulation of the liberal individual because they recognise that 'he' is to be understood as male and middle or upper class. William James's definition of a man's selfhood is to be understood entirely as a masculine phenomenon bolstered by the materiality of class privilege: in his terms, not only does no woman (of whatever class or race) have any significant selfhood to speak of, large numbers of unprivileged men are also excluded from the definition of the liberal-individualist self. There has therefore been a move to widen the definition of the individual to include some of those others who also make up a society, and in particular, to extend personhood to middle-class women. While there is a sense in which such a stretching of the meaning of individualism to include women is politically significant, it is also problematic because it leaves the basic structures of oppression (including those of class and race, for example, as well as of gender inflected by class/race disprivilege) intact. Nonetheless, the significant successes of feminist activism have been in the realm of extending individualism to include some women. In particular, the opening up of higher education and the professions to (bourgeois) women at the end of the nineteenth century, the extension of the franchise to women in the early years of the twentieth century, and the more recent institution of equal-rights legislation, maternity rights, the availability of safe and reliable contraception, have been successes of feminisms in its liberal guises. There are ongoing battles to achieve affordable child-care for working parents, and to undo the prejudice that still prevents some women from reaching the heights of their professions. These legislative and cultural changes are the logical correlative of a philosophical position that divorces sex from gender, and that insists that biology need not be destiny. The changes are very significant, and have made real differences to real people's lives. But liberal feminisms sometimes forget that their allegiance to the liberal individual is also an alliance with competitive capitalist economics, and that wherever there is competition, there are losers as well as winners.

Mary Wollstonecraft: vindicating the liberal-individual woman

When an early feminist writer like Mary Wollstonecraft (1759–97) examined the society in which she lived, a society in which liberal individualism was becoming the dominant ideological formation of (male) personhood and social organisation, what she uncovered was the systematic inequality of women in all areas of life – the family, work, culture, economics, the law, education – as well as the inconsistency of the ideological positions that held this inequality in place. Her *Vindication of the Rights of Woman* (1792) is a response to that inequality. She examines the 'naturalness' of women's inequality and discovers that it is not in fact natural at all – natural, indeed, may be one of the most ideologically loaded words in the English language. Women's inequality, says Wollstonecraft, is socially constructed to shore up the position of the privileged liberal-individualist male. Either, she says, 'Nature has made a great difference between man and man, or ... the civilisation which has hitherto taken place in the world has been very partial'; furthermore, she argues that 'women, in particular, are rendered weak and wretched, by a variety of concurring causes', amongst which are inadequate parenting, bad education, the lack of property rights, and exclusion from the political sphere, as well as the negative effects of literary-cultural life: the ideology of romantic love which makes women mere creatures of sentiment, and bad novels which reproduce a false picture of reality rather than an intelligent analysis of it (Wollstonecraft 1992, 79).

A small, but important example of her analysis is from her discussion of Dr Gregory's *A Father's Legacy to his Daughters* (1774), a conduct manual which focused on properly feminine behaviour. In his book, as Wollstonecraft describes it, Gregory advised his daughters to:

> cultivate a fondness for dress, because a fondness of dress, he asserts, is natural to them. I am unable to comprehend what either he or Rousseau mean when they frequently use this indefinite term [natural]. If they told us that in a pre-existent state the soul was fond of dress, and brought this inclination with it into a new body, I should listen to them with a half-smile, as I often do when I hear a rant about innate elegance. But if he only meant to say that the exercise of the faculties will produce this fondness, I deny it. It is not natural; but arises, like false ambition in men, from a love of power. (111–12)

The argument is that if something is natural, then one will do it naturally, without the advice to cultivate the position advocated. If the 'fondness for dress' is *not* a natural attribute of women, why should they be encouraged to cultivate it? The answer – the 'love of power' – comes from the larger context of the book, in which Wollstonecraft suggests that while women are denied other forms of power (political, educational, legal), they will make use of whatever power is left to them: in particular their sexual power to attract men because they are taught, and have learned their lesson well, that they can only draw power from sexual relationships rather than having any autonomous potency of their own. This sexualisation of femininity, noted also by de Beauvoir's comment that women are often designated '*the* sex', supports male privilege in two distinct ways: firstly it shores up a position that emphasises the attractiveness of masculinity and its potency; secondly, it keeps women actually weak, while pretending to offer them (very limited) power.

This short passage shows the inconsistency of the ideological positions which insist that women are unequal to men. On the one hand, their liking for clothes is labelled 'natural', and the word 'natural' is heavily invested with positive value. In culture, however, women are routinely disparaged for liking clothes too much, a trivial, unimportant preference. So when they are told to cultivate their 'natural' taste for clothes, they can be once more labelled as trivial unimportant people, incapable of serious thought. Ideology has a circular logic, and it is difficult to break the spell.

While Wollstonecraft herself could not have used the words 'ideology' and 'liberal individualist', her critique demonstrates the constructedness of social formations, and the inherent bias towards masculinity in those constructions. What she seeks is to improve the situation of women within the existing structures of society. Her work suggests that society is to blame for female oppression and for the general weakness of women. Women are not educated to do or know any better. Society has created women's foolishness and has then proceeded to blame women for their weakness, indeed has come to regard women's weakness as natural.

For all her anger at the systematic oppression of women, however, Wollstonecraft is not quite a revolutionary writer, and her insights remain within the limits proposed by a liberal-individualist version of the world. What she proposes is an extension of (male) individualist privilege to women. She does not propose to undo the very notion of privilege *per se.* Neither *The Vindication* nor Wollstonecraft's fiction demand a dismantling of contemporary social structures. Instead *The Vindication* is basically a plea for bourgeois woman's equality with bourgeois man in the areas of educational, legal and political systems. It is also an attack on an ideal of femininity that constructs female inequality as 'natural'. What is being demanded, therefore, is not so much a revolution towards an ideal of equality as a reapportioning of privilege to ensure that some (middle- and upper-class) women get some share of the spoils usually reserved to some (middle- and upper-class) men. As such her works dramatise the pervasiveness of ideological formations. On the one hand, her writings diagnose a social problem; on the other, they articulate that problem within its own terms. Wollstonecraft could not, in her social critique, imagine a world in which women might be equal to men in a different social formation from the one in which she lived, in which other kinds of inequality (the inequality of class, for example) would continue to exist. She addresses herself specifically to women of her own class, women who recognise the attractive power of male privilege because the males with whom they associate are privileged. A feminism derived from the experience of a working-class woman would very likely have different aspirations. And this is a point that liberal feminisms have had to adapt to cover. Liberal/materialist feminisms, which generally originate from bourgeois positions of relative comfort have had to stretch their remits, and to notice the structures of oppression that afflict women who occupy positions of multiple marginality by virtue, for example, of class and gender, race and gender, sexuality and gender, or any combination of these facets.

The class, race and sexuality biases of Wollstonecraft's writing have to be taken into consideration when thinking about the symptoms she uncovers (femininity is a kind of sickness) and the diagnoses she produces in the *Vindication,* not least because of the significant space she apportions to literature in the formation of the attenuated femininity she so deplores. In an age before widespread literacy, writing was necessarily addressed to the privileged few who could read. Her feminism is historically determined, depending on the ideological positions she deplores. It is also class determined, addressed not to 'ladies' (81),[3] but to middle-class women, with some education, but who did not suffer the debilitating effects of the excessive femininity of dependence, invalidism, frailty and false modesty that she suggests is cultivated by the aristocracy of the late-eighteenth century.

In her fictions, *Mary: A Fiction* (1788) and *The Wrongs of Woman* (1798), left a fragment at her death, Wollstonecraft dramatises the material effects of male-dominated liberal individualism on female subjects. The novella, *Mary*, describes the dissatisfaction of her heroine with the role models and opportunities that life offers to her. Despite her relatively comfortable social position – Mary becomes the heiress to a substantial fortune following the death of her brother – the heroine is trapped in the social roles that society has mapped out for her. Her father is tyrannical and adulterous; her mother, described by the narrator as a 'mere nothing' (Wollstonecraft 1980, 2), is a shadowy figure who has retreated into the invalidism she associates with attractive aristocratic femininity. For all their patent inadequacy as parents, however, Mary is both obedient and sincerely dutiful to them. She obeys her father, and marries against her own inclination; and when her parents die, she sincerely mourns them both. Her mother's long illness 'called forth all Mary's tenderness, and exercised her compassion ... continually' (5); and her father's death produces real grief: 'he was not a friend or protector; but he was her father' (18). On the one hand, then, Mary has the intellectual capacity to see that there is quite a lot that is wrong with her world; on the other, the affection for and obedience to her parents that has been instilled in her, and that we might read as oppressive ideological formations, prevent her from making real judgements of them or of what they represent. Sensibility – the cultivation of feeling – is both the require-ment of femininity, and a tool that also oppresses women: Mary remains obedient to her father even when he is wrong because 'he was her father'. Coupled with this doubled vision – *knowing* there is a problem, and yet *feeling* that to act would be wrong – Mary's social context would, in any case, prevent her from acting on any judgement of her own. The novella thus traces social circumstances as the causes of psychic discomfort in its heroine who is caught between intellect and sentiment within the realm of a social and historical specificity.

The projected novel, *The Wrongs of Woman: or, Maria*, is structured around the repeated telling of stories, the life-stories of the three major characters. These narratives eventually explain how they all come to be inhabiting the madhouse which is the novel's setting. The two upper-class characters, Maria and Henry Darnford, are there as inmates/prisoners; Jemima, the lower-class woman, is the keeper. In many ways, it is Jemima's story that is most pertinent to a liberal feminism that is more inclusive than exclusive. Jemima belongs to the most oppressed of all classes, being poor, female and illegitimate; her weak social and economic position is exacerbated by the fact that she has also lost her 'respectability', having worked for some time as a prostitute. Her degradation represents the logical conclusion of the social constructions of femininity and legitimations of male power versus female weakness within a framework of liberal individualism that does not recognise Jemima as an individual with rights. She has no stake in society, having been 'an egg dropped on the sand, a pauper by nature' (106), and consequently she preys on society, by thieving and prostitution – she dramatises what happens to liberal individualism when no rights are guaranteed and no responsibilities are required of the individual. Her story touches Maria as analogous with her own, though, of course, the details are different because of the different social positions of the two women. Maria speculates that 'Jemima's humanity had rather been benumbed than killed, by the keen frost she had to brave at her entrance into life' (120). The recognition of a common humanity is a partial recognition of the constructedness of the class system that oppresses Jemima more keenly even than it oppresses Maria herself. Jemima is attacked on many different fronts. Maria's main source of dis-ease is her gender.

Wollstonecraft's middle-class heroines are 'innocent', by which she means uneducated, unprotected by family or law, subjected to tyrannical family life and inappropriate marriages to unsuitable husbands, from which there is no escape. This is the argument also of the *Vindication*. If women are not educated, and if marriage is not reformed, the results spiral: women have no choice of career bar marriage, no realistic choice of marriage partner, no escape from bad marriages. Moreover, even within marriage, they are unfit even for their very limited role as mothers. Rich women, Wollstonecraft described as not working as mothers at all, since they had no care over their infants. Babies were sent out to wet-nurses, and children were left in the care of servants. The rich woman who did care for her children was so ill-educated that she could teach them nothing except for coquetry and false modesty. Her argument is that women, deprived of real social functions, have no stake in society, are 'mere nothings', who live bored and wasted lives. Thus Mary's story ends with the heroine waiting for death as a blessed relief from the disappointments of female life. *The Wrongs of Woman*, left unfinished at

Wollstonecraft's death, ends either with the legal demolition of
Maria's divorce case against her husband or, cheerfully, with a cata-
logue of disasters: 'Divorced by her husband – Her lover unfaithful –
Pregnancy – Miscarriage – Suicide' (202).

For Wollstonecraft, literature has to be understood as a powerful
tool – a tool both of social control and oppression, and a tool which
enables the transformation of a painful reality. In the *Vindication*, she
rails strongly against novels, which she sees as a mode of writing that
invokes sensibility and sentiment in their female readers at the
expense of intellect and analysis: 'There are women who are amused
by the reveries of the stupid novelists, who, knowing little of human
nature, work up stale tales, and describe meretricious scenes, all
retained in a sentimental jargon, which equally tend to corrupt the
taste, and draw the heart aside from its daily duties' (Wollstonecraft
1992, 313). In that reading, the novel text is dangerously powerful. It
leads to stereotyped writing by unimaginative writers, which leads in
turn to infantilised readers. On the other hand, she does not believe
that women should never read novels. Indeed, reading novels is better
than not reading at all (314); and the habit of reading even light work
can be seen as the foundation for a habit of reading more weighty
matter. It is the simple acceptance of unrealistic fictional dreams to
which she really objects, the 'stale tales' of stereotyping which bolster
up prejudice. Moreover, she shows the inequalities of the roles
proposed for male and female readers in her discussions of Rousseau
and Dr Fordyce's sermons. Women, she argues, are always presented
as angels, limited to one view; men, on the other hand, can be whatever they want to be:

> Men are allowed by moralists to cultivate, as Nature directs, different
> qualities, and assume the different characters, that the same
> passions, modified almost to infinity, give to each individual. A virtu-
> ous man may have a choleric or a sanguine constitution, be gay or
> grave, unreproved; be firm till he is almost overbearing, or, weakly
> submissive, have no will or opinion of his own; but all women are to
> be levelled, by meekness and docility, into one character of yielding
> softness and gentle compliance. (197–8)

Literary representation is a straitjacket for femininity, limiting women
to very narrow social roles and insisting on a uniformity of good qualities.

Her own fictions are diagnostic pieces rather than cures for social ills. The stories are even rather depressing, and she holds out little hope for social transformation, while at the same time producing the arguments which ought to lead to it. In the 'Advertisement' to *Mary*, however, she puts forward an ideal of what a literary text might be when it is acting as a political document. Her heroine, she says is no Richardsonian Clarissa Harlowe, no Rousseauian Sophie – not a male-defined, passive version of pleasing femininity. Texts like Richardson's or Rousseau's are not about transforming reality. They merely reproduce the unthinking acceptance of ready-made models. Such authors stay on the 'beaten track, solicitous to gather expected flowers, and bind them in a wreath, according to the prescribed rules of art'. The stereotypes, she suggests, are deathly – both to the reader and to the art of fiction itself. Her intention is different, and it might operate as a first model for feminist readings and writings of literature:

> In an artless tale, without episodes, the mind of a woman who has thinking powers is displayed. The female organs have been thought too weak for this arduous employment; and experience seems to justify the assertion. Without arguing physically about *possibilities* – in a fiction, such a being may be allowed to exist; whose grandeur is derived from the operations of its own faculties, not subjugated to opinion; but drawn by the individual from the original source. (Wollstonecraft 1980, np)

First, Wollstonecraft eschews 'art', since art has rules which would keep her tale on the 'beaten track'; and anyway, artists 'wander greatly from nature' when they merely impersonate the rules laid down by greater artists. Second, she states (not quite truthfully) that this is a fiction without episodes:[4] the events here are in the female mind, derived from a woman's imagination rather than from a male-defined reality. There is then the irony of her agreement that women are probably too weak to think in reality; but this tale is a fiction, and in a fiction, anything can happen, even things that received opinion would object to. She is appealing, she suggests, to her own experience, which implies both that her experience is some kind of guarantor of authenticity, and that it is an idiosyncratic version of reality, rather than a totalising one.

Having castigated the unreality of representations of women by other writers, Wollstonecraft is perfectly prepared to admit that her own fictions draw on a kind of fantasy life. While others do not represent the real, Wollstonecraft herself insists on the fictionality of *Mary*. This is a contradiction in her work, but it is an important contradiction. If literature can be one of the sites of the oppression of women, it can also be the site of an imagined alternative. Fiction is powerful because it is liberated from the necessity of telling observable truths. Instead it can tell any possibility. Wollstonecraft herself does not fulfil the promise of her Preface in the novel she writes. Mary is so hemmed in by her social limitations that despite her 'thinking powers' she proves unable to do anything to better her own situation. Wollstonecraft's writing – both her fictions and her more obviously political work – does, however, signal two of the important directions of feminist thinking that will be undertaken during the next two centuries within the framework of liberal, individualist and materialist thought. The *Vindication* provides an analysis of women's material oppression and psychic repression. The Preface to *Mary* holds out the promise of the literary expression of a different world in which women with 'thinking powers' exist, in which women can be imagined as bourgeois individuals.

Analysing materialism: reading as a socialist feminist?

What Wollstonecraft's writings show above all is that social formations have both practical and psychic effects on their subjects. Under certain kinds of social organisation people can be hungry and dispossessed; their hunger and their aspirations are formative of their worldview. For this reason, the analysis of social structures and their effects has been one of the most important approaches to literary texts in recent times. Marxist and socialist critics, following on from Marx's insight that Man is an economic animal whose attitudes are constructed in relation to his economic needs and his class position, have sought to see the literary text not as the product of transcendent individualism, but as the result of a matrix of social forces. The book is a product. It requires labour, materials, knowledge, a market, a distribution network, a technology of printing, to exist. Treating texts as if they were the outpourings of the individual's soul, as many traditional humanist approaches to literature tend to do, disguises the economic imperatives that lie behind the writing and the reception of the book.

This is true on both the macro level of economic systems and on the micro level of the individual writer's work processes. Writing, after all, is not a natural attribute. Unlike the learning of spoken language which takes place almost by a process of osmosis, learning to write requires a deliberate investment of time and effort. It also requires a technology: the biros we write with today may not seem like very technical instruments, and the paper on which we write is taken for granted, but both are the products of capitalist industries. The prerequisites for writing, then, include investment in some kind of educational system, the personal investment of time, the very small investment (for Western societies) in writing materials.[5] When Virginia Woolf argued that for the woman writer to write, what was necessary was a private income and a room of one's own (Woolf 1993a), she registered her own very privileged position. Before the income and the room, what one needs to write is to *learn* to write, and to have the materials for writing. The income and the room are luxuries on the grander scale of things.[6]

One of the key examples of the bringing together of Marxism, feminism and literature is Terry Lovell's 1987 book, *Consuming Fiction*, the very title of which emphasises that the novel is a consumer commodity invented in a capitalist system. Lovell's text is a history of literature that rewrites earlier histories, in particular Ian Watt's *The Rise of the Novel* (1957), with both gender and class as key terms of the analysis. She criticises Watt's book on several grounds, including the sociological, the historical and the idea of literary value. *The Rise of the Novel* was written in the wake of F. R. Leavis's establishment of a narrowly defined canon of English literature. When Watt looked at the eighteenth century, he admitted that the vast majority of novels published in the period were by women. But his own focus is on Defoe, Fielding and Richardson, since his definition of the novel derives from what he calls the properties of 'formal realism', the properties of writing that eventually informed the ideals of literary value found in Leavis's *The Great Tradition*. His finding that Fielding *et al.* were the founders of the novel is historically inaccurate, based not on the facts of what was being published in the period, but on the later establishment of the criteria of 'literariness', criteria which somehow always excluded women writers.

Watt also hypothesised that the rise of the novel was the direct result of the rise of the middle-class woman reader, a reader who had both the ability to read and the leisure in which to do so. Lovell's text provides a corrective explanatory gloss on this view. She argues that reading was the leisure activity that interfered least with domesticity as a marker of class, and with the domestic middle-class woman's other occupations, the unpaid labour of housework and child-care:

> It is doubtful whether middle-class women ... had more leisure time than middle-class men. What is true is that the ways available to them of deploying their leisure time were very much more restricted, and that the pattern of work/leisure was less differentiated for women. Women read in their leisure time because reading was cheap, and because it is a leisure activity which is most readily adapted to an undifferentiated work/leisure routine. A novel could be picked up and put down, read as and when, unlike the leisure pursuits of husbands and brothers which typically required blocks of free time which women, once married, did not usually have. (Lovell 1987, 39)

These factors, Lovell argues, also had their effects, not only on women as readers, but also on women as writers. Novel-writing was also an activity that could be presented as an occupation that did not interfere with domesticity. The woman writer could be self-assertive and economically independent in her fictions, while continuing to function as wife, mother and domestic manager. But self-expression was mediated through the lens of whatever ideologies of femininity were current at a given moment. Lovell identifies, therefore, specifically feminine modes of address in fiction. Taking the example of Elizabeth Gaskell's 1848 novel, *Mary Barton,* she shows how Gaskell worked creatively within the discourses of Victorian ideologies of domestic femininity. Gaskell occupied an apparently subordinate feminine position when she disclaimed any knowledge of political economy in her preface to *Mary Barton;* but she simultaneously claimed the feminine authority to tell her audience about how people feel, and argued that the analysis of feeling was just as important as particular knowledge of official politics and economics through the plot and structures of the novel. She addressed a male audience from a woman's position, with powerfully subversive results.

Lovell seeks to complicate the ways in which social constraints are both felt and evaded, and argues through the lenses of both feminism and Marxism to show how both gender and class are implicated in the structures adopted by women's writing:

> the ideology of domesticity in the nineteenth century could not be seen
> as an alien and oppressive imposition upon the middle-class woman –
> a narrow straitjacket which men forced her to wear. Neither could it be
> seen as a set of garments willingly donned by the silent sisterhood and
> worn with no consciousness of the tight corsets and constricted feet.
> Rather the ideology set the terms within which or against which
> women had to negotiate their sexed identity and their social relation-
> ships. And it was backed by punitive legal and social sanctions which
> made open defiance a costly and painful business. (95)

For Lovell, the intersections between class and gender and culture at
large mean that no single formation provides a complete explanatory
framework in its own terms. She argues that women experience life in
terms of 'a systematic ambiguity more or less deeply felt by all women
engaged in the business of constructing a sense of self and social
identity' (70). The markers of gender and class may even be in conflict
with each other, exposing the extent to which neither is a complete
explanation for women's generally subordinate positions in life, literature and culture.

A rather different example of a Marxist-inflected feminist approach
to literature is Mary Poovey's *Uneven Developments: The Ideological
Work of Gender in Mid-Victorian England* (1989). Like Lovell, Poovey
is interested in uncovering the intersections of various discourses in
the formation of individual experiences. She describes herself as a
literary critic first and foremost, with an interest in how textuality
mediates experience. And, indeed, *Uneven Developments* contains
some very interesting and challenging readings of literary texts,
including *Jane Eyre* and *David Copperfield*. But alongside that focus
on textuality, Poovey also provides a *con*textuality. The literary texts
are to be read in the light of medical discourses, legislative changes,
and the competing languages of gender, class and national identity. In
this kind of reading, the literary text is resolutely not to be understood
as transcendent individual self-expression. Rather it is to be seen as
the mediated product of the individual's responses to the various
formations of his or her own identity. Thus, while Poovey argues
strongly that class is one of the fundamental sites of the individual's
identity, she resists the possibility that either class or gender act alone
to produce identity or, by extension, textual meaning. In this, she
signals her departure both from the classic Marxist position, and the
classic feminist position:

> I do not think that class position is always or at all times more impor-
> tant than other constitutive categories, such as gender, race, or
> national identity ... My object here has been to examine the relation-
> ships among such categories. It seems to me that plotting the chang-
> ing interaction of these determinants within a culture and within
> individual texts is more important than relentlessly subordinating
> any combination of these factors to an ahistorical master category.
> (18–19)

The master categories (class or gender), Poovey suggests, are not
universal or trans-historical. They are inflected by time and place. The
obligation of a Marxist-feminist textual approach, therefore, is to pay
serious attention to the specific history and contexts of production of
the text that one examines. For Poovey this means an attention to all
the discourses that formed both masculinity and femininity (gender
refers to both men and women). Her literary critique takes place in
the contextualising frameworks of discussions of the Victorian
medical establishment's view of femininity, and of the Matrimonial
Causes Act of 1857 (the first act of Parliament that made divorce
possible for those other than the very rich). Moreover, she does not
focus entirely on the ideology of femininity, but shows the extent to
which masculinity was also the result of ideological formation.

Given that social and economic disprivilege are often felt more
acutely by women than by men, a Marxist/socialist approach to the
analysis of literature is a fruitful space for feminist thinking, too.
Linking the effects of capitalist production and class structures to
issues of gender provides a range of possible analytical tools with
which to diagnose the problems of oppression that are specific to
women, and thence enable the development of hypotheses that might
relieve the effects of oppressive structures. Moreover, since social-
ist/Marxist approaches to literature are both explicitly politically-
engaged critiques, what should happen by bringing the two
approaches together is that the politics of feminism and the politics of
the left learn from each other, modify each other, and together
change the world. That is the ideal.

The relationships between socialism/Marxism and feminism,
however, have not always been happy. Elaine Showalter, in 1979,
suggested that:

> The most natural direction for feminist criticism to take has been the
> revision and even the subversion of related ideologies, especially
> Marxist aesthetics and structuralism, altering their vocabularies and
> methods to include the variable of gender. I believe, however, that
> this thrifty feminine making-do is ultimately unsatisfactory. Feminist
> criticism cannot go around forever in men's ill-fitting hand-me-
> downs, the Annie Hall of English studies ... (in Showalter 1986, 139)

She argued that the feminist appropriation of Marxism was a form of
dependency on male models; and she suggested that feminism added
to Marxism tended to modify feminism more than Marxism, that the
'conversation' between the two discourses was 'one way': Marxism
spoke and feminism listened. It was a discomfort that was often
repeated, as Cora Kaplan has shown. She quotes the critic Heidi
Hartmann who saw the 'marriage' of Marxism and feminism as being
like 'the marriage of husband and wife in English common law:
marxism and feminism are one, and that is marxism' (quoted in
Kaplan 1986, 147). It appears as a very unequal marriage.

Nonetheless, Kaplan argues passionately for a feminism that takes
the analysis of social formations seriously, and which makes intelligent use of those pre-existing models. Masculinity and femininity, she
writes:

> are always, already, ordered and broken up through other social and
> cultural terms, other categories of difference. ... Class and race
> ideologies are ... steeped in and spoken through the language of
> sexual differentiation. Class and race meanings are not metaphors for
> the sexual, or vice versa. It is better, though not exact, to see them as
> reciprocally constituting each other through a kind of narrative invo-
> cation, a set of associative terms in a chain of meaning. To under-
> stand how gender and class ... are articulated together transforms our
> analysis of each. (149)

Identity is complicated by the different places in which it resides. In
the nineteenth century, for example, femininity meant different
things depending on the class position of the female subject. A
middle-class woman inhabited one set of structures of femininity, a
working-class woman inhabited rather different structures. A feminism that does not take the classed differences of gender into consideration is missing quite a large part of the plot.

Other problems for the alliance of Marxism and feminism as an approach to literary texts have to do with the category of the aesthetic. If Marxists and feminists both seek social transformation, both have equally often found the realms of the arts and literature of rather marginal concern. The revolution does not come through books and pictures, particularly if the emphasis on the 'great' books and pictures is on the unquestioning acceptance of their 'value' and of the values that they impart (2). Wollstonecraft's passionate view that revolutionaries have to take literature seriously often gets lost in Marxist approaches that do not wish to invest too much time in examining the conventional pieties, and which dismiss the possibility that the aesthetic (the definitions of beauty and value in art) is also political. Kaplan argues that the aesthetic is not just to do with taste and feeling, with a subjective view of what is beautiful. Rather it is also socially constructed, and the ways in which it operates can be analysed in the service of understanding the exclusions of the aesthetic – what do the 'great' books have in common? what are the ideals of feminine beauty through the ages? what kinds of book and kinds of beauty are excluded from the definition of greatness, and why? The answers to these kinds of questions will expose the ideological contents and the historical specificities of aesthetic judgements. Instead of allowing the category of 'great literature' to be unquestioned and unexamined, instead of tamely allowing it the privileged positions of universality, truth and transcendence, an approach to literature that focuses on gender and class, on modes of production and points of exclusion, could actively subvert the ideal of literary greatness that is a part of the underpinning of current systems of oppression. It is an approach that requires historical as well as literary research, that has to focus on contextuality as well as textuality.

But reading texts in relation to social contexts may not quite be enough. Cora Kaplan's important collection of essays, *Seachanges* (1986), is remarkable for the ways in which she seeks to combine social and psychological/psychoanalytical perspectives, so that a politicised criticism could also account for the illogicality of human responses to texts. Material conditions have psychic effects: feminist literary theory has to account for both. It has to be able to say, argues Kaplan, why one can be an intelligent grown woman with impeccable feminist politics and still like to read 'trashy' romance novels, commodity fiction that makes no real claim of literariness or value, fiction, indeed, that is overtly hostile to one's consciously held beliefs. A Marxist-feminist critique cannot concentrate on the content of books; it cannot only be interested in the economic networks that make book production possible for some and impossible for others. Kaplan describes with glee and also embarrassment her readings of Margaret Mitchell's *Gone with Wind* and Colleen McCullough's *The Thorn-Birds*, neither of which are 'respectable' from either the point of view of Marxist-feminism or of liberal humanist definitions of 'literature'. She explains her attraction to these texts in terms of her context: an adolescent in the gender-repressive 1950s who also lived in a liberal, left-wing household. She could feel herself being called to ape the models of femininity that society provided for her, and her attraction to them was at least in part because such slavish conformity to lipstick and petticoats was actually also an act of rebellion against her progressive parents. In addition, the block-buster romance, with its hundreds of pages and cast of thousands 'invite[s] ... the female reader to identify across sexual difference and to engage with narrative fantasy from a variety of subject positions and at various levels'. A novel like *The Thorn-Birds* 'confirms not a conventional femininity but women's contradictory and ambiguous place within sexual difference' (120). Kaplan speaks of identifying with both male and female characters, of imagining herself in different times, places, classes and genders. It may be politically-conservative commodity fiction: but readers do not always read the obvious content and do not always buy the 'proper' political message. For Kaplan, in other words, approaches to literature have to deal with the pleasure of the reading subject in the commodity of the text. That requires a psychic as well as a social analysis. Oppression and repression are not separate spheres.

There is always another side, always ... widening the view

Kaplan's guilty pleasure is a pleasure that I have shared, though in my case, the book also has a claim to literary value within the traditional academy: Charlotte Brontë's *Jane Eyre*. I read it first when I was ten, the same age as the heroine when the book opens. And although I cannot claim equivalence between Jane's childhood and my own, I decided there and then that she and I were soul sisters, both of us hideously oppressed (in my case, only by the relative powerlessness of childhood, not by any 'real' structure of oppression – no one ever threw a book at me, and I was always faintly disappointed by this since it meant I had no consequent necessity to develop Jane's heroism); both of us far more significant and attractive personalities than anyone else had noticed; both of us cleverer and nicer than our peers; both prepared to put up with many tribulations; both of us ready for and deserving of the inevitable happy ending with our ugly-duckling prince charming. I do not suppose for a moment that this is a unique experience. Indeed, *Jane Eyre*, with its structural similarities to the fairy story is probably a common transitional text for girls moving between childhood and puberty towards ... whatever the endpoint is. It's a guilty pleasure I continue to indulge, having reread the book probably around once a year since that first reading, in the beginning for pleasure, increasingly now for work (though pleasure is still part of it).

Like the narrator of *Middlemarch*, despite all the important differences between them, Jane Eyre's narrative voice speaks as one individual in conversation with another – her reader. Her experience validated mine. But as time went on guilt became attached to pleasure because it became increasingly evident to me that Jane's wonderful success in life was bought at the expense of the lives of all the other women in the text. The bad Reed family, mother and sisters, are disposed of, as is Jane's putative rival for Rochester's affections, Blanche Ingram. The foolish but harmless Adèle Varens, Rochester's daughter from an illicit liaison, is sent to school to have her nasty French ways trained out of her. Mrs Fairfax is sent into retirement. Rosamund Oliver is left disappointed in her love for St. John Rivers and fades from the story. Even the more positive figures that Jane has met have no part in the triumph of her story: Miss Temple and the Rivers sisters are happily married off, and in the process they are cut off from Jane. Helen Burns dies. It is as though there is only the space for one bourgeois liberal-individual woman's triumph in this society.

Most spectacularly, Jane's success is a function of the utter defeat of Bertha Rochester Mason, who is killed as she leaps from the tenements of Thornfield Hall, trying to escape from the fire that she has herself set. Because for Jane happiness equals Rochester, she can only achieve happiness if Bertha is dead. Chillingly, for all the apparent perfection of her future life with her husband, Jane's freedom is thus built on the mangled body of her predecessor, as well as on Rochester's mutilation. Moreover, the text presents this outcome as both inevitable and desirable, because Jane's insistent narrative voice so invades the consciousness of the reader that any other ending than the one that satisfies her desire to be happy is unthinkable.[7] Naive readings of the novel, such as my first readings were, never notice this, never dignify the other women in the text with a consciousness and individuality that equal Jane's. Indeed, many very sophisticated readings take Jane's point of view as the only view of significance in the text. As Gayatri Chakravorty Spivak has noted, there is a tendency to take Jane for a real person, rather than as an ideologically constructed character operating within a very specific set of literary conventions and historical circumstances. Marxist critics might concentrate, therefore, on her anomalous social position as a governess; and feminist critics, anxious to assert the significance of Jane's subjectivity, read the text as a psychological parable in which Bertha functions only as Jane's dark double. The text operates by making the reader into Jane's accomplice, and to do this it requires us to see Jane as an individual like ourselves (Spivak in Gates 1986, 262–7). We forget therefore the uncomfortable underlying facts (facts of class as well as of gender, of the history of imperialism as well as the history of the individual) that make Jane's position what it is, and we take her at her own assessment of herself.

In other words, one of the fundamental problems attendant on a literary critique grounded on material conditions of the individual is that such a critique permits us – encourages us, even – to forget that the individual does not arise naturally as a function of 'human nature', but that the meaning of the individual is historically and culturally specific, created out of material conditions, and is a construction rather than a naturally occurring phenomenon. Because the individual in the fiction appears to be more or less 'like us', questioning that construction is tantamount to questioning our own motivations. In the case of *Jane Eyre*, we take a sample of one, Jane herself, and use her as the evidence for unquestioning support of our own extra-textual norms. If we question Jane, we question the basis of our certainities about our own identities, and we are forced to confront some rather uncomfortable questions about our own position. What are we saying if we say that we are happy when Jane marries Rochester? That we sanction her triumph even though it depends on another woman's grisly death? That we do not care about that death much because we have not recognised that other woman as human? That even in a book so clearly dedicated to one version of feminism, victory for one woman necessitates defeat for another? What price sisterly solidarity now? No wonder my 'pleasure' is 'guilty'.

As Rosemary Hennessy comprehensively argues in *Materialist Feminism and the Politics of Discourse* (1993), a narrow version of materialist feminism, one that talks about equal-rights legislation for women in the West for example, is inadequate as a model. Hennessy's book is very dense and theoretically sophisticated, using models from Marxist and post-Marxist theories alongside psychoanalysis to mount a critique of conventional materialist positions, and to suggest ways in which materialist ideas can be used in feminist thinking. Her focus is not primarily literary, but political. But because literature is one of the privileged discourses in political formations her commentary is very useful for thinking about the ways in which texts call their readers into unquestioning allegiances to particular points of view. In the case of *Jane Eyre*, one of the reasons that the novel has been so often discussed in feminist literary criticism and theory is that it appears to announce a possible female victory under the restrictive and related conditions of patriarchy, capitalism and imperialism. The costs of Jane's victory are disguised. But the logic of imperialism in the nineteenth century, like the logic of the capitalist global economy of today, suggests that there must be connections between the comfort and privilege of (some) Western women (and men) that are largely borne by women (and men) in other places. At its most basic, I can buy mangetout in the supermarket all year round because suppliers in Africa have put aside their own more immediate need for food in order to supply a cash crop. My varied diet is supported by the low wages paid to African workers and by the inequality of economic conditions between Western Europe and South West Africa. The problem is thus both individual and systemic. My privilege is subsidised by the labour of African women. I know this; I'm often ashamed of it; and yet – there is still mangetout, airfreighted from Zambia, in my fridge because, bourgeois liberal individual as I am, the systems in which I live do not encourage me to look too closely at the whole picture.

The literary sphere, argues Hennessy, is connected to these economic conditions in part because literature is very often a representation of reality; it represents the economic sphere, though it often does so implicitly rather than explicitly. Moreover, literature is also a commodity within that self-same economic system, a circulating discourse, just as mangetout is a circulating product. The literary text with its claims to transcendence likes to pretend that it has no real truck with capitalism, just as I like to pretend that I am not implicated in a global economy that exploits other people's labour and disrupts their cultures and ecologies. The radical requirement of Hennessy's book is that we need to start to examine more closely those networks of social, economic and cultural relations. To understand their forma-tion is a prerequisite for changing them; and the goal for all kinds of feminisms must be the liberation of all women, not just the ones we happen to know, who live nearby, or who share our views of selfhood, not just the ones who appear to be like us.

Jean Rhys's 1966 novel *Wide Sargasso Sea* provides a striking example of tracking the relations – both economic and personal – between one character's triumph and another's defeat. The novel tells the story of Bertha Mason Rochester, largely from her point of view. It takes Bertha's ending as written by Charlotte Brontë as a 'given'. The reader knows from the outset that Bertha, now known by her 'real name', Antoinette Cosway, will set fire to Thornfield House, and will die leaping from the roof. In the sense that the ending has already been written, over a century before, then, it is inevitable. But the telling of the story from Antoinette's perspective demonstrates that her madness and death are not inevitable in other terms. Her life might well have turned out differently, had circumstances been differ-ent, and her death becomes a tragedy, not the supplementary neces-sity in someone else's plot. In *Jane Eyre*, Bertha's story is one of tainted heredity; she is 'the true daughter of an infamous mother' (Brontë 1996, 345) who inevitably inherits her mother's madness. *Wide Sargasso Sea* rebukes the trusting reader of the earlier narrative. As Antoinette tells Rochester, 'There is always another side, always' (Rhys 1985, 106).

The very structure of Rhys's novel implies that different discourses intersect in the making of subjects and of lives. The novel has three parts, the first narrated by Antoinette Cosway, the second by Rochester (though he remains unnamed in the text), and the third again by Antoinette. This structure dramatises the fact that the impe-rialist project was a two-way process in which both coloniser and colonised were materially affected by exposure to the other. Although it is a story about imperialism, however, its emphasis is not primarily on the relationships between White imperialists and their Black victims. Antoinette Cosway is white, 'a Creole of pure English descent', and she is therefore a racially suitable mate for Rochester. But she is also a native of the Caribbean, and is therefore culturally unsuited to him. As her Black servant, Christophine, tells Rochester,

Antoinette will not be satisfied with him because 'she is Creole girl, and she have the sun in her' (130). Consequently, she lives a life based on feeling, and has no understanding of the abstract concepts with which Rochester orders his world – law, justice, measured time mean nothing to her. But her version of the world, if Rochester would only listen to her 'side', would provide a useful corrective to his cold certainties. The novel offers not only a critique of *Jane Eyre*, but also a critique of the whole perspective of realist narrative which cannot admit that there is always another way of seeing things, that there are many subject positions that might have equally significant views but which nonetheless realism excises from its 'authorised' version of the truth. There is a sense in which Antoinette is neither quite white nor black, and her existence shows that the process of seeing things in black and white with which Jane's narrative presented us, is dangerously prescriptive and inaccurate: a blinkered view, not a clear one.

The materialist experience of living in one place as opposed to another is one way in which a subject position might begin to be formed. But the problem that the novel addresses is that it is highly likely that any individual will take the evidence of her own specific subject position as evidence for universal laws. On their wedding day, Antoinette and Rochester discuss where they come from – England and the Caribbean, and cannot reconcile the two at all:

> 'Is it true,' she said, 'that England is like a dream? Because one of my friends who married an Englishman wrote and told me so. She said this place London is like a cold dark dream sometimes. I want to wake up.'
> 'Well,' I answered, annoyed, 'that is precisely how your beautiful island seems to me, quite unreal and like a dream.'
> 'But how can rivers and mountains and the sea be unreal?'
> 'And how can millions of people, their houses and their streets be unreal?'
> 'More easily,' she said, 'much more easily. Yes a big city must be like a dream.'
> 'No this is unreal and like a dream,' I thought. (67)

These two perspectives cannot meet, in part because they cannot see the other side, in part because the power relations between the couple are so unequal. In law (that dangerous abstraction),[8] Rochester owns all Antoinette's property and has complete control over her person. Why would he want to modify his own perspective when the view he already has is what sustains his power? By the end of the novel, Antoinette's only resistance to his point of view is to insist that Thornfield is a 'cardboard house where I walk at night', and to refuse to believe that it is in England (148). England is a dream built on paper: no wonder it burns so easily.

For all its interest in dreamscapes and the chimerical nature of reality, however, the novel is nonetheless founded on rationalist and materialist explanations of how Antoinette Cosway came to be Rochester's mad wife Bertha. For Rhys, the story arises out the historical specificity of the aftermath of the abolition of slavery in the Caribbean. Slavery was certainly wrong. But those who had owned slaves were often financially ruined by its abolition. It is not easy to feel sympathy for the slave-owners, but the loss of caste and property is nonetheless the immediate context of Antoinette's mother's descent into insanity, and Annette is presented as a figure worthy of sympathy. The Cosway family are forced to live with the very natural hostility of the Black population whom they had once owned. They have no money with which to leave, or buy protection; they have no contacts or friends. Both Annette and her daughter are lonely and isolated and afraid. The simmering resentment of the former slaves only spills over into overt violence when the family fortunes are restored by Annette's marriage to Mr Mason. Now they are no longer among the dispossessed, no longer 'white niggers', and resentment grows until a mob attacks their home, setting it on fire, killing Antoinette's younger brother, and driving her mother to a degraded insanity in which she is abused by her keepers. It is this insanity that Antoinette will relive when she is rejected by Rochester. But she goes mad not because she is the 'infamous daughter of an infamous mother', as he calls her, but because she has lived through many of the same experiences as her mother, has lived with the aftermath of the abolition of slavery and the deadly logic of imperialism. Finally she has lost the apparent security of Rochester's love. She becomes mad from a combination of causes, in other words, including the material and social deprivations of her childhood, the betrayal of her friends and family, the failure of her husband to try to understand her, and his decision to take revenge on her for what he perceives as the trickery of his marriage. Had any of the links in this chain of cause and effect been broken, Antoinette need not have become Bertha.

As Rosemary Hennessy argues:

> the discourse of political equality is often unevenly articulated within one social formation, empowering some women at the expense of others, and ... the systemic workings of power are invariably not dismantled by campaigns aimed solely at the redistribution of political liberties. (Hennessy 1993, 26)

If the power relations between the West and the rest of the world remain intact, to put the same point in reverse, Jane's campaign for personal liberty will always be at the expense of Bertha Mason/Antoinette Cosway, and indeed, at the cost of Christophine, Amélie and Hilda, the women who service Antoinette's existence. The materialist analysis that Hennessy advocates requires the political commitment to uncover systemic injustice in our favoured narratives; it also – perhaps even more radically – requires the reader continually to question her own position in relation to the systems she discusses. By uncovering the buried stories of material oppression, Hennessy suggests, we diagnose the problems and begin the process of finding solutions. But when we face towards others, we must also rethink and reassess the materiality of our own existences, presumably with the goal of changing ourselves as well as the systems. This is a materialist feminism that takes the position of the individual (bourgeois and liberal, or otherwise) and the systems in which individuals function equally seriously. It is, perhaps, utopian. But it certainly provides us with tools to examine the relationships between oppression and what is/is not expressed.

Notes

1. For a more thorough investigation of the term 'ideology' in relation to materialist readings of literature, see Moyra Haslett's *Marxist Literary and Cultural Theory*, London: Macmillan, 1999. In addition James Decker's forthcoming book *Ideology* (London: Macmillan) provides a very useful explanatory discussion of the term.
2. Dorothea, for example is consistently compared with St Theresa of Avila, an epic figure who founded and reformed religious orders, and who found a suitable outlet for her gifts in the religious life. This comparison is itself also ironic; Eliot suggests that a figure like St

Theresa, living in contemporary England, would probably be something of a pain in the neck to live with in ordinary life. This self-
conscious irony, however, does not quite extend to the view of
Dorothea's material privileges.

3.   'Lady' is a designation of class as well as of gender. From the context in
     A Vindication, Wollstonecraft sees the lady as one who is outside the
     realm of economic necessity. Middle-class women, she argues, are
     more in touch with reality, because although they are not in actual
     material want, they nonetheless have 'useful' work to do in the sphere
     of the home (where the work of the lady's home is delegated to
     servants), and sometimes they may also be involved in their
     husband's/father's business. This version of the middle class is very
     probably derived from the mercantile classes, the authors and benefi-
     ciaries of the individualism that Williams argues arose side by side with
     capitalism. At later points in history, 'lady' will mean other things.

4.   In fact, the *Fiction* is packed with incident. Mary loses first her brother,
     whose death makes her an heiress, and therefore a person of some
     importance; next she loses her mother, having first married an
     unwanted suitor at her mother's deathbed. The husband conveniently
     disappears onto the continent to pursue his education. Her family is
     finally wiped out by the death of her father. She has a very close
     emotional friendship with Ann, a poor girl from the neighbourhood
     who suffers from consumption. On acceding to her fortune, and having
     gained her husband's permission, she takes Ann to Portugal for her
     health, where Ann eventually dies, having tested Mary's faith in her to
     the limit. Mary also falls in love with another man, Henry, while in
     Portugal. Their relationship remains platonic, and when they return to
     England, Henry also dies of consumption, leaving Mary alone, awaiting
     death. So, whilst there are no incidents in the sense of a traditional plot,
     where action begets action, there are lots of incidents.

5.   When I was on holiday in Egypt some years ago, the profoundest
     culture shock I suffered came from the realisation that most of the chil-
     dren I met begging wanted neither money nor food; they wanted pens
     and paper. What was/is for me a small investment was/is for them a
     wild aspiration towards the luxurious necessity of education.

6.   For a detailed exposition of Marxist approaches to literature, see Moyra
     Haslett's *Marxist Literary and Cultural Theories* .

7.   In fact, it is not quite unthinkable. Jeanette Winterson's *Oranges Are Not
     the Only Fruit* (1985, London: Vintage, 1991) has a striking rewriting of the
     novel at its centre. The heroine's mother, a zealous Evangelical Christian,
     rewrites the ending of Jane Eyre so that Jane does not return to Rochester,
     but marries St. John Rivers and becomes a missionary in India.

8. As Gayatri Spivak points out, when Antoinette is taken to England and is
    visited by her brother, she attacks him when he tells her that he cannot
    interfere legally between husband and wife. The word 'legally', which
    represents a lying abstraction, makes Antoinette mad. See Gayatri
    Chakravorty Spivak, 'Three Women's Texts and a Critique of
    Imperialism' in Henry Louis Gates, Jr. (ed), *"Race", Writing and
    Difference*, Chicago: University of Chicago Press, 1986, pp. 262–280, p.
    269 and Jean Rhys, *Wide Sargasso Sea* [1966], Harmondsworth:
    Penguin, 1985, p. 150.

2   Images of Women Criticism

In a world ordered by sexual imbalance, pleasure in looking has been split between active/male and passive/female. The determining male gaze projects its fantasy onto the female figure, which is styled accordingly. In their traditional exhibitionist role women are simultaneously looked at and displayed, with their appearance coded for strong visual and erotic impact so that they can be said to connote *looked-at-ness*. Woman displayed as sexual object is the *leitmotif* of erotic spectacle: from pin-ups to strip-tease, from Ziegfeld to Busby Berkeley, she holds the look, and plays to and signifies male desire.

Laura Mulvey, 'Visual Pleasure and Narrative Cinema'

Woman becomes plant, panther, diamond, mother-of-pearl, by blending flowers, furs, jewels, shells, feathers, with her body; she perfumes herself to spread an aroma of the lily and the rose. But feathers, silk, pearls and perfumes serve also to hide the animal crudity of her flesh, her odour. She paints her mouth and her cheeks to give them the solid fixity of a mask; her glance she imprisons deep in kohl and mascara, it is no more than the iridescent ornament of her eyes; her hair, braided, curled, shaped, loses its disquieting plant-like mystery.

In woman dressed and adorned, nature is present but under restraint, by human will remoulded nearer to man's desire. A woman is rendered more desirable to the extent that nature is more highly developed in her and more rigorously confined: it is the 'sophisticated' woman who has always been the ideal erotic object.

Simone de Beauvoir, *The Second Sex*

Given, as I've already suggested, that the word 'theory' derives from a root that has to do with looking and spectacle, it should perhaps come as no surprise that modern feminist literary theory began as a critique of images, and began especially as a critique of the stereotypical images of femininity that literary texts present. One of the things that Simone de Beauvoir's comments above suggest is that woman is the object of obsessive looking (usually, but not exclusively, she is looked at by men). By extension, one might also say that woman has had to be concerned with her own image, has had to spend time looking at herself and at other women to see whether or not she measures up. She looks at herself because her cultural value is bound up in her looks, her image. This concentration on images of femininity, however, is potentially destructive. It limits the female subject to the status of object; and it makes ideal images that are not often congruent with reality, into powerful ideological tools for the control of women who have been devalued if they do not have 'good' looks; and devalued, too, as surface over content, as brainless but lovely, vain fools, if they are too concerned with image. In other words, the image is one of the places in which the double bind of proper femininity can be seen at work: woman is damned if she does, and damned if she doesn't pay attention to her look, to her image, to how she looks and how she is seen.

And if literature is one of the privileged sites of representation, if the images presented in literary and artistic texts are powerful because of the power accorded to literature, images of women are an obvious starting point to begin a critique of the place of women in society at large. Representation is not the same thing as reality, which is, of course, part of the problem. It might also be seen, however, as a part of the solution. The analysis of literary representations of women and their differences from real women's lives might well be a fruitful place to begin a politicised analysis of that reality, through the means of representation. Furthermore, representation might not be the same thing as reality, but it is a part of reality. The images we see or read about are part of the context in which we live. If we can read these images differently, against the grain, as it were, we can go some way to altering our perceptions of reality, we can see a need for change: and when we have seen the need, perhaps we can bring it about.

For Mary Wollstonecraft, the prevalence of misconceived representations of women as meek, obedient, passive and pretty, was an evil because such representations had real effects in the development of real women's lives. Her criticism of the literary representation of femininity was firmly placed in a wider political context: representation was part of the larger picture. This emphasis on the troubled relationships between images and realities has remained a significant feature of feminist criticism. More than a hundred years after Wollstonecraft's *Vindication*, for example, Viriginia Woolf, began to make similar points. She took as the apotheosis of femininity the female wife-figure from Coventry Patmore's poem *The Angel in the House* (1854–62). Patmore's poem speaks of the impossibility of expressing woman's true perfection in words:

> No mystery of well-woven speech,
>> No simplest phrase of tenderest fall,
> No liken'd excellence can reach
>> Her, the most excellent of all ...
> For she's so subtly, simply sweet,
>> My deepest rapture does her wrong.
>
> 'The Paragon', ll. 24–36

Nonetheless, he has no higher wish than to 'live her laureate all my life', and in the writing of his poem, he seeks to have an effect on the world beyond the text:

> I'll teach how noble man should be
>> To match with such a lovely mate;
> And then in her may move the more
>> The woman's wish to be desired,
> (By praise increased,) till both shall soar,
>> With blissful emulations fired.
>
> 'The Paragon', ll. 43–8

His apparent inability to fix and define feminine perfection in poetry is no bar to his sense that his poems might teach both men and women to emulate his own version of the ideal. But the positions of male and female readers and their aspirations are very different. Man must learn to be worthy of female perfection; woman must learn to be more desired and more desirable. Woman's own desires have no place here. Her position is certainly that of a docile and dependent figure, although Patmore could not quite say so even in his 'deepest rapture.'

Like Mary Wollstonecraft, Virginia Woolf remarked on and disapproved of the incapacitating effects of such docile images on the woman who aspired to be a writer, something that Patmore's Angel would never have sanctioned as an appropriate role for a woman.[1]

The terms of Woolf's hatred for the Angel precisely mirror Wollstonecraft's criticism of Rousseau's image of idealised woman-hood, though her suggested remedy is more violent and self-assertive. Woolf knew that she had to kill the Angel in the House if she were to enjoy any career of her own – though her narrative throws some doubt on whether she actually succeeded in suppressing the mode of life that the Angel represented:

> [The Angel in the House] was intensely sympathetic. She was immensely charming. She was utterly unselfish. She excelled in the difficult arts of family life. She sacrificed herself daily. ... [S]he was so constituted that she never had a mind or a wish of her own, but preferred to sympathise always with the minds and wishes of others. ... And directly I came to write I encountered her with the very first words. ... Directly ... I took my pen in my hand ... she slipped behind me and whispered: 'My dear, you are a young woman. ... Be sympathetic; be tender; flatter; deceive; use all the arts and wiles of our sex. Never let anybody guess that you have a mind of your own.' (Woolf 1993a, 102–3)

This particular image demonstrates the extent of women's interpellation into constructed ideas about gender.[2] Woolf's murderous fantasy ('She died hard. Her fictitious nature was of great assistance to her. It is far harder to kill a phantom than a reality' [103]) shows how insidious ideal femininity can be: it appears to be sympathetic and charming – usually positive terms, supposedly virtues to which women should aspire. At the same time, as Wollstonecraft also noted, this version of femininity is hypocritical, dishonest, deceptive. It twists a woman's mind.

The image has also mattered a great deal *inside* works of literature by women where the critique of the ideology of idealised femininity has often been a significant part of the plot in poetry and novels. Charlotte Brontë, for example, deliberately chose women who were not conventionally attractive as her heroines in *Jane Eyre* (1847) and *Villette* (1851). Her point is that the emphasis in fiction on physical attractiveness need not imply that a plain woman cannot be interesting and attractive in other ways. Of Jane Eyre, she wrote, 'I will show you a heroine as small and plain as myself who shall be as interesting as any' extant heroine in fiction. Jane indeed represents herself as a 'Governess, disconnected, poor and plain' in contrast to the portrait of an 'accomplished lady' she sets herself to paint when she fears that she is becoming presumptuous in her attraction to Rochester. The images of the governess and the lady are supposed to act for her as lessons in humility, in knowing her own place which is defined by her apparent lack of physical attractions (Brontë 1996, 183–4). The novel itself, of course, belies the supposed message of this lesson in feminine submission and humility for the plain woman, since it is Jane who marries Rochester in the end, not the accomplished beauty, Lady Blanche.

Images of women serve an even more didactic purpose in *Villette*, when Lucy Snowe ventures out alone and attends Villette's art gallery, where she muses on the meanings of the representations of femininity that she sees there. The first picture she sees is one which represents Cleopatra in voluptuous half-undress. Lucy's disapproval of this image is presented as being practical and also funny: Cleopatra's image is unrealistic, it does not match the reality of women's bodies and women's lives that she has observed. Cleopatra is painted as larger than life, semi-nude despite the 'seven-and-twenty-yards' of material in which she is draped, reclining on a sofa ('why, it would be difficult to say; broad daylight blazed around her'), and surrounded by scattered objects (pots and pans, Lucy calls them, before modifying her remark to 'vases and goblets, I should say') that suggest that she is a poor housekeeper with no proper sense of tidiness (Brontë 1979, 275). The picture, she thinks, is indecent; Cleopatra is excessive, larger than life, extremely well fed, and like no woman that Lucy has ever seen in either physique or apparent temperament.

Her thoughts on this picture are interrupted by the arrival of M. Paul, who will one day be her lover. M. Paul does not want her to look at the picture of Cleopatra because it might put sexual ideas into her head. (He is also shocked, by the way, that she has wandered the town alone, without a male chaperone, suggesting the practical limitations that proper femininity might impose on a woman in the mid-nineteenth century.) He moves her on to examine pictures of women that seem to him to be more in keeping with what a woman should know of her sex. He shows her a set of pictures entitled 'La vie d'une femme' (the life of a woman). Lucy, however, objects to these four images of proper femininity with more indignation and less good humour than she showed in responding to the Cleopatra:

> They were painted ... in a remarkable style – flat, dead, pale and
> formal. The first represented a 'Jeune Fille,' coming out of a church-

door, a missal in her hand, her dress very prim, her eyes cast down, her mouth pursed up – the image of a most villainous little precocious she-hypocrite. The second, a 'Mariée' with a long white veil, kneeling at a prie-dieu in her chamber, holding her hands plastered together, finger to finger, and showing the whites of her eyes in a most exasperating manner. The third, a 'Jeune Mère,' hanging disconsolate over a clayey and puffy baby, with a face like an unwholesome full moon. The fourth, a 'Veuve,' being a black woman holding by the hand a little black girl, and the twain studiously surveying an elegant French monument, set up in the corner of some Père La Chaise. All these four 'Anges' were grim and gray as burglars, and cold and vapid as ghosts. What women to live with! insincere, ill-humoured, bloodless, brainless nonentities! As bad in their way as the indolent gipsy-giantess, the Cleopatra, in hers. (277–8)[3]

As with the Cleopatra, Lucy objects to these pictures on both aesthetic and moral grounds. The quality of the painting is one problem, and its 'flat, dead, pale and formal' lines imply also something of her response to the content of the pieces. These are didactic pieces, deemed by M. Paul as appropriate images to present to a young lady: indeed he instructs Lucy to sit and observe them until someone should come and chaperone her back home, as though these pious pictures will keep her pure by their very nature. The pictures of a woman's life emphasise piety, domesticity and dependence, qualities that Lucy clearly neither has nor wishes to have.

These images all depend on the woman's supposed relationship with the male. The absent male figure to whose love the young girl aspires, who marries the young wife, fathers the young mother's baby and dies leaving the widow, suggests the extent to which femininity is supposed to exist only in terms of its dependent relationships with the male. His presence is deathly, imaged in his metonymic presence/absence in the funeral monument. He hems in and frames femininity and creates it in his own ideal image. Like Wollstonecraft and Woolf, Brontë presents us with a critique of images of women that are based on hypocrisy, vapidity and stupidity. The various pictures represent the angels in opposition to the whore Cleopatra whose overflowing sexuality also disgusts Lucy Snowe. But the story she makes these pictures tell is about her resistance to being framed into these images of the either/or of femininity. She seeks a third way. She is called by these images, and she rejects the interpellation into the roles they depict.

The pictures that Lucy Snowe sees are not merely literary representations of pictorial art. The four images that make up 'La vie d'une
femme' had their real counterparts in mid-nineteenth-century painting, as Lynda Nead has shown, and these 'real' pictures were powerful
ideological tools. In *Myths of Sexuality*, Nead discusses a triptych of
paintings by George Elgar Hicks, entitled *Woman's Mission*, which
were exhibited in 1863 in the Royal Academy exhibition in London.
The paintings depict in turn a woman in her roles as *Guide to
Childhood* (a woman guides a child along a wooded path),
Companion to Manhood (the same woman supports her husband
when he has received bad news, though she also signals her dependency by leaning on him) and *Comfort of Old Age* (she ministers to her
sick father). Woman's mission, that is, is entirely bound up with her
familial role as mother, wife, and daughter. As such, they appear to
typify Victorian views about proper femininity:

> *Woman's Mission* re-forms and re-works already familiar moral
> values and social relationships; it invites its audience to make a moral
> as well as an aesthetic judgement – to recognise the truthfulness of
> this representation of femininity and to approve of its picturing of
> female virtue ... it would appear that Hicks's picture is a straightfor-
> ward confirmation of bourgeois definitions of respectable femininity.
> (Nead 1988, 14)

These images are, in other words, a direct call to the banner of proper
femininity. But as Nead goes on to show, contemporary responses to
these images were not necessarily positive, and reviews of the exhibition even criticised Hicks's pictures for their vulgarity, sentimentality
and emphasis on 'millinery' and furnishings. Nead suggests that one
reason for hostility towards such images in some sections of the press
was that 'the definition of respectable femininity was far from
resolved; the ideal of "woman's mission" was frequently contested
and this instability posed a potential problem for any representation
of the contemporary woman in high art' (16). The single idealised
version of a woman's life was undermined by the multiplicity of realities of real women's lives.

The point that I want to derive from this brief excursion into nineteenth-century art and literature is that images are not simple
messages transmitted between canvas or text and viewer or reader.
We may each respond very differently to a given image. And it would

be naive to assume that because a given set of images exist or were once prevalent, that they map easily onto either the experiences of real women's lives, or onto their own sense of what they should strive to be or to become. Admittedly, Lucy Snowe is a somewhat unusual character; but her responses to the 'brainless nonentities' represented in 'La vie d'une femme' are presented by the text as common-sense responses that any intelligent woman might share. Images, I repeat, are not quite the same thing as reality. 'Looking' is after all, an ambiguous concept. The way a woman looks might mean either a description of her own appearance, or a description of her act of looking at others; the two kinds of looking might even be modified by each other. As such, the images at which one looks can be simultaneously both a call towards or a warning against a particular way of looking ('La vie d'une femme' versus Cleopatra), and an opportunity to look differently, to criticise or refuse that look in favour of another way of looking.

The ways we looked – then

The early feminist classics of the post-war era, like Simone de Beauvoir's *The Second Sex* (1949), and of the 1960s such as Mary Ellmann's *Thinking About Women* (1968) and Kate Millett's *Sexual Politics* (1969), though very different kinds of book, all share a commitment to pursuing the image as a way of analysing the ideological force of literature, and as a method for pursuing political analyses in the worlds beyond the text.

De Beauvoir's *Second Sex* is a thoroughgoing politicised discussion of the place of women in society and culture. Her discussion is extremely wide-ranging as a sample of chapter titles suggests. She writes of biology, psychoanalysis, history, literature, politics, myth, of 'woman's life today', of the various roles of women from childhood to marriage to maternity and old age, and she ends by positing a future for the 'independent woman'. Her argument begins from the premise that there is no natural reason why women should be regarded – or should regard themselves – as inferior to men in society. That in almost every known society women are seen as lesser beings is a function not of nature but of a mode of thought in which Man is taken as the norm and the ideal, and Woman is his defining 'other', the being who validates his importance because of her differences from him.

humanity is male and man defines woman not in herself but as relative to him; she is not regarded as an autonomous being. ... she is
simply what man decrees; thus she is called 'the sex', by which is
meant that she appears to the male as a sexual being. For him she is
sex – absolute sex, no less. She is defined and differentiated with
reference to man and not he with reference to her; she is the incidental, the inessential as opposed to his essential. He is the Subject, the
Absolute – she is the Other. (de Beauvoir 1997, 16)

This kind of thinking has, however, to be understood as a habit rather
than as a fact of life. De Beauvoir suggests that it is more difficult for
women to analyse their own situation because they are dispersed
through society, and they therefore have very little sense of themselves as an alienated, oppressed group. Unlike the Jew in the anti-
Semitic culture, or the Black man in the racist society, or the worker in
a hierarchical capitalist system, women are not oppressed into a
geographical ghetto which makes their oppression visible, and this
makes it more difficult to recognise the terms of their oppression
since they are without a strong sense of either individual or collective
subjectivity:

> Proletarians say 'We'; Negroes also. Regarding themselves as subjects,
> they transform the bourgeois, the whites, into 'others'. But women do
> not say 'We', except at some congress of feminists or similar formal
> demonstration; men say 'women', and women use the same word in
> referring to themselves. ... women lack concrete means for organizing
> themselves into a unit which can stand face to face with the correla-
> tive unit. They have no past, no history, no religion of their own; and
> they have no such solidarity of work and interest as that of the prole-
> tariat. ... They live dispersed among the males, attached through resi-
> dence, housework, economic condition, and social standing to
> certain men – fathers or husbands – more firmly than they are to
> other women. If they belong to the bourgeoisie, they feel solidarity
> with men of that class, not with proletarian women; if they are white,
> their allegiance is to white men, not to Negro women. (19)

Passages such as this suggest the complexity of de Beauvoir's argument, where a concept such as subjectivity – apparently a personal,
even private, sense of selfhood – is shown to stand in an important
relation to communal politics, to public life, and to ideas such as
history, religion, work, race and class.

For de Beauvoir, representation, whether it be the representation of the self to the self on a private, individual basis, or whether it is how one represents or is represented in or by a larger social group, is crucially bound up with subjectivity. If women do not see themselves as subjects, either individually or communally, they are robbed of the ability to represent themselves. In *The Second Sex*, the image of woman comes from outside her. Woman is a myth, an object of male fantasy created out the minds of male subjects who represent her as it suits their purposes, as objects within their fantasies (174–5). As such, femininity is a profoundly contradictory state. It is the apotheosis of both nature and culture, as the epigraph to this chapter suggests, in its evocation of the superabundance of apparently natural supplements which make up the cultured body of the sophisticated woman who is the erotic ideal of male fantasy. It is precisely the contradictions in the edifice of femininity which deny women individuated subjectivity, since the subject is supposed to exist as self-consistent and coherent. Thus a subject who inhabits contradictions is not quite a subject at all. This, de Beauvoir suggests, is the technique of 'othering', of rendering someone as 'other'. Patriarchal thought has created an incoherent version of femininity, in which the women who live it are trapped, and for which they are blamed. Their 'nature' is culturally constructed; but the construction is disguised – and, after all, nature is precisely the thing that one cannot change.

In her readings of 'The Myth of Woman in Five Authors', de Beauvoir writes about five male writers and their various evocations of femininity in fiction and poetry. For Montherlant, woman is a danger; the Eternal Feminine is a threat to virile masculinity. For D. H. Lawrence, both men and women are 'animal' – but woman is somehow more 'animal' than man, and is the willing object of his phallic animality. In the works of Claudel, Woman is a mass of contradictions: she is at once the dangerous siren who brought about the Fall from the Garden of Eden, but she is also a figure of redemption who brings about the possibility of Heaven. For Breton, woman is a concrete figure who represents the abstractions of poetry and love, but who has no subjectivity of her own. And for Stendhal, women are 'flesh and blood' (268), and are to be understood in relation to the social limitations placed on them, not as abstracted figures in an imaginary landscape. Of all the writers, Stendhal's view is to be preferred since it 'presupposes that woman is not pure alterity: she is subject in her own right. ... he gives [his heroines] a destiny of their own'. Her conclusion from these discussions is, unsurprisingly, that the majority of male writers recreate woman in their own image. She is presented as Other to the 'self' that they privilege: 'When he describes woman, each writer discloses his general ethics and the special idea he has of himself' (282). And she objects to the majority of these representations because they are not realistic, because they say more about the male writer than about Woman or women, and because they insist on constituting femininity as the mystery which foregrounds the knowability and coherence of male selfhood – this despite the fact that each man 'still needs to learn more fully what *he* is' (277, my emphasis). Woman's mysteriousness and inconsistency relieves the male writer from having to recognise woman's humanity and subjectivity. The image of women – in life as well as in literature – de Beauvoir suggests, is man-made; and it is less a representation of reality than the icon of an unrealisable ideal.

The Second Sex is a classic and important book because of its insistent connection of apparently disparate ideas. Politics and literature, history and anthropology, sociology and culture are shown to be part of a network which contribute to the making of meanings about women. No single aspect of life is isolated; everything is presented as interdependent: the personal *is* political, as the feminist slogan of the 1970s was to put it. This process of thinking through the connections between discourses is possibly the most important legacy of de Beauvoir's text to subsequent generations of feminist readers and thinkers.

Like de Beauvoir, Ellmann's book *Thinking About Women* pursues the image relentlessly as the articulation of what she sees as an untenable sexual analogy in which the supposedly natural relationships between men and women and relative positions of the sexes permeate every aspect of life. The sexual analogy refers primarily to the idea that superior male physical strength and the prolonged nurturing role of women in the bearing of children are metaphors for every human action, even when these 'facts' have no apparent bearing on the matter in hand. Given the 'natural' facts of physiology, Ellmann ironically suggests that:

> [a]n utterly practical (though not an ideal) society would be one in which these facts were of such importance that all men and women were totally absorbed in their demonstration – that is, in the use of strength and the completion of pregnancies. Both sexes would live

without intermissions in which to recognise their own monotony. (Ellmann 1968, 2)

In other words, if the sexual analogy really held true – if women were mere childbearing machines, and men were simply physically strong – the whole of society would revolve around war and reproduction: childbearing would have as its sole function the supply of more soldiers. Given that this is not actually the case in the Western societies to which Ellmann limits her observations, the views that derive from this analogy must be stereotypes, images which reproduce and are themselves reproduced by a false sexual analogy.

Ellmann's focus is primarily on literary texts (which are a relatively small part of *The Second Sex*), and she announces that she will focus on 'women as *words* – as the words they pull out of people's mouths' (xv). Her assumption seems to be that the words that the idea of 'woman' produces are themselves the product of lazy stereotypical thinking, a laziness she seeks to expose and deflate. She considers a number of stereotypes of femininity as they appear in contemporary (1950s and 1960s) fiction. These include: formlessness, instability, confinement, piety, materiality, spirituality, irrationality and compliancy; she ends her discussion with a focus on two 'incorrigible stereotypes' of the feminine, the shrew and the witch.

The book is wonderfully funny in its demolition of the logic of the sexual analogy as it is dramatised by these stereotypes. For example, Ellmann mocks the assumption that image and substance are the same thing by mounting an attack on the view that regards women's bodies as softer and rounder than those of men: 'soft body, soft mind' is the analogy, but what have bodies actually got to do with brains? (74). Or, elsewhere, her discussion of piety disentangles the argument that women are more likely to be pious than men because they are less intellectually curious or able: 'To prove this stereotype [of piety], religions must work like washing machines: men construct them and women run them. To found a religion is inventive, but to keep its rules is pious' (93). In other words, women are socially constructed to concentrate on immediate duty, whilst men are licensed to search for variety and excitement. The limitations placed on women are socially constructed, but although they are trapped by these limitations, women also show themselves to be socially responsible. After all, if no one runs the washing machine, then the male adventurer will have to be inventive in dirty smalls. The tone of the text is elusive and ironic.

Ellmann does not state her objections directly – indeed one might even go so far as to suggest that she is 'ladylike'. Rather than become the stereotype of the shrew in her objections to the sexual status quo, she juxtaposes incongruous images and allows the reader to make up her own mind: the result is bewitching, though not witch-like or monstrous (terms very often used against clever women). Piety, for example, she suggests, is a mainstay of fiction, without which 'we would lose that store of short stories and novels which faithfully and regularly bring our attention to women's special vulnerability to religious enthusiasm'. This appears a gentle statement, but look at the words in which she writes: 'faithfully' is a word that ironically registers a *male* author's piety, as well as that of the female character; 'regularly' implies that the male author is not nearly so inventive as he would like to claim. She does not say that the loss of such a 'store' of fiction would be a great loss, indeed rather implies that the world might be better for it, since this store is so full of stock notions. Her parting shot on piety is that in robust male writing, 'the Henry Miller solution is standard: if the woman is nubile, she can be redeemed from piety by copulation' (94–5). The juxtaposition of redemption and copulation suggests, but does not quite state, that she does not think much of either, and that Henry Miller is hardly to be viewed as a good example.

This is image criticism of a very sophisticated kind. Ellmann takes the examples she has uncovered, and uses them as the springboard for a critical but also creative performance of her own. *Thinking About Women* exemplifies extremely careful writing and its poise and irony unsettle the reader's certainties. It is a text that probes the connections between nature and culture, between sex as biology and gender as behaviour determined by social rules. Indeed, it uses those rules against the grain. Ellmann's prose is 'feminine' in that it is elegant and poised,[4] strangely well-mannered considering its revolutionary implications. It is moreover possible to read it 'straight', to miss its irony, so that like a revolutionary feminist version of Woolf's Angel in the House, it flatters to deceive. It treads a fine line, and not all 'images of women' criticism has such suppleness and subtlety.

Thinking About Women is a short book which created little stir when it was first published. In Janet Todd's words, it 'mocked assertive masculine criticism' and found 'female experience in a kind of *style* rather than in the choice of peculiar experience' (Todd 1988, 21, my emphasis). In other words it is a very 'literary' book, taking literature as its subject, and reading literature through the medium of a style inflected by literature. In contrast, Todd reads Kate Millett's *Sexual Politics* as a 'socio-historical' text, which takes literature as source material for a hypothesis about the relationships between the sexes in the non-literary world from the late-nineteenth century to the present. Millett assumed that literature was 'mimesis', a relatively transparent reflection of life as it is lived; and she used this assumption to develop an idea of gender 'as a culturally acquired sexual identity, not a natural given, as women had been hoodwinked into thinking' (Todd 1988, 22). And *Sexual Politics* became a 'World Best-seller' as a red banner on my edition announces. Compared to Ellmann's book, it caused a massive stir, and it probably did so for two related reasons. It is a sensationalist book which focuses primarily on the sex scenes of a number of male-authored texts; and it is an angry book, which is infuriated by the misogynistic images of women it finds in these scenes. In other words, both its tone and its content are a vigorous assault on conventional ways of thinking about literature, and they found a new way of thinking about women.

In the Introduction, I suggested that literature is often defined as a kind of 'polite' writing, 'fine' writing; a correlative of that view of literature is that literary criticism is supposed equally to be polite and in some sense 'objective'. Millett's criticism upsets these positions in its insistence that literature is often not polite at all, and her criticism takes place in a tone of outrage at the material that is being presented under the guise of 'literature'. Her first chapter exemplifies her rhetorical strategies; she extracts three sexually explicit passages from novels by Norman Mailer, Henry Miller and Jean Genet on which she comments in order to demonstrate that there is some relationship in all three writers between sex and power. Her argument is that the apparently private sexual relationships between men and women (or between macho and feminised males in the case of Genet) 'can scarcely be said to take place in a vacuum'. In defining what she means by sexual politics, she broadens the definition of the political away from merely meaning party-political or governmental structures, to a meaning which refers 'to power-structured relationships, arrangements whereby one group of persons is controlled by another' (Millett 1977, 22). In other words, she shifts definitions of power and politics towards the private and personal sphere, as well as considering politics in terms of its more public manifestations. In examining sexually graphic excerpts from novels, Millett connects the assumptions that regulate apparently private activity with the assumptions that govern the wider world. Her move from literary text to real world can be criticised as under-theorised (how are the text and the world related?); but the book's importance, as Toril Moi notes, is in its insistence that 'social and cultural contexts must be studied if literature was to be properly understood, a view she shares with all later feminist critics regardless of their otherwise differing interests', and in its proposal that the (woman) reader's point of view had equal value to the male author's supposed intentions (Moi 1985, 24).

Sexual Politics, like both *The Second Sex* and *Thinking About Women*, concentrates its attention on writing by men. The images of women in sexual relationships that Millett uncovers are images inflected by her sense of the inequality of power in these relationships: the women are largely seen as passive and helpless in the clutches of the strong male lovers/writers, who control both the sexual encounters and the points of view from which they are written. Millett is angry about these repeated representations which she sees as perpetuating a misognynistic patriarchy; but because the images of which she disapproves are repeated, so are her arguments. The book depends on a rhetoric of anger at least as much as it depends on argument. Moreover, Millett decisively rejected psychoanalytic theory as a tool with any value for feminism, seeing Freud's works as simply another foundation for the edifice of patriarchy. Because of this rejection, it is not possible for her to account for the ways in which women, both as beings in the world and as readers of literary texts, can be called into the roles that she sees as so degrading. There are, after all, women readers who enjoy the works of Mailer, Lawrence and Miller. How can that happen when, for example, Henry Miller merely expresses: 'the yearning to effect a complete depersonalisation of woman into cunt, a game sexuality of cheap exploitation, a childish fantasy of power untroubled by the reality of persons or the complexity of dealing with fellow human beings and, finally, a rude species of evacuation hardly better than anal in character' (Millett 1977, 313)? *Sexual Politics* is an important book because it spotted a certain set of stereotypes, because it tried to explain those stereotypes, because it insistently placed literary texts in social and historical contexts, and because it championed the woman reader. But feminist literary criticism and theory still had more to do than the models offered by de Beauvoir, Ellmann and Millett.

Looking again at looking

As Toril Moi argues, certain types of image criticism are bound to lead to a critical dead end. She takes as her example a collection of essays edited by Susan Koppelman Cornillon, and entitled *Images of Women in Fiction: Feminist Perspectives*, first published in 1972. This volume contained 21 essays about various nineteenth- and twentieth-century male and female writers. The book is important, as Moi suggests, because of its influence on a whole generation of American college graduates for whom it defined what might be meant by a feminist perspective on literature. The definition it offered had certain key assumptions: that literature is supposed to be a more or less unmediated reflection of life; that experience and fictional representation ought to map onto each other; and that the purpose of literature for the (woman) reader is to find her own experience replicated in the fictional world – she should be able to 'identify' with the characters in the books she reads. These are also the assumptions that partially underlie the works of de Beauvoir (insofar as she deals with literature), Ellmann and Millett. But to limit feminist approaches to these ideas would lead, as Moi suggests, to a cul-de-sac. The critic would read a novel, look at its women characters and say either: 'that is accurate, it is like my life, this is a good book'; or, alternatively, 'that woman is like no one I've ever met, she's certainly not like me and this is a bad book because of it'. A literary criticism that relies only a 'reality test' has several potential problems. It could only be a repeated critical gesture, looking for the same things over and over again; the critic assumes that her own reality (if such a thing can be categorised), stands for a kind of universal reality; such a criticism does not itself lead to an analysis of the social context in which certain views about women came about; it offers little in the way of a political future – it does not attempt to answer the question of how the situation of real women might be changed for the better; and in its concentration on content, it forgets the literariness (the forms and languages) of the literary text (Moi 1985, 42–9).

This is not to say, however, that images of women are unimportant, nor that they cannot provide a focus for feminist theories of literature. On the contrary, looking at looking can be a fruitful exercise, depending on how it is done. Useful examples for feminist literary theory can be found in the fields of feminist art history and feminist cultural history, both of which are very much concerned with images of women, but which are also significantly focused on placing images in contexts, and on historicising representation. In their insistence that images of women are not autonomous, art and cultural historians have traced developments in ideas about representation. They show that ideal images of femininity have a history that maps onto cultural changes through time; the ideal is not then a fixed entity, timeless and immutable, but something that has changed through differing social and historical circumstances, and something, therefore, that can change again: perhaps this time through the agency of female subjects reclaiming their images for themselves.

I have already briefly mentioned Lynda Nead's important book on images of women in nineteenth-century art and literature, *Myths of Sexuality* (1988). Her method in this book is to examine the relationships between social constructions of femininity and its representation in the 'high' cultural spheres of paintings and literary texts in the context of more 'ephemeral' forms of contemporary writing such as journal and newspaper articles. The detailed historical research which is the foundation for this work enables her to demonstrate an historicised consciousness that complicates our contemporary view of the Victorian age. It is not simply the case that women were uniformly oppressed in the 1860s. Oppression took place, but would have been felt differently by different groups and individuals: working women had very different experiences from middle-class women. Indeed, when one looks closely at the context of art production in the period, one can discern the tensions and contradictions inherent in the separate spheres ideology of the period. The apparent dominance of one view of male female relations ('Man for the field, Woman for the hearth', as Tennyson put it), is belied by the raging debates current in the mid-century, that were taking place in contemporary journals, in political articles, in art criticism and in literary commentary. Those debates also find their way into the contradictory representations of women in books and pictures of the time. Nead demonstrates a relationship between text and context which moves in both directions: paintings, for example, helped to form artistic taste and political allegiances, but were themselves formed out of a radically unstable context. In the end, they did not create a homogenous audience, in which everyone more or less agreed that femininity was to be understood as 'this' and not 'that'. The complications thrown up by historicising our understanding of a particular period show the extent to which 'looking' at images is itself determined by context. It also suggests that we are ourselves historicised beings who may be looking for what we want to find, subject to our own contexts of looking.

Similarly, some of the works of cultural history produced by a writer like Marina Warner can help to politicise the image, and render looking more than something passive. In books such as *Alone of All Her Sex: The Myth and Cult of the Virgin Mary* (1976) and *Monuments and Maidens: The Allegory of the Female Form* (1985), Warner looked at ideal images of femininity as they have changed across time and place. Her argument in the latter book is that the prevalence of female forms to represent nations (Britannia, the Russian Motherland, the French *République*) and abstract nouns (Justice, Liberty, Freedom, Immortality, Democracy) is strangely at odds with the subordinate positions of real women in western and other cultures. As she ruefully notes, 'Liberty is not represented as a woman ... because women were or are free' (Warner 1985, xix–xx). Instead, the allegory of the female form is a kind of double-speak, a hypocritical raising of femininity onto a high pedestal that disguises women's real place in culture. Femininity may be an ideal, but real women are not. In diagnosing the distinctions to be drawn between image and actuality in different times and places, she shows us why we should not accept the space of the pedestal at face value. Indeed, idealising Woman may be little more than a confining strategy that judges and limits real women in relation to an impossible standard. The 'allegory of the female form' displaces the multiple realities of female forms, and tries to have us scrabbling after an image that we cannot replicate because we are too fat or too thin, to black, too muscular – too different. Once we know that it's a trick, once we have a diagnosis, we can see the images through different eyes, and stop listening to their siren calls. Well – if only...

The ways we look now?

It would be nice to think that images can no longer interpellate women into untenable roles or positions. It would be heartening to believe that the rigorous analysis of the image has freed the female viewer from the need to conform to the impossible. The real case is rather different and more complex than that. As non-literary books like Naomi Wolf's *The Beauty Myth* (1991) amply demonstrate, women are still called to ideal images, and still respond to the call.

Knowing that there is something wrong with an image does not necessarily mean that we are not attracted to it, not tempted by it. Because of the proliferation of images around us, from television, an expanded print media, from film and advertising hoardings, more than any previous generation, we can see what we are supposed to be: we are even sold the products that are alleged to enhance this image – advertisements in women's magazines are all about clothes, make-up, perfume and cosmetic surgery. Simone de Beauvoir's evocation of the eroticised female ideal, supplemented by fur, feathers, perfume and kohl, is still there: and we still buy it, or the products that promise that we can attain it. Image criticism has largely shifted away from discussions of the representations of women in literature, and focuses instead on the image-rich media. As Wolf suggests, we are living in a time of '"beauty pornography" – which for the first time in women's history artificially links a commodified "beauty" directly and explicitly to sexuality.' While many of the material battles of feminism – the vote, reproductive rights, equal pay, equal access to education – appear to have been 'won', at least partially, and only in Western countries, 'eating disorders rose exponentially, and cosmetic surgery became the fastest growing medical specialty' in the United States (10–11). The image obviously still matters.

It is probably unreasonable to expect that any theoretical approach to literature can bring about absolute changes in human conditions. And a critique that exposes a problem is still worth doing, even, it cannot change the world. It is a tool, a part of an ongoing process – not an answer in itself. What is still needed is a better explanation of how images produce their calls; and of why viewers continue to respond to them. Image criticism, if it is to retain its usefulness, needs to combine the ideas of psychoanalysis with the more materialist sociological views about why and how the image counts.

Notes

1. There are, of course, at least two kinds of image. There is the negative image which limits feminine sensibilities; and there is the 'positive' image, the role model, who imaginatively opens up alternative versions of female life which may then be taken up by women in the real world.
2. 'Interpellation' is a term derived from the writings of the Marxist thinker Louis Althusser. It literally means the process of being 'called into' a

particular set of social conventions and beliefs. Althusser does not simply argue, however, that people are called and that they respond unproblematically to the call. Rather, he suggests that whilst interpellation is a powerful tool of social control, people nonetheless have some capacity to resist insistent conformity. For more information on this, see Moyra Haslett's *Marxist Literary and Cultural Theories*, London: Macmillan, 1999.

3.   The four women in turn are a young girl ('jeune fille'), a bride (mariée), a young mother ('jeune mère') and a widow ('veuve'). The use of the word 'anges' (angels) is clearly ironic.

4.   This is, of course, a very dangerous thing to say. But I mean 'feminine', not female – indeed ladylike, the term I used earlier, might be a better word. I'm obliged to qualify my position because of Toril Moi's strictures on the ways in which Ellmann's book has been read. In *Sexual/Textual Politics*, Moi argues that to see *Thinking About Women* as 'feminine' is to fall into exactly the trap of 'ad feminam' criticism, fuelled by the sexual analogy, that Ellmann is attacking. It's a fair point, given that Patricia Mayer Spacks, the critic Moi cites as saying that Ellmann has developed a technique of 'feminine elusiveness', does not differentiate between femininity and femaleness. When I say 'feminine' though, it is in the light of the argument that there is a distinction between sex and gender. It seems to me that Ellmann has very deliberately adopted the mask of a particular version of femininity in order at once to disguise and to express her views. Her femininity is a kind of masquerade, a performance, that defuses criticism (we cannot say she is a bitter old harridan) whilst still allowing her to make her point. In other words, femininity need not just be a trap; it can be creatively harnessed for subversive effect. See Toril Moi, *Sexual/Textual Politics: Feminist Literary Theory*, London: Methuen, 1985, 31–41, and Patricia Mayer Spacks, *The Female Imaginaion: A Literary and Psychological Investigation of Women's Writings*, London: George Allen and Unwin, 1976.

3 The Woman as Writer: Forging Female Traditions

At its most naive, image criticism leaves feminist literary theory at an impasse. It is very noticeable that all of Millett's and de Beauvoir's main literary case studies, and a large majority of Ellmann's examples, were taken from male-authored texts. They noticed the dishonesty of the images, but their works did not interrogate the *literary quality* of the models they examined. There was no question that the works of Lawrence or de Montherlant or Mailer deserved to be read *as* literature. While each of the three feminist critics mounted a critique of the *content* of the works they described, they did not suggest that women readers might be better off reading the works of female writers in the hope of finding 'better' content. Their works thus risked merely reiterating that men do not write well or accurately about women. They did not, in other words, expand the canon of works that are supposed to be worth reading to texts authored by women. Why not?

The answers are many. For de Beauvoir, in particular, literature was not her main focus after all, and she can hardly be blamed for not taking a revisionist attitude to the question of the meaning of literariness. But fundamentally, the problem for women writing in the 1940s and at the end of the 1960s about literary texts was that what 'counted' as literature was an inherited concept, derived from humanist and New Critical traditions of Great Britain and the United States. The emphasis was on the inherent qualities of literature, which were presented as being self-evident to any attentive reader. Western Europe had its canon of 'great' writers, to whose glories the sensitive reader was attuned. As Terry Eagleton puts it, the humanist critics and the New Critics established a map of English literature 'from which criticism has never quite recovered ... "English" included two and a half women, counting Emily Brontë as a marginal case; almost all of its authors were conservatives' (Eagleton 1996, 28). Not to put too fine a point on it, Ellmann and Millett belonged to a generation for whom women did not write literature – or rather, only very exceptionally were they admitted to write literature, if they were women such as Jane Austen, George Eliot, and, 'exceptionally', Emily Brontë. In order to write about women writers, and remain respectable as critics, a new definition of literature was going to have to be established. 'English'[1] needed a new map. On top of that, it requires a different conception of the practice of criticism to take the sex of the author into consideration. Image criticism emphasises the reader's interpretation; as such it represents a creative threat to the autonomy of the text, which can no longer be said simply to pass down a transparent meaning to its audience. Moreover, it unsettled the assumption that the reader was 'man', that generic category of humanity that is supposed to include women, but often radically excludes them. By positing a woman-reader image criticism offers a new point of view. But it does not inherently threaten the status of the literary text as a special kind of writing, as important, as having a certain 'quality' that defines its literariness. If, on the other hand, we are encouraged to read a text simply because it is by a woman, what might we end up reading? There's no guarantee that it will be 'literature', that it will have those ineffable qualities which have defined literature since around, say, the early nineteenth century, when many of the key assumptions about literariness were articulated by Romantic theorists such as Wordsworth, Coleridge, Hazlitt and Lamb.

Now, it would not be true to say that no one wrote about women's novels or plays before 1970; but it was rare that the woman writer was treated *as a woman writer* (unless the term was used pejoratively) or that she was placed in the supportive context of other women writers, rather than always being measured up against the men. The uncovering of a women's tradition in literature offered the opportunity to locate the significance of 'literature' elsewhere. It suggests that instead of being 'sensitive' readers, we might choose to be politicised readers. Instead of looking for value in the autonomous text, we could search out new values in a contexualised historicised text. Indeed, we might even ask whether the study of literature needs a concept of value at all.

The 'problem' of quality

> Silly Novels by Lady Novelists are a genus with many species, determined by the particular quality of silliness that predominates in them

– the frothy, the prosy, the pious, or the pedantic. But it is a mixture of all of these – a composite order of feminine fatuity, that produces the largest class of such novels, which we shall distinguish as the *mind-and-millinery* species. The heroine is usually an heiress, probably a peeress in her own right, with perhaps a vicious baronet, an amiable duke, and an irresistible younger son of a marquis as lovers in the foreground, a clergyman and a poet sighing for her in the middle distance, and a crowd of undefined adorers dimly indicated beyond. Her eyes and her wit are both dazzling; her nose and her morals are alike free from any tendency to irregularity; she has a superb *contralto* and superb intellect; she is perfectly well-dressed and perfectly religious; she dances like a sylph, and reads the Bible in the original tongues. (Eliot 1990, 140)

These words appeared anonymously under the title 'Silly Novels by Lady Novelists' in the *Westminster Review* in October, 1856. The anonymity was merely a journalistic convention of the time – most articles were unsigned during most of the nineteenth century. The original readers of the article, unless they were somehow 'in the know', would have assumed that it had been written by a man, since most articles in journals would have been assumed to have been written by men, though anonymity could, of course, have masked a woman's voice as much as a man's. In this case, though, the tone of the piece is deliberately constructed to imply male authorship. The two terms 'silly novels' and 'lady novelists' suggest infallible masculine judgement. The objections to such texts, their piety or pedantry,[2] their focus on hats, the unrealistic attainments of the heroine, and the proliferation of unlikely lovers who pine at her feet, conspire to suggest that no man would write such a thing as a *mind-and-millinery* novel. Moreover, since such novels are allegedly specifically aimed at a female audience, an audience which presumable enjoys their escapist fantasy, the seriousness of the critique of such silly novels tends to presume male authorship.

These words were, however, written by a woman, albeit a woman who went to great lengths to disguise her gender at the beginning of her novel-writing career, under the conspicuously masculine pseudonym, George Eliot. The article is not exactly a sisterly gesture on the face of it, though Eliot does go on to argue that plain-speaking criticism will result in improvements in women's writing; and that undeserved panegyrics are as dangerous to female literary achievements as critical indifference and hostility. And while the article ends with the exhortation that women writers must think before they write, Eliot also suggests that women can (and, indeed, already do) achieve at the highest level in the writing of fiction:

> Fiction is a department of literature in which women can, *after their kind*, fully equal men. A cluster of great names ... rush to our memories in evidence that women can produce novels not only fine, but among the very finest ... No educational restrictions can shut women out from the materials of fiction, and there is no species of art which is so free from rigid requirements. (162, my emphasis)

The novel, relatively speaking a 'new' genre, was something that anyone who knew how to write could, in theory, write: it did not require a classical education and women could write novel fiction because its content was the content of their own lives. Eliot's warning is against the assumption that knowledge of life constitutes a knowledge of how to write about life – technique in fiction matters just as much as technique in playing the piano, she argues. But the phrase that seems important here is 'after their kind'. Women write in their own way, achieve in their own way. They 'fully equal men', but they are different from them because of different opportunities for the observation of life, because of different educational experiences, because of sexual (and/or gendered) differences.

Two consequences follow on from Eliot's view that women write after their kind, though equal in quality to men. First: the critic who seeks to consider texts largely or exclusively by women writers will find differences in the kinds of writing produced by women when they are compared to writings by men, who presumably also write 'after *their* kind'. Eliot's comments imply, that is, that women writers share feminine content or feminine coding in their works. This femininity of writing is the quality that the feminist critic of women's writing might seek out and analyse. Second: if writing exhibits femininity as opposed to masculinity, the critic may well be required to define different criteria of value in women's writing from those that are supposed to inhere in male writing of the so-called Great Tradition. In this way a concentration on women's writing might be expected to call into question assumptions that have traditionally defined the category of literature as a whole. Thus might the canon of important works be expanded to include rather more than the two and a half women identified by Eagleton; indeed, thus might the very idea of a canon of great writing be called into question. If images of women criticism opened up a space for the woman reader to interpret texts from a politicised position, reading women's writing potentially gives reader and writer a more equal stake in interpretation in relation to the issue of gender. Most radically of all, it permitted women readers to claim literary qualities for texts by women that might otherwise have been dismissed.

In an important essay first published in 1979, entitled 'Towards a Feminist Poetics', Elaine Showalter surveyed the current state of play in academic literary criticism's response to feminist interventions. She suggested (with considerable corroboratory evidence) that universities and academic journals had been very hostile towards feminist criticism. On the one hand, it was attacked (usually by men) as phallus-obsessed and insufficiently academically or theoretically grounded; on the other, it was attacked by activist feminists outside the universities precisely for being too theoretical and insufficiently political. Showalter's essay does not, in fact, seek to answer either objection in this double bind (feminist criticism is not academic, feminist criticism is too academic). Instead, she sets out to describe possible practices for feminist criticism, of which she argues that there are two basic kinds:

> The first type is concerned with *woman as reader* – with woman as the consumer of male-produced literature, and with the way in which the hypothesis of a female reader changes our apprehension of a given text, awakening us to the significance of its sexual codes. I shall call this kind of analysis *feminist critique* ... Its subjects include images and stereotypes of women in literature, the omissions of and misconceptions about women in criticism, and the fissures in male-constructed literary history. (in Showalter 1986, 128)

This is the kind of criticism that I have already designated as 'images of women criticism'. Showalter argues that although feminist critique is powerful and necessary in diagnosing what we might call 'the woman problem',[3] it has two basic difficulties: it is 'male-oriented' because it focuses particularly on the representation of women by men; and, more importantly, it has 'a tendency to naturalize women's victimization by making it the inevitable and obsessive topic of discussion', and it therefore comes dangerously close to being 'a celebration of victimization, the seduction *of* betrayal' (130–1).[4]

In contrast, she advocates that academic feminism could concentrate its energies on writing by women, on '*the woman as writer*'. The focus would then be on:

> woman as the producer of textual meaning, with the history, genres and structures of literature by women. Its subjects include the psychodynamics of female creativity; linguistics and the problem of female language; the trajectory of the individual or collective female literary career; literary history; and, of course, studies of particular writers and works. (128)

To describe this new discipline in literary studies, Showalter coined the term 'gynocritics' (a word she derives from the French language, meaning criticism about women and by women). Gynocritics, she argued, 'begins at the point when we free ourselves from the linear absolutes of male literary history, stop trying to fit women between the lines of male tradition, and focus instead on the newly visible world of female culture' (131). This is George Eliot's point – that women write 'after their kind', and that they write as well as men, but differently from men – rewritten in different terms. The problem that gynocritics set itself, then, was to invent or to discover an alternative but coexisting literary tradition for women writers. This would be a tradition in which the values of feminine culture and female biology (the early critics did not distinguish rigorously between gender and sex) could be explored and valued on their own terms, and with as little reference as possible to pre-existing male traditions, since such references would represent a dependency on men and on male approval that feminist criticism needed to resist.

Early makers of female traditions: Patricia Mayer Spacks and Ellen Moers

One of the first writers to attempt to map a specifically female literary tradition was Patricia Mayer Spacks. Her book *The Female Imagination: A Literary and Psychological Investigation of Women's Writing* was first published in 1972. The stated aim of the book was find out whether there were aspects of women's writing that were trans-historical – that remained as constants despite the vagaries of time, history, geography, or social class. Spacks set out to 'look for evidence of sharing, [to] seek persistent ways of feeling, [to] discover patterns of self-depiction that survive the vagaries of change ... to investigate how women use their creativity to reveal and combat their characteristic difficulties' (Spacks 1976, 3). And she began with the assumption that such evidence *would* exist: 'there appears to be something that we might call a woman's point of view – except that that sounds like a column in the *Ladies Home Journal* – a vague enough phenomenon, doubtless the result of social conditioning, but an outlook sufficiently distinct to be recognisable through the centuries'. Since men and women 'represent separate cultures', it is reasonable to assume that a twentieth-century woman writer such as Doris Lessing will have more in common with an eighteenth-century writer such as Lady Mary Wortley Montagu than either writer is likely to have with 'a male writer even from her own time and space in history' (4–5).[5] The assumption is that women do indeed write *after their kind*, and that their *kind* produces identifiable patterns of gendered difference.

There are problems with some of Spacks's assumptions, and I will return to them at the end of the chapter. But one of the things that is most interesting in the text is Spacks's method of investigation. In the preface, she writes that not only is she trying to find a female tradition of writing, but she is also interested in how the problems of the woman as writer affect the woman reader. This claim is dramatised throughout the book by constant references to the responses to texts from the female college students that she has taught. Often the students are not saying anything particularly profound; instead, they are responding very personally to the texts, empathising with characters and situations, discussing what they would do if similarly placed, trying to analyse how they feel when they read about a given heroine. The text juxtaposes these often naive, but nonetheless heartfelt responses, with the measured, academic musings of Spacks herself. Those student voices are a kind of revolutionary gesture in *The Female Imagination*. Their opinions are valued, given space in a serious published work, making the individual untheorised, uncritical response important in the academic field of literary criticism. Spacks's book focuses on the woman writer, but her method dramatises the ways in which readers and writers are related through the texts that the one writes and that the other consumes.

The book itself examines a range of different kinds of text. It opens with a discussion of the current state of feminist thinking about literature, and provides readings of Virginia Woolf's *A Room of One's Own*, Simone de Beauvoir's *Second Sex*, Ellmann's *Thinking About Women* and Millett's *Sexual Politics*, to suggest that woman-centred criticism[6] often finds itself in various double binds which dis-able its effectiveness. Woolf, for example, disapproved of female anger in literature and criticism, seeing it as a distortion of her measured, controlled aesthetic sense; she moves towards an ideal of androgyny which is not quite, suggests Spacks, what a *female* tradition might need. De Beauvoir's method is seen as playing the men at their own game by amassing vast heaps of scholarly evidence in support of her argument. In doing so, however, her impersonation of a masculine mode risks excising femininity completely. Ellmann's technique is that of ladylike irony: it is devastating as a critique if the reader sees the irony, but elusive and impotent if she does not. Spacks then moves on to Millett, of whose method she strongly disapproves, feeling that her polemic outweighed her judgement. Millett's anger provoked anger, and was widely read, but it generated more heat than light and was of relatively little service in thinking through the features of a female tradition. The implication is that there needs to be a new method for woman-centred criticism, a method that takes women seriously; which does not make women disappear into androgyny or masculinity, a criticism which is neither ladylike propriety nor unladylike fury.

The student responses are part of this new method. These are voices that are not usually heard, or rather, not heard as if they have anything important to say. When Spacks reads her various texts, she intersperses relatively traditional (if woman-centred) practical criticism with these other voices in an argument that is more accretive than explicit. She notes over and again how femininity – for characters in novels, for the women writers of novels and for the women readers of novels – is a double bind. In the next three chapters, 'Power and Passivity', 'Taking Care' and 'The Adolescent as Heroine', through commentaries largely on well-known books by nineteenth- and twentieth-century women writers, she demonstrates this. Passivity, for example, is to be understood as both attractive and dangerous to women (as characters, writers and readers). It is attractive because it provides a way in to power over men in marriage, since the proximity to men it grants to women is a prerequisite for manipulating them. On the other hand, it is also deceptive, and may not in fact produce the power it appears to promise, as say, Gwendolen Harleth (a major protagonist in George Eliot's *Daniel Deronda*) is to find out to her cost when she discovers that her husband has no intention of permitting her power in their marriage, indeed, intends rather to 'break' her, as a trainer breaks a horse. This passivity is very dangerous. Similarly, the femininity of adolescence is also double, and is acutely felt by young women as the choice between childishness and adulthood is played out. Spacks contrasts the ways in which the heroines of Jane Austen's novels (especially Elizabeth Bennet in *Pride and Prejudice*) achieve maturity, whereas many later writers (her examples are taken from Emily Brontë, Doris Lessing and Sylvia Plath) arrest their heroines' development and sink them into madness and/or death. She laments the fact that there is no female equivalent to James Joyce's *A Portrait of the Artist as a Young Man* (1916), or J. D. Salinger's *Catcher in the Rye* (1951), 'no literary work by a woman that *celebrates* female adolescence' (Spacks 1976, 157–8), because adolescence is more ambiguous for girls than for boys. Sex and sexual aspirations mean very different things for women and for men.

The next two chapters, 'The Artist as Woman' and 'Finger Posts', concentrate on women's autobiographies, a genre that had not received much critical attention at this period in the early 1970s. In these chapters Spacks invokes the double bind that women who claim the role of artist (for example, Isadora Duncan)[7] are unattractively self-centred, but women who live more ordinary lives see life as a service to others to such an extent that they abnegate their selves. They are 'finger posts' in that they point out the way for others (especially their children and husbands); they live through others in contrast to the woman artist who lives for herself. She concentrates on ideas of feminine propriety which make the woman artist a dangerous or monstrous figure in her egotism, and which simultaneously create ordinary women into vicarious and contingent beings who depend on others for their self-definition. There appears to be no middle course in the autobiographies of the Duchess of Newcastle (Margaret Cavendish, 1623–73), Mrs Thrale (1741–1821, Bluestocking friend of Fanny Burney and Samuel Johnson), Charlotte Perkins Gilman, feminist and activist, and Mabel Dodge Luhan, friend and financial sponsor of D. H. Lawrence. Spacks excavates the hidden anger about their social positions, displaced rather than expressed in their writings, and sees this displacement as a female strategy imposed by social constraints: anger cannot be expressed by any proper lady. Marriage, too, is a traditional limitation on women, and it too is a double bind, as Chapter Seven, 'The World Outside', demonstrates. Marriage appears to be a private contract between two people, but its attendant duties (hostessing, taste, taking care of children, guests and husbands) are all socially oriented and socially conditioned, leaving no space for the private individual woman. Across history, Spacks argues, women have chosen different solutions from men to the problems they live with because the problems themselves are different given the social set-up that prescribes such different lives for men and women.

Spacks's book is one example of a gynocritical method in action. A good fifteen years before Showalter attempted to define feminist poetics, Ellen Moers had also begun to write the essays that would eventually be collected into her gynocritical book, *Literary Women: The Great Writers* (first published in 1976). The book is very wide-ranging, describing writer's biographies, historical contexts, networks of literary influence (often in quite surprising places), the significance of finance in women's writing; it also elaborates a theory of the 'female gothic' which is both an explanation and a celebration of women writers' propensity to 'scare' their readers. The essays were written over a ten-year period, but what unites them, despite occasionally disparate subject matter, is their concentration on the woman as writer – 'gynocritics' before there was a word (at least in English) for it. Moers's introduction opens with the bold statement: 'The subject of this book is the major women writers, writers we shall always read, whether interested or not in the fact that they happened to be women' (Moers 1985, ix). The statement is bold because of its uncompromising assumption that great women writers do indeed exist. It is, of course, an old accusation thrown at feminists that women have produced neither a Shakespeare nor a Beethoven, that they are incapable of 'greatness'. Virginia Woolf, indeed, in *A Room of One's Own*, notably agreed that the bishop who said that women could not write the plays of Shakespeare was right, though she went on to suggest that this was not a congenital failure of femaleness, but a socially, educationally and economically constructed failure of the social constructions of femininity (Woolf 1993a, 42–5). But while Moers says unequivocally that great women writers exist, she is careful throughout the book never quite to align herself with any political feminist cause: the fact that these 'major women writers' 'happened to be women' is disarmingly presented as irrelevant to their greatness.

On the other hand, a little later in the introduction, Moers is

anxious to signal the importance of women writers being in the world
as women, and suggests that the fact of their sex is a matter that criticism might legitimately seek to consider:

> Being women, women writers have women's bodies, which affect
> their senses and their imagery. They are raised as girls, and thus have
> a special perception of the cultural imprinting of childhood. They are
> assigned roles in the family and in courtship, they are given or denied
> access to education and employment, they are regulated by laws of
> property and political representation which, absolutely in the past,
> partly today, differentiate women from men. If they denied their
> bodies, denied whatever was special about being a woman in their
> time and place, they would be only narrowly human and could hardly
> be much good as writers. (Moers 1985, xi)

In this passage, several ideas that will recur through the development
of feminist theory are brought together. Moers suggests that social
conditioning, legal, political and economic rights and the various
positions of women in the family and wider society, matter in the
formation of both women's humanity and their writing. More significantly, but less polemically, she also points to physical differences
between men and women, who because of their different bodies are
likely to perceive the world differently, and are therefore likely also to
represent it differently. The implication of the book as a whole, in its
juxtapositions of different themes and writers and strands of thought,
is that women's writing will reflect the social formations and biological givens of femininity and femaleness. There are links between
women writers *because* they are women, *Literary Women* suggests,
sexed as female, gendered as feminine.

Moers's examples, however, tend to suggest that female responses
to social and/or biological limitations are, in fact, very varied. It is the
social limitations that are shared by women (and they are a matter of
biography, how women have been made to live), rather than the
woman writer's responses to them (literary responses, what women
have chosen to write). Chapter One, for example, 'The Literary Life:
Some Representative Women', takes the French novelist George Sand
(1804–76, pseudonym of Aurore Dupin) and the English poet
Elizabeth Barrett Browning (1806–61) as women writers who represent two possible modes of life for women writers. Moers describes
how Barrett made a space for herself to write by retreating into a

convenient invalidism, 'a luxurious scholarly idleness', that allowed her to evade the feminine domestic responsibilities that would have taken away from her writing time (7). She closed her world to one room in her father's house, where she was utterly shielded from the mundane cares of housekeeping, and where her illness protected her from the social duty of receiving visitors. Her way of life was a virtual parody of the domesticity and dependency that characterised Victorian femininity: but it was an apparently submissive performance that had unexpectedly subversive results in that it produced a major poet who was also a woman. George Sand, on the other hand, could scarcely have led a more public life, a life she achieved by practising both a literal and a literary transvestism.[8] In contrast to Barrett's exaggerated physical debility, Sand was physically very strong, with an 'extraordinary physical robustness' that allowed her to live a full life during the day, to entertain her lovers in the evening, and to write her novels well into the night (12).[9] The point here is that these are quite contradictory ways of dealing with the 'problem' of being a woman writer in a constricted society. The examples are fascinating, but they do not demonstrate that the two writers in question shared anything but their sex and perhaps a certain deviousness.

Again, in Chapter Three, 'Women's Literary Traditions: The Individual Talent', Moers argues that networks of female influence, where one woman writer influences another, are not often direct. She writes that George Eliot's *Adam Bede* was written 'not because of what Jane Austen wrote but because of what she chose not to write' (51–2). The character of Adam Bede is Eliot's version of Robert Martin, the tenant farmer who loves Harriet Smith in Austen's *Emma*. Moers describes how Eliot breaks out of the highly cultivated but narrow fictional garden made by Austen, and is negatively inspired by her female precursor, reacting against her narrow aesthetic, implying that this is not so much a tradition of female writing as willed iconoclasm by Eliot. If Eliot and Austen belong to the same tradition, then, it is a tradition of disruption and reaction, not one of continuity or unquestioning obedience to a pre-existing standard: 'tradition', indeed, might not be quite the right word to describe this process.

Probably Moers's most influential point in *Literary Women* is her identification of one specific strand of a female tradition: she terms it 'the female Gothic' as it appeared in nineteenth-century fiction (and occasionally poetry) by women. Her definition of the female Gothic is bound up with a physical bodily response. She interestingly begins her discussion by quoting a description of a new-born baby from Benjamin Spock's influential book on child-care. This description, she quite rightly suggests, makes the child monstrous – scary because naked, pink, hairy and screaming. This emphasis on the 'monstrous body' is feminine in that women are generally closer to it than men because of the biology of maternity (they give birth to children, and they care for the monstrous infant); but they are also closer to it because of social constructions in which the female body is both idealised and demonised because of its proximity to unacculturated child. Women inhabit, that is, a body that is both fetishised as perfect and excoriated as vile. This ambivalent body informs Moers's definition of the female Gothic:

> what I mean ... by 'the Gothic' is not so easily stated except that it has to do with fear. In Gothic writings, fantasy predominates over reality, the strange over the commonplace, and the supernatural over the natural, with one definite authorial intent: to scare. Not, that is, to reach down to the depths of the soul and purge it with pity and terror (as we say tragedy does), but to get to the body itself, its glands, muscles, epidermis, and circulatory system, quickly arousing and quickly allaying the physiological reactions to fear. (70)

This concentration on the body is decisive for Moers in her thinking about the Gothic in general, and about the female Gothic in particular. This is not a cerebral literary mode; it doesn't make the reader think; it makes her feel physical sensation – it makes her flesh creep. In an age when female education was often inadequate, the high emotions of pity and fear produced by tragedy, were not available to women writers, just as the classical authors who taught pity and fear were closed books to them. But their bodies, their physical sensations, were available to them. So Moers reads the female Victorian gothic tradition inherited from Mary Shelley's *Frankenstein* (1818) as arising either from the feminine situation of domesticity and pregnancy, or from the feminine experience of sexual repression in which their bodies experienced desire in a social context where female desire was understood as monstrous. She argues that novels like Emily Brontë's *Wuthering Heights* (1847), or a poem such as Christina Rossetti's *Goblin Market* (1862), bear the mark of feminine domesticity experienced as both desire and terror. In particular, the domestic space of the nursery loomed large for Victorian women writers: 'it was the *only* heterosexual world that Victorian literary spinsters were ever freely and physically to explore' (105). It is represented as a time of innocent physicality, before the ravages of puberty absolutely separated male and female experiences, and it is represented with both passion and nostalgia. The fear that the female Gothic expresses is the fear of the unruly female adult body. For Moers, 'nothing separates female experience from male experience more sharply and more early in life, than the compulsion to visualize the self' (107). She suggests that visualising the self, especially through puberty, makes women peculiarly aware of their own potential for monstrosity. It is this potential that the female Gothic both articulates and displaces: the stories of the female Gothic tell of the fear, but keep it in the world of fiction, where fear is safe.

The importance of this argument is that it defines a female tradition as the result of both physiology and of cultural mores. Biology and sociology are the combined explanation of a strand in women's writing in the nineteenth century. Moers's discussion of the female Gothic fulfils many of the conditions of Showalter's gynocritics, with its emphasis on the woman writer, an analysis of the genre and structure of writing by women, the psychodynamics of the choice of that genre, and its attempt to map a history of a collective female literary career. But there is another focus to Moers's work. She concentrates explicitly on the woman as writer; but it is implicit that the *readers* of the texts of female Gothic are also women, who experience a pleasurable physical *frisson* when they read and are scared. After all, the same conditions of repression, poor education and domesticity apply to women readers as well as to women writers. There is an underlying belief here in the commonality of all women's experiences, whether they are writers or readers – or even characters. The commonality of female experience – a sisterhood of suffering – is perhaps an attractive proposition; but it is not without its problems, as we shall see later.

Developing the female tradition: Elaine Showalter, Sandra M. Gilbert and Susan Gubar

In 1977, Elaine Showalter produced her own gynocritical book, entitled *A Literature of their Own: British Women Novelists from Brontë to Lessing*. The title has two reference points. First, it is a quotation from

John Stuart Mill's 1869 essay, 'The Subjection of Women' in which Mill argues that women do not have a literature of their own because of the social situation that forces them to be either pale imitators of male writing, producing only pseudo-masculine writing which palls because of the paucity of their education and experience in comparison to the education and experience of their male models; and in addition, they have no literature of their own because women have to kow-tow to a male-defined view of appropriate matter and manner in their writing – there were so many things that a nice girl could not think about, let alone write about or publish in the late 1860s. Second, the title is an allusion to Virginia Woolf's 1929 essay *A Room of One's Own*, in which Woolf argues that a woman writer must have a certain level of income and a private space (the room of her own of the title) if she is to be able to write. The two sources of the title indicate the two points of emphasis in the book; the sense of a larger tradition into which a woman writer might place herself and against which she can measure her own achievement, and the individual, practical needs of the woman writer. Showalter sets out to investigate, that is, a larger historical narrative, and to place individual social and psychological situations into that larger context.

From that brief description, it is already clear that Showalter's book represents a development from the idea of tradition outlined by either Spacks or Moers. Rather than a trans-historical idea of the female imagination, *A Literature of their Own* is a more nearly historicist approach which identifies historical phases in women's writing: if Showalter describes various kinds of continuity, she also identifies historically specific changes in the kinds of writing that women produced between the 1840s and the 1970s. Broadly, she names these phases the feminine phase (from 1840 to the death of George Eliot in 1880), the feminist phase (from 1880–1920) and the female phase (from 1920 to the present, with a resurgence in the wake of second-wave feminism in the early 1960s). Instead, then, of seeing women as linked by sex, she pronounces herself 'uncomfortable with the notion of a "female imagination"' because it risks 'reiterating the familiar stereotypes' and suggests permanent deep differences between men and women in writing. And if the differences are permanent and sex-determined, then analysing them and describing them probably merely fixes them further. Instead, the emphasis here is 'not on an innate sexual attitude, but [on] the ways in which the self-awareness of the woman writer has translated itself into a literary form in a

specific place and time-span', suggesting the possibility of change
and development (Showalter 1978, 12). For if the differences between
men and women writers are culturally, historically, geographically
and socially constructed, they change through time and those
changes suggest something quite different from a fixed structure.
For Showalter, women constitute a sub-culture within literature in
much the same way as Black, Jewish, Anglo-Indian, Canadian or even
American writers began their existence as members of literary sub-
cultures in relation to a dominant literary mode (in this case the mode
favoured by the white, heterosexual, English male). Her three phases
of the female tradition – feminine, feminist, female – map onto the
three phases identified by the historians of other kinds of sub-culture:

> First, there is a prolonged phase of *imitation* of the prevailing modes
> of the dominant tradition, and *internalization* of its standards of art
> and its views on social roles. Second, there is a phase of *protest*
> against these standards and values, and *advocacy* of minority rights
> and values, including a demand for autonomy. Finally, there is a
> phase of *self-discovery*, a turning inward freed from some of the
> dependency of opposition, a search for identity. (13)

For women writing in the specific circumstances of Victorian England
and its long aftermath, the female sub-culture was characterised by
secrecy, in particular the secrecy of the physical experience of being a
woman – '[p]uberty, menstruation, sexual initiation, pregnancy,
childbirth and menopause – the entire female sexual cycle – constituted a habit of living that had to be concealed'. Women could not
write directly about these experiences, but they could encode them
into their texts for other women to notice and understand, as secret
markers of shared femininity, as a 'covert solidarity that sometimes
amounted to a genteel conspiracy' (15–16). The relationship of the
sexed body to the contingencies of a particular historical period and
its social mores is what Showalter tries to trace: sex and gender at
work together in forming modes of women's writing at different
times.

As well as her commitment to some kind of historicisation of
women's experience, though, Showalter's book also attempts to
widen the terms of the debate around women's writing and literary
quality. Spacks and Moers focused on writers who were more or less
accepted as writers of some limited literary quality, as the subtitle of

Literary Women – The Great Writers – attests. *A Literature of their Own*, although it concentrates on Charlotte Brontë, George Eliot, Mrs Gaskell, Dorothy Richardson and Virginia Woolf, already writers with established literary reputations, also opens its pages to the works of far less well-known women writers, in particular those of the mid-nineteenth century whose names had (at least in 1977) virtually vanished from serious discussion of nineteenth-century literature. There has been, notes Showalter, a tendency for women writers to disappear. Even those who were successful in their own times drop out of sight in the histories of literature, so that women writers have very often found themselves 'without a history, forced to rediscover the past anew, forging again and again the consciousness of their sex' (11–12). Trying to work out what might make a female tradition, therefore, involves historical excavation work which must include writers who seem to subsequent generations 'irreparably minor. And yet it is only by considering them all – Millicent Grogan as well as Virginia Woolf – that we can begin to record new choices in a new literary history, and to understand why, despite prejudice, despite guilt, despite inhibition, women began to write' (36). True to her word, she does indeed examine the works of forgotten women, tracing patterns and relationships between the so-called Great Tradition of Jane Austen, George Eliot and half a Brontë sister, and the writers of pot-boilers, best-sellers and prim religious tracts who were their contemporaries.

A Literature of their Own is a very important signpost book that attempts to offer a theory and a methodology for reading women's writing in its own terms. It does however have its blind spots. Probably the most important of the blindspots is the elision of differences between women, and the failure to see women as inhabiting sub-cultures within sub-cultures. When she sees women's writing as a literary sub-culture as equivalent to Black, Jewish, Canadian or American sub-cultures, she forgets that these sub-cultures are also made up of women: the Black or Jewish woman writer does not fit into the tradition that she forges, even though, like the white woman, these women are excluded from the traditions of their race. This is an important failing in the book to which I will return later.

Another of those blind spots relates to the issue of value in relation to any female tradition. In describing the novel *Lady Audley's Secret* (1861) by Mary Elizabeth Braddon (a forgotten novel in 1977, remembered now at least partly because of Showalter's championship),

Showalter saw it is a book that has been much underrated by twentieth-century critics:

> *Lady Audley's Secret*, though it is often brash and hasty, has been
> much underrated. It is not only a virtual manifesto of female sensa-
> tionalism,[10] but also a witty inversion of Victorian sentimental and
> domestic conventions, certainly equal to the work of Wilkie Collins
> and Charles Reade. In Braddon's novels generally, women take over
> the properties of the Byronic hero. The bigamist is no longer
> Rochester, but the demure little governess. Readers responded by
> making the novel one of the greatest successes in publishing history;
> there were eight editions in the first year alone, and it was never out
> of print in Braddon's lifetime. (164–5)

Braddon's book is clearly a text that Showalter has enjoyed, for all its
brashness and hastiness, which are presumably terms of disapproba-
tion. It was also a subversive book, undermining the ideal of proper
femininity in its treatment of 'the demure little governess' who is not
only a bigamist, but also a forger, an arsonist and a potential
murderer. *Lady Audley's Secret* can quite easily be read as a feminist
protest against the limitations placed on women; indeed, as
Showalter also notes, the physician who eventually commits Lady
Audley to a madhouse, argues that she is not mad – her actions are all
rational so that her real secret is 'that she is *sane*, and, moreover,
representative'. But the feminist protest of this book remains
disguised by the feminine proprieties that constrain the author. At the
end of the novel, Lady Audley is treated *as if* she were mad 'to spare
the woman reader the guilt of identifying with a cold-blooded killer'
(167). Moreover, the protest is also contained in a book that, for all its
'faults' in literary 'quality', is a rip-roaring, page-turning, good read.

In other words, *Lady Audley's Secret* has political content, but it is
not overt. Showalter clearly favours this 'disguise' of protest over
almost every production of the 'feminist phase' she discusses, in
which she argues that the protest *is* the fiction. In the feminist phase,
'[f]eminist ideology temporarily diverted attention from female experience to a cultist celebration of womanhood and motherhood'; '[t]he
high spirits and comic exuberance of the sensationalists were soon
submerged in the portentous anthems of the feminists' (181). There is
a clearly stated view in *A Literature of their Own* that political writing
is not literary writing, that protest overwhelms quality, and that it is

for this reason that the New Woman writers between 1880 and 1920 'have not fared well with posterity' (193–4). In her discussion of Olive Schreiner's 1883 novel *The Story of an African Farm*, she quotes George Moore's contemporary view of the book, that he had found in it 'more than he wanted to know about sandhills, ostriches and women, "but of art, nothing; that is to say, art as I understand it – rhythmical sequence of events described with rhythmical sequence of phrase"' (199). Moore's misogynist confusion of ostriches and women passes without comment, and Showalter endorses his view of 'art' as a kind of ineffable quality even as she uncovers a forgotten history of New Woman writing. In her introduction she laments that the Great Tradition has left its residue on English criticism and literary history; she is not quite untouched by its residual ideals of value and quality herself.

Only two years after the publication of *A Literature of their Own*, when Sandra M. Gilbert and Susan Gubar produced their massive and very influential tome *The Madwoman in the Attic: The Place of the Woman Writer in the Nineteenth-Century Literary Imagination*, the idea of a female tradition in writing was apparently secure. In their Preface, they cite the works of both Moers and Showalter as having established without doubt that 'nineteenth-century literary women *did* have both a literature and a culture of their own – that ... by the nineteenth century there was a rich and clearly defined female literary sub-culture, a community in which women consciously read and related to each other's works' (Gilbert and Gubar 1979, xii). *The Madwoman in the Attic* sets out to chart both the patterns of plot and metaphor in nineteenth-century women's writing and the psychological reasons for women's recurrent choices of certain images, stories and fantasies of escape, confinement and madness. Their theoretical impetus derives not only from Moers and Showalter, but also from the aggressively masculist critic Harold Bloom, in particular his 1973 book *The Anxiety of Influence*. Bloom's argument here is that writers situate themselves in a tradition through violent reactions against their literary forebears. A poet is validated by his (Bloom's examples are all male writers) hostile rewritings of the texts of the past. The male writer is always engaged in a quasi-Oedipal struggle with his literary fathers for supremacy and value. The terms of Bloom's book imply that poets are never women, that they have no mothers (either literal or figurative), no significant relationships with women as women, or with women as writers that their works have to address.

The Madwoman in the Attic adopts this virtually psychoanalytic model, but attempts to apply its logic to the position of the woman writer, who is clearly differently situated in relation to the 'family romance' that Bloom's masculinised idea of tradition suggests.[11] Gilbert and Gubar's text opens with the faintly shocking rhetorical question, 'Is the pen a metaphorical penis?' It answers the question with a quotation from a letter by Gerard Manley Hopkins, who 'seems to have thought so', writing that the artist's 'most essential quality':

> ... is masterly execution, which is a kind of male gift, and especially marks off men from women, the begetting of one's thoughts on paper, on [sic] verse, or whatever the matter is ... on better consideration it strikes me that the mastery I speak of is not so much in the mind as a puberty in the life of that quality. The male quality is the creative gift. (Hopkins, letter to R. W. Dixon, 1886, quoted in Gilbert and Gubar 1979, 3)

Gilbert and Gubar view this statement as a common nineteenth-century opinion, and conclude from it that 'male sexuality ... is not just analogically, but actually, the essence of literary power. The poet's pen is in some sense (even more than figuratively) a penis' (4). For the woman who seeks to write, this conflation of male biology and creativity, will clearly be a problem.

Through a reading of the story of Little Snow White, Gilbert and Gubar argued that the woman artist always found herself in a creative double bind. She was permitted to be the object of the male-authored literary text (the passive, dependent image of male desire, figured in Snow White's incarceration in a glass coffin); but she was not supposed to be the author of her own destiny, or the active subject-author of her own text. The creative assertive woman in the Snow White story is the 'wicked' stepmother, who creates her own image before the mirror, and who also, in a literary metaphor, 'plots' her daughter's downfall, but who is herself destroyed at the end of the tale, dancing herself to death in red-hot iron shoes at Snow White's wedding to her handsome prince. Snow White's story is an allegory of women's social and psychological positions under patriarchy. Snow White has to choose a role model – either her 'good' natural mother, who pricks her finger while sewing and conforming, and dies; or her 'bad' unnatural stepmother, who is assertive, creative, plotting and non-conforming – and who also dies. It's not much of a choice.

Interwoven with this reading, Gilbert and Gubar set out to show that art depends for its definition on patriarchal authority, on the father's silent approval. Only what patriarchy views as art is seen as art. At the same time, outside certain rigidly defined spheres, female creation is improper. For the nineteenth century, prevailing definitions of femininity resided in passivity and dependency, and insisted that a woman's proper sphere was the home. The woman who chose to assert her active intellectual mind, and her economic independence, in writing, and in writing for money, could be labelled as an improper woman – as unladylike, unfeminine, unwomanly. To attempt to write was to usurp what was regarded as a male sphere. The woman writer, then, would necessarily fail as an artist because she was a woman and therefore lacked the patriarchal authority of art; she would fail also as a woman because she was arrogating a male power, failing through the impropriety of her female creation. Because the standards of literary value against which the woman writer had to compete were male-identified as well as male-defined, the works she produced were in turn defined as 'less than' art. The woman writer suffered therefore a double-pronged attack: as a woman and as an artist.

Gilbert and Gubar took Bloom's model from *The Anxiety of Influence* and rewrote it from a feminist perspective. They discovered, not surprisingly, that in the male tradition of aggression against the father, 'a woman writer does *not* "fit in". At first glance, indeed, she seems to be anomalous, indefinable, alienated, a freakish outsider' (48). For the woman writer, they suggest, the anxiety of influence is rewritten as the 'anxiety of authorship' – the fear that literary writing is impossible for a woman; that she has no models against which to define herself, and that she will not herself become the model against which future generations of women writers will define themselves in their turn. The model of influence is therefore different in the female tradition than in the male. The woman writer actively seeks precursors, a tradition into which she can insert herself, not to define herself against her foremothers, but in order to find a model who 'proves by example that a revolt against patriarchal literary authority is possible' (49). At the same time, the woman writer is engaged in a struggle for valuation with the male tradition that deliberately excludes her. The consequences of social and psychological limitations imposed on the woman writer are summarised as a literary timidity (I'm only a woman, and I only write about women's things), or competitive protest (I'm as good as a man). The limitations lead 'an obsessive interest in these limited options ... [and an] obsessive imagery of confinement that reveals the ways in which female artists feel trapped and sickened both by suffocating alternatives and by the culture that has created them' (64).

After the first three chapters that set up the problematic of female literary creativity, Gilbert and Gubar turn their attention to nine-teenth-century novelists and poets – there are sustained and impressive readings of the works of Jane Austen, Mary Shelley, Emily Brontë, Charlotte Brontë, George Eliot, Christina Rossetti and Emily Dickinson. There is not the space here to discuss all their readings which remain very important documents of feminist criticism. Instead, I will concentrate briefly here on their reading of Emily Brontë's *Wuthering Heights* (1847) to highlight their typical mode of argument.

Chapter 8 of *The Madwoman in the Attic* occurs as the third chapter in a section entitled 'How are we fal'n?: Milton's Daughters', which contains also chapters on 'Patriarchal Poetry and Women Readers' and on Mary Shelley's *Frankenstein*. These two preceding chapters provide a double context for the reading of *Wuthering Heights*. Brontë's novel is seen as a feminist myth to rival the myth of origins contained in Milton's *Paradise Lost*, the archetypal patriarchal poem that keeps woman 'in her place'; and it is read as a different, though related, feminist myth to that written by Shelley in her fantasy of male scientific creation, also written as a direct and explicit response to Milton. Brontë's novel is thus placed into two distinct traditions: a tradition of male-defined literature, and a tradition of women's revisions of male writing. The chapter focuses on the nature/culture binary inherent in all *Bildungsromane* (novels of development or formation). A child is born as nature incarnate, but must learn the rules of culture in order to function properly in the world: in this kind of story, nature represents a dangerous anarchy which has to be suppressed. In the reading of *Wuthering Heights*, however, Gilbert and Gubar see the novel as a 'Bible of Hell',[12] as a novel which validates the natural over the cultural, the anarchic over the world of organised repression. Wuthering Heights, the house of the title, is hellish by conventional standards, but for the first Cathy and Heathcliff, her double, it represents the kind of non-hierarchical social space in which they are permitted a degree of power which would be denied them elsewhere, since she is female and he is illegitimate, and they are both thereby excluded from power in the conventional world. Thrushcross Grange across the moor, home of the Linton family, represents the standards of patriarchal culture which will be triumphant at the end of the story, but which the novel itself, through its sympathies for Cathy and Heathcliff, implicitly attacks.

Embedded in this argument about the reversals of structured meanings in the novel, the chapter also tries to establish relationships between *Wuthering Heights* and other kinds of text, both male- and female-authored. Byron and Blake provide constant sources of reference, with Thrushcross Grange, for example, being seen as a 'Urizenic' realm – a reference to Blake's unpleasantly righteous God figure, Urizen; and with Heathcliff and Cathy's relationship being read in terms of Byron's verse drama *Manfred* (1817, a story of quasi-incestuous brother–sister love). The chapter opens comparing the structures of *Wuthering Heights* (its use of letter and frame narratives) with the structures of Shelley's *Frankenstein*. There is no evidence in fact that Brontë had read either Shelley or Blake (though the Brontë sisters certainly read Byron compulsively). The logic of a female tradition, however, does not require this kind of absolute knowledge, since the female tradition is constructed both consciously in relation to known models and precursors, and also unconsciously, in relation to the shared experiences of oppression, and the shared desire to protest, of the woman writer. Gilbert and Gubar's version of female tradition looks both backwards and forwards: backwards to an American Indian myth from the Opaye tribe, that reflects the shape of the *Wuthering Heights* plot, but which Brontë could not have known; and forwards to the poetry of Sylvia Plath whose images of confinement, starvation and madness might or might not be explicitly derived from Brontë's model.

The reading is a *tour de force*, which mixes a traditional approach of close reading of the text and wide citation from other critical sources with an accumulation of more eclectic detail. Its sheer weight of allusion makes it very persuasive. For all its potency, however, this version of the female tradition is actually produced through parallel quotation and allusion. The readings of individual texts are fascinating and important, but the conclusions about the nature of a female tradition drawn from the larger contexts are open to question. In particular, as Nancy Armstrong has persuasively argued in *Desire and Domestic Fiction*, Gilbert and Gubar's approach is dangerously ahistorical, and inasmuch as they deal with history, it is a history that takes place outside of women's sphere:

They argue that women authors, in contrast with their male counter-parts, had to manage the difficult tasks of simultaneously subverting and conforming to patriarchal standards. But when understood in this gendered frame of reference, the conditions for women's writing appear to remain relatively constant throughout history because the authors in question were women and because the conditions under which they wrote were largely determined by men. ... Gilbert and Gubar virtually ignore the historical conditions that women have confronted as writers, and in so doing they ignore the place of women's writing in history. For Gilbert and Gubar ... history takes place not in and through those areas of culture over which women may have held sway, but in institutions dominated by men. (Armstrong 1987, 7–8)

In other words, the story Gilbert and Gubar write is not quite a tradi-tional history, but nor is it quite a feminist history. By concentrating on literary protest *inside* the text, they do not account for historical, social and geographical differences beyond the text. While they rewrite women's literary history, they take history itself as a prede-fined grand narrative.

In their second major collaboration, the three-volumes of *No Man's Land: The Place of the Woman Writer in the Twentieth Century* (1988–94),[13] Gilbert and Gubar moved away from the more strictly gynocritical approach of *The Madwoman in the Attic*. Although their central concern remains with the woman artist, the literary history of the twentieth century is figured as a battle of the sexes, of action and reaction by men and women working against each other, and in order to tell this story, they are obliged to investigate the writings of both sides. If *The Madwoman* opened with one shocking rhetorical ques-tion, *The War of the Words* opens with another: 'Is a pen a metaphori-cal pistol? Are words weapons with which the sexes have fought over territory and authority?' The question is answered with a quotation from the British poet, Ted Hughes, widower of Sylvia Plath, and author of a poem with the ironic title 'Lovesong':

> His words were occupying armies
> Her laughs were an assassin's attempts
> His looks were bullets daggers of revenge
> Her glances were ghosts in the corner with horrible secrets
> His whispers were whips and jackboots
> Her kisses were lawyers steadily writing. (Gilbert and Gubar 1988, 3–4)

For Gilbert and Gubar this poem represents the fundamental relationship between men and women in literature in the twentieth
century: literary words are will-to-violence, weapons in a war that
crosses and recrosses the same territory, alternatively imagining male
victories, male defeats, female victories, female defeats. Like
Showalter, they offer a chronology of the battle which begins in the
mid-nineteenth century, and brings us to the present day. In this
battle, women were defeated in the nineteenth century, but became
more powerful in the modernist period. The immediate post-war
years saw the reimagination of male victory; second-wave feminism
brought about a new conception of feminine triumph (4–5). This is
also a sweeping story, founded on extrapolation from the particular
literary text to the general picture of literary history. It is also a rather
exclusive version of literary history, notwithstanding the massive
sweep of three large volumes, concentrating on major figures and on
the literary movements already validated by the academy.
Armstrong's critique of Gilbert and Gubar's masculist view of history
is scarcely answered by their writing of a history of war.

The limits of one female tradition

> When you asked me to speak about women and fiction I sat down on
> the banks of a river and began to wonder what the words meant. They
> might mean simply a few remarks about Fanny Burney; a few more
> about Jane Austen; a tribute to the Brontës and a sketch of Haworth
> Parsonage under snow; some witticisms, if possible, about Miss
> Mitford; a respectful allusion to George Eliot; a reference to Mrs
> Gaskell, and one would have done.
>
> Virginia Woolf, *A Room of One's Own*

In *The Madwoman in the Attic*, Gilbert and Gubar had elaborated a
story of the woman writer that depended on her embattled relationship with male tradition, and on her desperate search for grandmothers, for a female tradition to which she could belong, through which
she would be validated, which would provide a support system that
allowed her to write. In the twentieth century, the story went on with
a continued battle against male supremacy in the literary battlefield,
but with an altered relationship for the woman writer with the female
tradition. If the male author in a well-established masculine tradition

is, in the Bloomian model, engaged in an Oedipal struggle with his forefathers, the woman writer, once her tradition has also been established has a not dissimilar problem. In Gilbert and Gubar's words, in the twentieth century the woman writer is 'not unequivocally energized by the example of her female precursor', and begins to suffer the same kind of anxiety that Bloom identified in his male texts:

> If she simply admires her aesthetic foremother, she is diminished by the originatory power she locates in that ancestress; but, if she struggles to attain the power she identifies with the mother's autonomy, she must confront ... the peril of the mother's position in patriarchy ... To have a history ... may not be quite so advantageous as some feminists have traditionally supposed. (Gilbert and Gubar 1988, 195–6)

In other words, *No Man's Land* tells a story not only of the battles between the sexes, but also of the battle *within* the female sex as well. The family romance of literary tradition with its powerful metaphors of maternity and paternity, inheritance and exclusion, has Oedipal complexities for both sexes. Mothers are ... well, both wonderful and terrible. Ask any group of women, no matter how good their relationships with their mothers are, whether they want to be like their mothers, and the majority will answer 'no'. Yet if we seek to be 'our own women', we are always in a sense defining ourselves against the model of the mother. The family, with its networks of physical and emotional resemblances and differences, with its apparent ideality and its often concealed monstrosity, is a useful metaphor for thinking about female traditions in life as well as literature. One of the problems of a female tradition, then, is its insistent recuperation of family resemblance: it behaves as if Jane Austen had Fanny Burney's eyes, Charlotte Brontë had inherited Ann Radcliffe's freckles, or Virginia Woolf was 'just like' her grandmother, George Eliot, in character if not in looks. The search for female family likenesses in a tradition of women's writing conceals differences. And just like the male Great Tradition, it tends to bastardise some of the female children, and disinherits some branches of the female family, just as patriarchy has always done.

This is not to say that seeking a tradition is unimportant or wrong. It is one of the key ways in which sub-cultures and marginalised groups seek out their own identities. For Black women writers, for lesbian women writers, for working-class women writers, finding voices that identify a community has been an early step in the process of achieving visibility. But in that sentence alone one of the major limitations of the female tradition so far outlined is exposed: where, in the works of Moers, Spacks, Showalter, and Gilbert and Gubar, are those 'other' women? De Beauvoir argued that woman was man's Other. It would seem that to one version of the female tradition, woman's other is any woman who is not educated, white, middle or upper class, straight. The female tradition attacked a male tradition made up of dead white European men, but it's a problem if it did so at the price of elevating only dead white women, and leaving those 'others' outside its validating frame. That problem is compounded by the recurrent names of the female tradition – the emphasis on nineteenth-century writing by an apparent female great tradition of Austen, the Brontës, and Eliot, with Virginia Woolf's twentieth-century writing being given the last word.

One way to combat this exclusionary bias is to propose not one tradition, but many, connected by the commonality of femaleness, but not limited to the Western white femaleness so far beloved of the academy. Plurality might mean unsightly, unfeminine competition; but more positively it could also mean creative coexistence between female traditions which inform and modify each other, and which have the valuable political results both of calling into question definitions of literature that depend on conservative versions of literary value, and of recovering and republishing works that have disappeared from view. One example is Mary Helen Washington's *Invented Lives: Narratives of Black Women (1860–1960)*, first published in 1987, a book which challenges older versions of literary history, whether masculist or feminist in origin. *Invented Lives* is a work of bibliographical research in the sense that it rediscovers texts that have been out of print, or that have never been published. It is a criticism that uncovers patterns in Black women's writings, and which also focuses on the position of the Black woman reader. If white women were searching for grandmothers for a literary tradition, as Elizabeth Barrett Browning put it, Black women had an even more difficult struggle, fighting not just against a definition of literature that absolutely excluded them, but also against a culture which kept them poor and largely uneducated – which, indeed, before 1860, kept them literally as slaves. The disease of femininity felt by white women was (and probably still is, in white-dominated societies) much more acutely experienced by Black women. And the common bond of being female did not feel much like a bond between, say, women who were slave-owners and women who were slaves. The idea of tradition evokes a sisterly solidarity; but it must not be allowed to do so at the cost of disguising the often appalling attitudes of white women to Black women.

Barbara Smith's landmark essay 'Towards a Black Feminist Criticism' discusses the implicit racism of an academy that simply ignores Black women, and argues for the political necessity of Black feminist criticism as a 'precondition' for the growth and visibility of Black female consciousness. She argues that where Black women writers are dealt with in current criticism (she wrote this piece in 1977), they are usually lumped in with Black men, with the consequence that the significance of sexual politics in their writing is ignored. She is disgusted and outraged by criticisms that simply don't see that Black women have important lives too. Her ideal is of a criticism that deals with the intersections of class, race, gender and sexuality in the formation of identity. As such it is a major challenge to the white woman tradition – for, after all, white women in white-dominated societies do not see themselves as having a race that needs analysis at all. Similarly, heterosexual women tend not to analyse their sexuality, taking it as a natural 'given'.

Smith argues otherwise, and asks her readers to consider how the connections between sex, race, politics, identity and class are mixed up in the writings specifically of Black women, but also in the writings of white women, even if they don't notice: the Black women, she suggests, don't have the choice of not noticing. She argues that Black feminist criticism has to take the existence of Black female literary traditions as its starting point. These traditions share something of the histories of Black male traditions and white female traditions, but 'thematically, stylistically, aesthetically, and conceptually Black women writers manifest common approaches to the act of creating literature as a direct result of the specific political, cultural, social, and economic experience they have been obliged to share.' Black women writers use common metaphors, common images, common fantasies, and write deliberately in the language used by Black women in the world beyond the page. The common ground of Black women writers 'takes their writing far beyond the confines of white/male literary structures' (Smith in Showalter 1986, 174). The consequence of this would be that the Black feminist critic 'would think and write out of her own identity, not try to graft the ideas or methodology of white/male literary thought upon the precious materials of Black women's art'. The consequence would be a Black feminist criticism that was both cause and result of Black feminist activism. The rather genteel disclaimers of Spacks and Moers that they were not really feminists, since politics and objective criticism could not go together, is very ungently and urgently rebuked in this clarion call for a truly radical, politicised critique.

Exclusiveness is certainly the most important criticism of 'tradition' formation as exemplified by the 'canon' in Moers, Spacks, Showalter, and Gilbert and Gubar. But there are others which are important too. Several feminist critics including Dale Spender (*Mothers of the Novel,* 1986), Janet Todd (*Feminist Literary History,* 1988 and *The Sign of Angellica: Women, Writing and Fiction, 1600–1800,* 1989) and Jane Spencer (*The Rise of the Woman Novelist, from Aphra Behn to Jane Austen,* 1986) implicitly and explicitly demonstrate that all these writers situate women's literary history almost entirely in the nine-teenth and twentieth centuries. Moers commented in her preface that 'The historical boundaries of the book have been set not arbitrarily but by the subject itself ... For all practical purposes, literary profes-sionalism for women began with the rise of the Richardsonian novel [which heralded] their chance to achieve, to influence, and to be decently paid' (Moers 1976, ix). Professionalism, however, is not the only criterion of 'greatness', whatever that is; moreover, the claim of Aphra Behn for the status of professional woman writer predates the Richardsonian novel, as do the works of several other eighteenth-century women. A tradition that takes 1800 as its real start date is something of a problem. As Marion Wynne-Davies suggests in her recent essay, 'Abandoned Women: the Middle Ages', there were quite a lot of women writing in the more distant past, and for all the diffi-culties of recovering their texts, patterns of female resistance can nonetheless be discerned, including the validation of personal experi-ence against abstract authority, and – in mystic writing – the love of God recurs as a trope that allowed the woman writer to evade or tran-scend man-made laws that confined her (Wynne-Davies in Shaw 1998, 9–36). Toril Moi wrote of her concern that there would come a time when the libraries were exhausted of new works for feminist critics to excavate. While that must be literally true, it has not happened yet, and female traditions go back further than Moers *et al.* suggest, and can be traced in wider social, racial and sexual commu-nities.

Residual Great Traditionalism is also a problem. In other words, the tradition critics measure depends on an ideal of value in women's writing. Even Showalter, who also wrote about less-valued women writers, measured their achievements in terms of the humanist ideals represented by the 'great women' writers. Literature – after all, a privileged term – preserves its privileges in a narrow definition of a woman's tradition. In *Consuming Fiction*, Terry Lovell noted that what she terms woman-to-woman fiction – that is, fiction written clearly from a female perspective for a female reader – tends to get 'coded out of "literature". ...Woman-to-woman forms are not permitted to become part of the general stock of cultural capital' (Lovell 1987, 132). Lovell is here writing about the politicised fiction of the New Woman writers of the 1890s; but her point holds true for other woman-to-woman forms, in particular the mass-market romance such as those published by Mills & Boon, or the fictions of Catherine Cookson, as well as for modern equivalents of the 'mind-and-millinery' novel, the sex-and-shopping blockbuster or the airport novel. These are traditions which have been very deliberately excluded from the academic studies that define 'literature'. A book like Rosalind Coward's *Female Desire: Women's Sexuality Today* (1984), which examines the reasons for women readers' interpellation into conservative fantasies of masculinity and femininity in romantic fiction, makes these apparently lesser fictions into important objects of study, and in the process calls into question the exclusivity of 'literature' as defined in terms of masculist humanist ideals of value. Coward's analysis shows that there is something important to say about women's compensatory fantasies of powerful ideal men: literature is about aspiration as well as about the accurate reflection of real authentic experience. Readers read to see themselves as they might be in different circumstances – they can see themselves as they are in any old realist mirror.

The question of form is another potential weakness of feminist tradition formation. As Gilbert and Gubar establish, the novel is the pre-eminent mode of women's writing. For reasons to do with the ways in which literary value is apportioned, poetry in particular has been a difficult form for women to write and achieve literary success. The concentration on fiction, however, is problematic because of the kinds of criticism it tends to attract. Before the twentieth century, novels tended to have extractable content – plots and characters could be paraphrased to produce a narrative of what the novel 'is about'. Criticism based on content alone though tends to privilege message over form, recovering a literary politics without uncovering more abstract literary structures. While this is indeed an important process in making a politicised literary critique, it is sometimes at the expense of the re-evaluation of the literariness of women's writing.

The attempt to establish traditions has been and continues to be an important foundational stage in different feminist traditions. For the student reader, it is the glue that cements the gynocritical courses that are now available in many universities. The patterns of female experience represented by feminine images and plots make sense of otherwise quite disparate materials. But traditions, like all histories, are founded on exclusions. A tradition is what it omits as well as what it includes. When we think about women's traditions, we must think in the plural, and not try to make one white woman's middle-class story *the* story of all women's experience. If female traditions merely replicate the strategies of exclusion enacted by conventional literary criticism, they are hardly radical. The onus on the feminist literary historian is to be aware of disruptions as well as continuities, to value those differences, and to be honest about what her own core definitions leave out, and why. Whatever commonality women share, the stories we tell of our definitions must be alive to our differences too. Tradition criticism, like image criticism, must not be naive. Perhaps, to paraphrase George Eliot, it would be truer to say that women writers write after their many kinds; that their kinds of writing fully equal the kinds of writing produced by the many kinds of men; and that if we are alert to their kinds, we may also be alert to differences that enrich the field of literature even as they also subvert its own traditional assumptions.

Notes

1. As most of my examples are drawn from English literature, I've stuck with that designation. But despite locally differing circumstances, similar points can be made about American literature, as well as about the canons of the major Western European languages. Eastern European women writers have faced exacerbated versions of the same problems of women writers in the West; and in any area where female

education has been slow to arrive (or has not yet arrived) the same implicit devaluation of women's writing continues to exist. The Third World woman writer has her own very specific problems.

2.   It's instructive to remember that Mary Ellmann, more than a hundred years later, identified piety as one of the feminine stereotypes presented by novels by men; *plus ça change,* as the French might say, *plus c'est la même chose* [the more things seem to change, the more they stay the same].

3.   The Woman Problem is a rather tongue-in-cheek phrase in this context. The phrase was used in the nineteenth century to discuss in turn, the problem of surplus women who could not marry because there were not enough men (from around the 1850s and 1860s), then the 'problem' of women's suffrage at the end of the century. Debates in and around feminism demonstrate the unwillingness of the problem woman to go away, even when she acquires education, training, employment and the vote.

4.   Showalter's reference here is to Elizabeth Hardwick's book, *Seduction and Betrayal: Women and Literature* (New York: Random House), first published in 1974, which considered women seduced and betrayed in nineteenth-century fiction.

5.   Lady Mary Wortley Montagu (1689–1792) was a travel writer, dramatist and political commentator for much of the eighteenth century. Doris Lessing (born 1919) is a writer of both political realist novels, and of politicised science fictions.

6.   I'm using this phrase rather than 'feminist criticism' because Spacks herself refuses the term, arguing that her focus is 'literary and psychological rather than political' See Patricia Mayer Spacks, *The Female Imagination: A Literary and Psychological Investigation of Women's Writing,* London: George Allen and Unwin, 1976, p. 7.

7.   Isadora Duncan (1877-1927), American dancer who published her autobiography, *My Life,* in 1927.

8.   Literal, because Sand actually did dress up as a man at various points in her life, in order to achieve the freedom to roam the streets at will, unencumbered by female clothing, unbothered by feminine propriety. And what is a pseudonym like 'George Sand' if not a kind of literary transvestism?

9.   Moers is here quoting the American novelist Henry James's assessment of Sand's physique.

10. Sensationalism is the term used to describe a genre of popular fiction in the mid-nineteenth century. The plots of sensation fiction were fast-moving and complicated; they involved dubious inheritances, powerful women, sinister men and quasi-gothic domestic settings. The

fashion for such fiction caused something of a moral panic in the 1860s, not least, as Lyn Pykett has argued, because these were books largely written by women for women, which had dubious moral content, and could be seen as threatening conventional pieties about 'proper femininity'. See Lyn Pykett, *The Improper Feminine: The Woman's Sensation Novel and the New Woman Writing*, London: Routledge, 1992, for more information on the genre. For information on the reception of sensation texts, in particular, women's enthusiastic readings of them, see Kate Flint's *The Woman Reader: 1837–1914*, Oxford: Clarendon Press, 1993.

11. Although Gilbert and Gubar adopt a psychoanalytical model in this book, *The Madwoman in the Attic* is nonetheless not really a psycho-analytically-informed critical model. The main technique of the book is a New-Critical attention to close reading. The family romance is the context for the reading of the woman writer's position, rather than the centre of attention, and the woman writer is seen more as a psycholog-ical than a psychoanalytic subject.

12. The full title of the chapter is 'Looking Oppositely: Emily Brontë's Bible of Hell'.

13. The three volumes are entitled: *The War of the Words* (1988); *Sexchanges* (1989); and *Letters from the Front* (1994).

Part II

(Psycho)Analyses

4   Psychoanalysis and/or Feminism?

The relationships between psychoanalysis and feminisms have been both fraught and fruitful. For many of the early writers in feminist criticism, the two modes of thinking were distinctly incompatible. The 'and/or' of this chapter's title represents the discomfort that the theories of Sigmund Freud and his followers in the field caused to a critique that was avowedly materialist, historical and politicised. In those early days, Freud was read as having only negative connotations for women in general, and for women as readers and writers. For Kate Millett, Freud was 'beyond question the strongest individual counter-revolutionary force in the ideology of sexual politics' of the twentieth century (Millett 1977, 178). Her critique is based on her sense that Freud's writings rendered biology as destiny, and forgot to account for the specificity of social acculturation in the Western European family of the late nineteenth and early twentieth centuries. She criticises his refusal to separate 'two radically different phenomena, female biology and feminine status' (190), objects strongly to his definitions of femininity as aligned with passivity, masochism and narcissism, and attacks his 'scientific' language (she calls it jargon) which renders what she sees as his Victorian views of masculinity and femininity into the powerful discourse of apparently objective science:

> Dressing the thing up in jargon ... one gives the old myth of feminine 'nature' a new respectability. Now it can be said scientifically that women are inherently subservient, and males dominant, more strongly sexed, and therefore entitled sexually to subjugate the female, who enjoys her oppression and deserves it, for she is by her very nature, vain, stupid, and hardly better than a barbarian, if she is human at all. ... psychoanalysis promised [female] fulfilment in passivity and masochism, and greater fulfilment, indeed, the very meaning of woman's life lay in reproduction, and there alone. (203)

She attacks in particular the theory of penis envy, in which the little girl, realising that she is 'castrated' and suffering from lack and loss, wishes for a psychic wholeness which is denied her because it is figured solely in the male sex organ. For Millett, this theory is problematic on logical grounds – why would the girl child assume that the penis is 'better than' her own sexual organs? But it is also discounted because it does not recognise that, in a patriarchal society, a girl may envy a boy on grounds other than those of biology – the social grounds of masculine privilege such as freedom, education, and status, rather than the biological grounds of possession or otherwise of a penis.

Millett is by no means the only critic of psychoanalytic theory in relation to a feminist critique of society. Mary Ellmann, whose stated interest in *Thinking About Women* was in 'women as *words*' (Ellmann 1968, xv), is disturbed by the potency of defining words about women derived from psychoanalytic discourse (21). Even some of the French feminist theorists most associated with pyschoanalysis in the minds of anglophone critics have had much to say about the problems of mixing up biology and culture that psychoanalysis appears to risk. Hélène Cixous, writing in 'Sorties', her contribution to *The Newly Born Woman*, proclaims that femininity is not defined by lack so much as by difference: 'not that I desire to stop up some hole, to overcome some flaw of mine', she says. Her version of woman is heterogenous and multiply-erogenous, not defined by a single lack (Cixous 1986, 89). And Luce Irigaray, herself an analyst, rails rhetorically against Freud's construction of the Oedipus complex:

> So we must admit that THE LITTLE GIRL IS THEREFORE A LITTLE MAN. A little man who will suffer a more painful and complicated evolution than the little boy in order to become a normal woman! A little man with a smaller penis. A disadvantaged little man. A little man whose libido will suffer a greater repression, and yet whose faculty for sublimating instincts will remain weaker. Whose needs are less catered to by nature and who will yet have a lesser share of culture. A more narcissistic little man because of the mediocrity of her genital organs (?). More modest because ashamed of that unfavorable comparison. More envious and jealous because less well endowed. Unattracted to the social interests shared by men. A little man who would have no other desire than to be , or remain, a man. (Irigarary 1985b, 26)

More recently still, Janet Todd has described herself as 'mystified' by the influence of Freud and Lacan on feminist thought, arguing that the concentration on psycho-linguistics is both ahistorical and apolitical (Todd 1988, 52–4), history and politics being precisely the things that she defines as essential to a feminist poetics. As Rita Felski suggests, psychoanaltyic feminism can risk overestimating 'the radical effects of linguistic indeterminacy'. 'The defamiliarizing capacity of literary language and form does not in itself bear any necessary relationship to the political and social goals of feminism' (Felski 1989, 5–6). It is very easily understandable that feminist criticism has objected to psychoanalysis as a tool for feminist criticism. From its content and assumptions, it represents precisely the kind of female dependency on male models of culture and philosophy that feminism supposedly exists to combat, and merely retells the old story of femininity in different words.

These are serious objections to the relationships between the avowedly political discourses of feminism and the apparently apolitical discourses of psychoanalysis, and they should not be trivialised. And yet, the materialist positions that the earlier part of the book charts do not quite explain everything either. For most people, sex and gender remain related to each other. Whilst on the one hand I can *know* that social formations have played a very great part in my construction as a female human being with some feminine attributes, in a different order of knowledge, I also *know* that the body I inhabit somehow also constitutes my selfhood. Sociological or materialist accounts of subjectivity are very important. After all, if feminisms are concerned with changing an unjust status quo in the material world, they have to be concerned with the things that *can* be changed: and the conditions of the material world are changeable as basic biological conditions are not. But even after the revolution, you and I will be men and women still, still experiencing the world through biologically sexed bodies even if definitions of gender have changed in the meantime. And it may just be that there are psychic consequences to the sexed bodies we live in, consequences which can be analysed, diagnosed, and perhaps even also changed. Psychoanalytic discourses offer radical ways of looking at how material conditions (both social *and* biological) have psychic effects, and in particular they provide us with ways of describing the distinctively gendered nature of those effects in which women are differently effected than men. In order to suggest why psychoanalysis has seemed so hostile and yet has also had very radical theoretical effects in feminist literary theory, it is probably a good idea briefly to revisit some of the key ideas of the discourse before we go on to look at what some feminist theorists have done with them.

Freud

At its most simple level, the two most significant things that the writing of Sigmund Freud offers to contemporary thinking are: his discovery of the unconscious, and his view that individuals achieve gendered adulthood through social processes rather than through innate biological ones. His description of the Oedipus complex provides a psychic as well as a social explanation for heterosexuality as an acquired, not an innate, sexual mode.

Freud argued that a newborn child is, in a sense, bisexual. He[1] has a biological sex but no gendered behaviour to go with it. Instead, the child is a bundle of oceanic desires, seeing himself as the centre of his own universe, and having no sense of differentiation (he does not yet recognise others in the world beyond himself); the child's mother is, at this stage, not recognised as a separate being, but is mis-recognised as a part of the child himself. His desires are polymorphous (many-shaped): for example, he takes pleasure in sucking, and this pleasure is sexual because it exists even when the child is not taking in milk; it is independent of the function of nourishment. He also discovers other pleasures in his body that originate in biological necessity (eating, defecating), but which are also pleasurable in their own right, and in bodily pleasures that defy biological necessity, such as mastur-bation, the pleasure of the penis. At this point, the child has no real sense of self, seeing the world and himself as continuous. Only at the point at which his desires are not immediately gratified (when the mother does not immediately provide milk on demand, for example), does he start to grasp that his world and himself are separate. His self-hood is therefore constructed on the grounds of a loss which ensures that the child recognises the mother as 'other' than himself rather than continuous with himself. Freud suggests that this sense of loss institutes desire (an 'I want' demand which is not met), and that desire produces language (the demand 'I want' has to be formulated in language).

For both male and female children, the first object of desire is the mother, the provider of nourishment, care and of the physical needs of the child. But in order to become separate selves, male and female children must split away from the mother, despite their desires to unite with her because she is the source of pleasure and comfort. The process by which this occurs is named, by Freud, the Oedipus complex. For the boy child, it begins at the moment when he first discovers that female people have no penises. This shocks him horribly, and he postulates to himself the idea that girls and women must have been mutilated by castration, which institutes a fear of a similar 'punishment' being enacted on his own body as the consequence of his powerful desire for his mother, a desire that eventually becomes recognised as forbidden because incestuous. Since, at the time when Freud was writing, and beyond, the father of the family was the source of punishment and power in the family, the boy child decides that discretion is the better part of valour. To protect his own sign of masculinity, his penis, he works to please his father, to identify with his father, and he relinquishes and represses his desire for his mother. The reward for this act of repression and abnegation is that the boy child will eventually come to share the power of the father as a reward for giving up his mother's body. Heterosexual orientation is established when the boy decides to be *like* his father, and to direct his desires towards women *like* his mother.

Now, straightaway, it is evident that the girl child does not have the same experience in the move away from the mother. Freud's pronouncements on the female Oedipus complex demonstrate a far more tortured path for the little girl to achieve an individuated personhood. Like the boy child, the girl is also a bisexual baby with polymorphously perverse tendencies, with oceanic desires and an inability to differentiate between self and other, in particular to differentiate between herself and her mother. Her only difference at this point from the male child is in the physical location of her pleasures – the masturbation of the clitoris, rather than the penis. And the process of differentiation begins at the moment when the girl child catches sight of a male anatomy and discovers that she has no penis, that she is, as it were, already castrated. Freud made it clear that this was a very traumatic experience for the little girl. What she has discovered is her own lack in comparison to the plenitude of the male body: 'She makes her judgement and her decision in a flash. She has seen it and knows that she is without it, and wants to have it', he wrote in his essay on 'Some Psychological Consequences of the Anatomical

Distinction Between the Sexes' (Freud 1986, 406). The consequence of this glimpse of the penis is that the girl child becomes angry with her mother, blaming her for what appears to be her own mutilation. Having decided that she 'wants to have it', the girl child turns her desire towards her father as the possessor of the penis, so that her desire becomes suitably heterosexual and passive, and her behaviour maps onto the femininity desired by the adult male. Eventually she will decide that it is not a penis that she wants, but a baby, thus instituting her female selfhood within the realm of heterosexual reproduction.

From that rather bald summary, it is perhaps no surprise that Kate Millett objected so strongly to Freud's account of female sexuality. Why, she wonders, would a little girl think that having a penis is better than not having one? With no experience of the penis, she might equally decide that it's comic, or ugly, not that attractive or desirable in fact (Millett 1977, 182–5). The manifest content of Freudian theory looks dangerously essentialist and positively misognynistic.

And yet: as literary critics, we do not read only the content of any discursive formation. There is context and mode of expression that should also be taken into consideration. In 1974, Juliet Mitchell published *Psychoanalysis and Feminism* as part of the process of recuperating Freud for contemporary feminist concerns. One of the first things that she points out is that Freud was *describing* the contemporary conditions of his own context, that he was thinking about the Western European family at a very precise time in history, and that his views are not therefore to be taken either as pronouncements on how psychic development always takes place, or on how it *should* or must take place. As a writer who began her critical career in Marxist/materialist discourses, Mitchell is very aware of the contexts of history, geography and economics. And she valued Freud's writing for its attempt to offer 'objective knowledge' of the subjective phenomena of the psyche in its social contexts (Mitchell 1974, 6).

Moreover, what Freud also offered to feminism, despite what Millett saw as his profound hostility to it, was a description of femininity that was not merely biological. From the account offered above, the body clearly does matter to Freud's theoretical interventions. But it is a body in a context (a content within a textual context), and it is a body which is naturally *sexed*, but not naturally *gendered*. Male and female may always already exist, but masculinity and femininity are presented as processes rather than givens; and if they are processes which take place in social contexts as well as in biological bodies, the processes and their meanings can be changed. The analysis and diagnosis of the symptoms of femininity could therefore be placed at the service of political ends. So while Janet Todd is right to be suspicious of the apparent depoliticisation and ahistoricity of psychoanalysis, that need not disable the feminist critic from using it for politically motivated and historicised ends. Feminisms forage amongst discourses, and use what they can for their own purposes. Freud gives us both the means to view femininity as socially constructed, and the means to analyse the ways in which women have internalised views of themselves which are harmful to their social and economic circumstances as well as their psychic well-being. Psychoanalytic theory is a tool to be used, not an idol to bow down before.

The second strand of Freudian theory that has been seized on by literary criticism in general, as well as by feminist theory in particular, is the concept of the Unconscious. The Unconscious is the psychic realm to which the forbidden desires for the mother are consigned during the Oedipus complex, when the child accedes to what Freud called 'the reality principle' – the realisation that his desires, if unchecked, would lead to disaster, because they would bring down punishment on him. The acculturated adult person has many desires of many kinds. But s/he realises that these desires must be reined in rather than acted on willy-nilly. As part of the Oedipus complex, the child modifies his/her desires to ends acceptable in his/her social context, or displaces those desires onto other objects than the forbidden mother. The desires, however, do not just go away, according to Freud. They are consigned to the unconscious, an unregulated psychic space which is not subject to conscious control. In dreams, slips of the tongue, neurotic symptoms or physical tics, the unconscious surfaces during everyday life. For Freud, then, a 'healthy' human being is one who has managed to put up a front of self-control, but also one whose unconscious motivations can and do surface from time to time to disrupt the carefully constructed self which is the result of the Oedipus complex. And since the Oedipus complex has to do precisely with constructing the gender of the self, the Unconscious may displace the mask of gender. A feminist criticism that takes the unconscious seriously, then, is a criticism that can see femininity as a performance, womanliness as masquerade as Joan Rivière put it in 1929. And if femininity is not innate, it can be rewritten, re-imagined, constructed along different lines.

As a clinical practice, pyschoanalysis is about the uncovery of the unconscious as it manifests itself to conscious life, and its subsequent regulation through analytic explanation. Psychoanalysis, like literature, is a kind of narrative structure. The analyst reads the analysand's texts; the patient speaks, and the analyst interprets both the content of the speech (sometimes the narrative of a dream, for example, since dreams are the 'royal road to the Unconscious'), but also the context of that speech (body-language, nervous tics), and the discourse of the speech (how it is put together, the hesitations, sentence structures, what is, or appears to be, missing, the images which may be metaphors of displaced desire). Freud identified two main modes of analysis in the patient's speech, which he named condensation and displacement. Condensation refers to a single image around which are clustered a whole range of unconscious desires and memories; displacement occurs when a single dangerous desire is displaced onto an apparently harmless single image. As Lacan was later to note, condensation and displacement work like the poetic figures of metonymy (comparison by contiguity or proximity) and metaphor (comparison of like and unlike). If the constructedness of gender identity in psychoanalysis maps onto the political analysis of feminisms, the realm of the Unconscious maps onto the realm of the literary theoretical concerns of feminisms. The analyst is a reader whose reading offers a model for literary-critical readings.

Early psychoanalytic readings focused on the biography of the author as if the text could be read as a simple manifestation of the writer's unconscious, or they focused on the analysis of literary characters within a text. More recently, psychoanalytic readings have tended focus on the unconscious motivations of the text itself – that is, they concentrate on the textuality of the text rather than on a purely thematic account of its workings. Such a reading can, and perhaps ought, to account also for textual contexts (of production and of reading), so that the text's psyche is understood as part of a matrix of meanings which include the social and economic realms as the formative background for what goes on in the head. The feminist critic making use of psychoanalysis must not forget her commitments to politics and history as part of the process.

Lacan

As the above summary suggests, feminist theory does not sit unprob-lematically with Freudian psychoanalysis, for there remains the underlying problem that Freud's account of gender development depends dangerously closely on the essentialist basis of biology. On the other hand, however, that concentration on bodies is exactly one of the things that feminism is bound to replicate since female bodies are part of its subject. It is perhaps for these reasons that much contemporary feminist psychoanalytic theory draws heavily on the writings of Jacques Lacan, despite the fact that, in some ways, his views on women are just as troubling as those of Freud himself. Indeed, as Jane Gallop rather mischievously puts it, Lacan was 'The Ladies' Man' who wanted to take a stroll 'as cock of the walk', and enjoyed staging his own masterful masculinity for audiences largely made up of women (Gallop 1982, 33–42). What Lacan offers, however, is a psychoanalytic critique which bases itself firmly in language – hence its attractiveness to *literary* theorists. Because his view of language is derived from Saussurean linguistics, moreover, taking account of arbitrariness and difference rather than fixing things by naming them, his description of identity as taking place in language also resists solidifying and essentialising selfhood in any terms, and perhaps especially the terms of gender. Moreover, the language in which Lacan wrote was French, a language which is absolutely gender inflected, so that the relationships between language and the body are ideas that can be pursued through a Lacanian lens.

Lacan's thinking is rigorously post-Freudian. It could not exist without Freud's descriptions of the psychic field; and yet it is no slavish recapitulation of Freud's views. Rather it is a development and a rewriting of them, a model of reading and rewriting that is also undertaken by feminist appropriations of psychoanalytic models. Lacan takes on many of Freud's fundamental concepts, and then reviews them through the prism of language studies, especially the version of linguistics developed by Ferdinand de Saussure. His most famous statement is that 'the unconscious is structured like a language', and the model of language he takes up is that proposed by Saussure's structuralist linguistics. Saussure's most important point was that words have no intrinsic relationship to the things they describe. The relationship between a word and a thing is arbitrary, maintained by conventional agreement rather than by a God-given link. He argued that signs (words or images) have two components: the signifier (a sound image or written/graphic equivalent) and the signified (that to which the signifier refers). While signifier and signified are apparently like two sides of a piece of paper (inseparable), their relationship is in fact arbitrary, signalled by the fact that different languages have different signifiers for the same signifieds. This view might imply that meaning is impossible. In fact, Saussure's position is that meaning is contingent rather than absolute – there are meanings, but they are not fixed. Meaning comes from differentiation, from the differences between words as sound or written images, and from differences of syntactical positioning. The consequences of this view of langauge for psychoanalysis are: that if the unconscious is structured like a language, it is structured in such a way that its structures are recoverable and describable, but also that it is structured in such a way that the meanings attached to its content (semantics) are multiple, contingent, unfixed, unstable.

Lacan's description of the process of human development, then, draws on the Freudian model of the Oedipus complex, but insists on its basis in language. Lacan's human infant (a word that derives from the Latin *infans*, meaning without speech) is in some ways much like Freud's, a creature of oceanic and undifferentiated desires. The child still sees the world and himself as continuous, with no separation between self and other. Lacan names this pre-linguistic, pre-Oedipal phase the Imaginary realm, signalling its non-realistic fantasmatic nature. As time goes on, the child passes through 'the mirror stage'; either actually or figuratively, he catches sight of himself in a mirror, and identifies the image as himself. This identification of self with image is labelled a 'misrecognition' by Lacan because the image is a substitute for the self, a signifier of the self, not the self itself. Nonetheless, on the basis of this misrecognition, the child begins to see himself as a separate individual, differentiated from the rest of the world. At this stage, he also begins to speak. The development of language, Lacan argues, is constituted by lack – a need is not met, and it requires language to formulate that need as a demand: 'I want'. This development, too, refers to Saussurean linguistics, since words are not the things they represent, but merely substitutes for them. The realisation of the separation of self and world is what produces language.

The entry into language is an entry into a realm with pre-existing rules (of grammar, socialisation, acceptable behaviour and so on). These rules are a form of prohibition: don't say that, don't do that.

And in many (perhaps most) societies, prohibitions are associated with the father, the locus of power and restraint within the family, and representative of the family in the world outside. The father here is both the literal father ('just wait till your father gets home!'), but also he is the symbolic father of society at large, representing the institutions of socialisation – the church, the law, education etc. The achievement of acculturation, then, depends on an identification with the laws of the father, named by Lacan the *nom du père*, a pun in French on the No of the Father/the Name of the Father. The father's name is the name the legitimate child takes when it starts the process of becoming a socialised being; and the No of the Father represents the prohibitions placed on behaviour by literal and symbolic fathers in social and psychic life. The realm the child enters through his acquisition of language is called, by Lacan, the Symbolic realm. It is the realm of consciouness, rules, order, differentiation, logic (*logos* is the Greek for word), power, in contrast to the Imaginary realm of the Unconscious with its anarchic, uncontrolled desires.

Lacan's ideas suggest a number of quite shocking things for our general sense of ourselves, as well as for feminist literary theory. Perhaps his single most important move is the shift from seeing the conscious self (the Freudian ego) as central to personhood, to seeing the unconscious as the 'kernel of our being'. His writings suggest that subjectivity takes place in words. What I am, and what I am able to imagine myself as being are linguistic features because they take place entirely in language. And if words are merely substitutes for something that is missing, my selfhood is as arbitrary, unfixed, unstable and contingent as the language in which I express it. Moreover, his discussions of the Symbolic and Imaginary realms tend to imply that the ordering of the one and the anarchy of the other coexist in the single self, which is always therefore more than one self at a single time. The word 'I' is multiple. It is at once the word I use to designate myself and the word that you use to designate yourselves. That marker of my unique identity is therefore always plural rather than single, a signifier that appeals to oneness, but which has infinite numbers of signifieds.

The significance of these views for literary theory in general lies in part in what they do to a humanist notion of self as unique and individual. Neither writers nor characters are as coherent or whole as the language in which they are written likes to pretend. Rather, they are functions within language: and, more worryingly, in the world beyond the text, so are we. It is not so much that we speak language as that language speaks us. Moreover, the Unconscious is structured like a language, so that even as we enter the Symbolic order of language, there is always a residue of that anarchic, arbitrary psychic space of the Unconscious and the Imaginary. Rationality and disorder coexist in the speaking subject.

The relationship between these ideas and the literary text is twofold. First, the Symbolic order is that mode of language which appeals to reason, and it here that one finds the discourses of power – science, philosophy, medicine, and the authoritative and valued literature of Realism. Poetry, with its creative disruptions of grammatical rules, syntax and vocabulary partakes of the Imaginary, even as it also functions within the Symbolic. The Lacanian critic, then, is concerned with investigating breeches in the Symbolic discourses of authority and with tracing competitive and creative relationships between the Symbolic and the Imaginary, seeing how each does and undoes the work of the other. Second, Lacanian thinking offers a way of rethinking the processes of reading and writing which rebound on the conception of subjectivity. If characters, and their writers, and their readers, are effects in language, then we can rethink our positions in the world. Language has underlying rules; but it also contains the possibility that those rules can be broken – deliberately or unconsciously – to creative effect within the literary text, to psychotic effect in real lives, producing alternative scenarios of selfhood for readers and patients in their worlds.

In *Thinking About Women*, Mary Ellmann spoke of her interest in women as words. The value of combining structuralist linguistics with psychoanalysis for feminist thinking is that it points out that words are not things even whilst the words have real material and psychic effects: thinking about language and minds, we have to recall that 'women' is a signifier, not a signfied, and meanings, as dictionaries demonstrate, can and do change. Although language may be related to reality, it is not identical with it. So, because words are not directly transcripted from reality, they can be used to open up new realms, to fantasise alternative futures in both material and psychic frames.

This section of the book, then, considers the relationships that psychoanalysis and postmodernisms ascribe to women and language, to women as spoken subjects, and to women as speaking subjects.

The next chapters consider the thinking of the three most influential French feminist theorists for the English-speaking world, Julia Kristeva, Luce Irigaray and Hélène Cixous. There are as many differences as similarities between these writers, but they each share a serious intellectual interest in language as a constitutive function of subjectivity, and they come to this position through an engagement (sometimes hostile) with psychoanalysis. Their interest in language is what has made them so usable in feminist literary theory. They dramatise the demand that the literary aspect of feminist literary theory has to approach the literariness of texts as well as their themes and contents. Politics is not just a matter of what is said but is also a question of form and language. This is an important point for the sexual politics of literature, for if feminism refuses any claim to the value attached to the word/concept of literature, it risks a repositioning of women readers and writers as somehow less important, more marginal to the claims of 'real' literature.

Postmodernist and post-structuralist accounts of texts (accounts to which contemporary psychoanalysis is often very much indebted which is why these chapters appear together), take the argument yet further. A theory that relies on psychoanalysis still has one key assumption in place – that we all know what a woman is, and that we are accustomed to being able to tell what one is, just by looking, as it were. But what if woman is more a word than a body? Thinking through the works of Marjorie Garber and Judith Butler, as well as through the insights of lesbian-feminist and Black-feminist criticism, the feminist critic is forced to confront the possibility that the feminist appeal to women's bodies, and their experiences in those bodies, might just be a false start. These are unsettling ideas which unstructure our habitual modes of thought, and there are reasons for resisting these ideas, as well as for embracing them. What these critics do is to resist even the most residual essentialism, even the essentialism that is a political strategy of feminism. For this reason, they remain controversial, and dramatise one of the key underlying positions of this book – that feminisms are pluralist not totalitarian.[2]

Notes

1. Freud starts his analysis with the presumption of a male child. This presumption has serious effects when he comes to describe the devel-

opment of girl children. But for the time being, I will stick with his
presumption of masculine gender.

2.   There are many kinds of psychoanalysis and psychoanalytic criticism
that I have not dealt with here. A notable omission in a book dealing
with feminist literary theory is the modification to psychoanalytic
theory made by some of Freud's own female followers, in particular,
Helene Deutsch, Karen Horney and especially Melanie Klein. Klein's
work in object-relation theory, and her partial relocation of the infant's
object of desire to the mother's breast and away from the (father's)
phallus, is clearly highly significant for feminist theory generally. My
emphasis, however, is on the 'fathers' of psychoanalysis, since it is the
modifications of their mthinking undertaken by writers like Irigaray,
Cixous and Kristeva that has been highly influential for feminist
thought in the last twenty years. And without their work, it is difficult to
imagine the writings of theorists like Judith Butler and Rita Felski. For
detailed discussions of the 'mothers' of psychanalysis, see: Janet Sayers,
*Mothering Psychoanalysis: Helene Deutsch, Karne Horney, Anna Freud,
Melanie Klein*, London: Hamish Hamilton, 1991. For a helpful descrip-
tion and discussion of Klein's object-relations theory, see Elizabeth
Wright, *Psychoanalytic Criticsm: A Reappraisal* (2nd edition),
Cambridge: Polity Press, 1998, and Andrew Roberts, *Psychoanalysis and
Literature*, in this series (forthcoming).

5   Julia Kristeva: Rewriting the Subject

The writings of Julia Kristeva bring together several discourses which are more usually separated, which tends to make her writing difficult to begin to read since she assumes a range of knowledge in her readers that we may not always quite possess. Her career as an academic began in the discipline of linguistics, the systematic study of language. Born in Bulgaria in 1941, she came to consciousness under an intensely politicised system of Communist government, and learned to think politically as a matter of course. She was profoundly influenced in her linguistic research by the thinkers of Eastern Europe (she speaks Russian), in particular the Russian Formalists who argued that literary language is a kind of double agent, a writing which at once advertises content and form. They attempted to analyse the 'literariness' of literary languages. On her arrival in France in the mid-sixties, she added to her knowledge of political and linguistic theory by an intense engagement with the psychoanalytic theories of Jacques Lacan. Her work is of particular interest to feminist literary theorists because it touches therefore on all three of the bases of such thinking established by Elaine Showalter, namely oppression, expression and repression.

The works of the Russian critic Mikhail Bahktin were formative in Kristeva's thinking, and some of her early published essays (in particular, 'Word, Dialogue and Novel' and 'Semiotics: A Critical Science and/or a Critique of Science', Kristeva 1986, 34–88) bear the imprint of Bahktin's ideas. Bahktin's importance lies in his critique of structuralist linguistics, and its assumption that the system of language (called by Ferdinand de Saussure, *la langue*) operates as a fixed structure that can be defined and analysed. He proposed instead that language must always be understood as *a process of making meaning*, dependent for its force on extra-linguistic features such as context or tone. As such, language is never a closed system, but rather a series of gestures towards meaning directed at an other – the reader or hearer of writing or speech. As such, it is the site of contradictions and struggle. Writers/speakers always communicate in a contingent way. Their meanings are never fixed or final, since their audiences are always heterogeneous (multiple) and hear or read in terms of their differences. Bahktin wrote of what he called the *dialogic* nature of language which he saw as doubled because it involves both hearer and speaker, reader and writer. Literary language is particularly 'doubled' because of its advertisement of the importance of form as well as content. For him, words are material things. They circulate in specific contexts, and they cannot be fixed to one catch-all, all-or-nothing significance precisely because words are oriented towards an audience that makes up its multiple minds about what the words 'really' mean in the various contexts of their reception.

In themselves, these ideas are significant for all literary theory in their dispersal of the possibility that any text is coherent or whole, that any piece of writing could act as an untouchable artefact containing pre-determined meaning. And for feminist theory, these ideas are important in that they open up the fissures in the apparently closed systems by which patriarchal thought dispossesses women. In refusing the stability of fixed significance, Bahktin's ideas provide leverage on any systematic and apparently unchanging, immutable set of ideas. In her own work, Kristeva helped to bring Bahktinian thinking to the West, and further developed and modified his thinking. Her 1977 book *Polylogue*, for example, gestures in its title towards Bahktin's notion of the dialogic nature of language, and takes it further, suggesting that language is multiple rather than only double. As she comments in an interview about the book, 'Talking about *Polylogue*': 'The theoretical work that interests me involves the analysis of the *work* of language, not as something possessing an arbitrary but systematisable nature ... but rather as a verbal practice whose economy is complex, critical and contradictory (poetic language offers the most striking example of such a practice)'. (Kristeva in Moi 1987, 115, my emphasis).[1] Her emphasis is on the '*work* of language', language as a process, something that does work, and as something that works, though its workings are complex, critical and contradictory. Her linguistic investigations, then, are investigations into a language system that is not really a system at all, since it cannot be described except temporarily and locally. Her work is a series of antitotalising gestures.

In these terms, then, for Kristeva the analysis of language is always also political. Her relationship with conventional politics in general, and with liberal feminist politics in particular, however, is not an easy one. As Leon Roudiez notes, 'her feminist position is no more orthodox than her other stands', and he quotes an interview between Kristeva and Jean-Paul Enthoven to demonstrate her heterodoxy. In the interview she says:

> I am quite dedicated to the feminist movement but I think feminism, or any other movement, need not expect unconditional backing on the part of an intellectual woman. I think the time has come to emerge out of the 'for-women-only' practice, out of a kind of mythicizing of femininity. ... I have the impression [some feminists] are relying too much on an existentialist concept of woman, a concept that attaches a guilt complex to the maternal function. Either one has children, but that means that one is not good for anything else, or one does not, and then it becomes possible to devote oneself to serious undertakings. As far as I am concerned, childbearing as such never seemed inconsistent with cultural activity, and that is the point I try to make when talking to feminist groups. (Roudiez 1981, 10)[2]

And in the Preface to *Desire in Language*, she writes that her function as an analyst of and in language is 'to describe the signifying phenomenon, or signifying phenomena, while analyzing, criticizing, and dissolving, "phenomenon," "meaning," and "signifier"' (Kristeva 1980, vii). If part of the process is always to criticise and dissolve the very subjects of study, the very tools which enable the study in the first place, as a political analyst, Kristeva's work is likely to undermine the very concepts that underpin activist political movements. In her comments on feminism, she is refusing the conceptual framework that makes feminism as activist politics possible. She will not see the culture/nature debate surrounding childbirth as the binary opposition that some feminists have claimed it to be. The so-called 'natural' process of childbearing is always already also a 'cultural' process, since its 'product', the child, will become a subject in culture, and since the woman who gives birth inhabits both poles of the opposition of culture and nature in her very being. In other words, she attacks the terms of the liberal feminist agenda because she sees them as reinscribing precisely the oppositions (between culture and nature, between subjectivity and materiality) that she believes it is the role of feminism to attack.

What, then, makes her an appropriate study for feminist thought? If Kristeva had gone no further than her study of language and its politics, she would remain an important thinker, whose contribution to linguistics was recognised by significant contemporaries such as Roland Barthes. But in her bringing together of linguistics with psychoanalysis she made her most significant move. As Toril Moi has noted, she arrived in Paris in 1966, the year in which Jacques Lacan's *Ecrits* were first published (Moi 1986, 1), which is, of course, just a coincidence. Similarly coincidental were the so-called *événements* of May 1968, when students and workers banded together in a short-lived attempt to overthrow the French state and to establish a more egalitarian society along Marxist lines. That revolution, however, never quite happened, partly because the French Communist Party had opposed it from the outset. The disillusionment of the idealistic young men and women and the workers of France was cemented by elections which returned a massive centre-right majority later that year. For those who wanted a leftist state of some description, the betrayal of the Communists was a turning point. At the same time, the Soviet Union invaded Czechoslovakia to end the revisions of Marxism that were taking place in Prague; and the French Left could not look to the United States because of its involvement in the Vietnam War, increasingly seen by Europeans as an imperialist and unjustifiable conflict.

The Tel Quel group of *avant-garde* writers in France, with which Kristeva was involved from the mid-sixties to the late seventies, looked to China for a different version of the state, one that was neither Stalinist nor Imperialist. For Kristeva, who had been brought up in a Communist state, China did not make an unproblematic third way. She was troubled by the intellectual poverty of left-leaning political groupings and their purely materialist explanations of the world, especially in what she saw as their omission of individual subjects from their political analysis. It was in order to re-place what she called the 'speaking subject' (Kristeva 1980, viii) into political and linguistic analysis that she turned to psychoanalytic theory. What interested her about the speaking subject was that individual emotions are not explicable merely by traditional political or philosophical formulations; or rather that they are not explicable by those formulations alone. She became interested in the ways in which the speaking subject disrupts explanations of cause and effect, and undoes the very structures of totalising explanation. The speaking subject is therefore always a political and politicised subject. The importance of psycho-analysis is that it is a discourse that gives space to the individual speaking subject, values his/her interventions, and can have 'real' effects, in that the psychoanalytic speaking subject may even get 'better', be cured of his/her neurosis or pain. One person's cure, however, does not amount to a once-for-all explanation; nor does it represent a cure for all speaking subjects.[3]

The move towards psychoanalysis did not mean that Kristeva abandoned her earlier subjects of study. The real importance of her work, on the contrary, is in her rigorous combination of different discourses. Not for nothing is she credited with introducing the concept of 'intertextuality' into critical discourse, a concept that depends on discourses competing with and modifying each other within a single text. As Michael Payne has suggested, her work 'is at once a major study in semiotics, psychoanalysis, philosophy and literary criticism', and its rigorous combination of these discourses into an intertext leaves none of these disciplines 'undisturbed' (Payne 1993, 163). In her essay 'Word, Dialogue and Novel', she praised Bahktin for being 'one of the first to replace the static hewing out of texts with a model where literary structure does not simply *exist*, but is generated in relation to *another* structure'. She argues that Bahktin's work is involved in tracing an '*intersection of textual surfaces*', not in tracking down a single point or fixed meaning. It makes his writing dynamic and energetic, as it seeks the traces of multiple other discourses within any textual formation. She writes:

> Bahktin situates the text within history and society, which are then seen as texts read by the writer, and into which he inserts himself by rewriting them. Diachrony is transformed into synchrony, and in light of this transformation, *linear* history appears as an abstraction. The only way a writer can participate in history is by transgressing this abstraction through a process of reading-writing; that is, through the practice of a signifying structure in relation or opposition to another structure. ... The poetic word, polyvalent and multi-determined, adheres to a logic exceeding that of codified discourse and fully comes into being only in the margins of recognized culture. Bahktin was the first to study this logic, and he looked for its roots in *carnival*. Carnivalesque discourse breaks through the laws of a language censored by grammar and semantics, and, at the same time, is a social and political protest. There is no equivalence, but rather, iden-

tity between challenging official linguistic codes and challenging official law. (Kristeva in Moi ed. 1986, 36, emphasis in original)

This passage articulates in linguistic, formalist and political terms the
concerns which Kristeva's interest in Lacanian psychoanalysis will
enable her to formulate in terms of the speaking subject – a subject
who is necessarily connected to language, to forms and to politics, but
who also experiences him/herself as transgressing the boundaries
between these discourses. Individuality is, as it were, the excess that
cannot be contained by any single system.

The speaking subject is a kind of text. But the meaning of an individual person, like the meaning of any text, is not a fixed point. Because
people are born into cultural and historical specificities of which they
have both collective and individual experience (they are members of
groups, as well as being individuals separate from those groups), they
are texts overwritten with traces of other texts or contexts. They bear
the marks of these traces, and have their meaning in their intersections. They cannot be simply be explained: and if they could, it would
be tantamount to being 'explained away', having their individual
subjectivity removed from them. It is for this reason that Kristeva
resists ideas such as 'feminine language', and argues instead that
women, overwritten by the traces of a dominant masculine culture,
must analyse that culture from within. In the interview, 'Talking about
Polylogue', she says that what is at stake in her writing is the 'fundamental re-examination of those identities and laws by which we live':

> how can the new values offered by the arts, the sciences and politics
> ... respond to the psycho-social characteristics of women, and so
> propose another ethics in which women could partake? Or in other
> words: how can an enquiry into the nature of motherhood lead to a
> better understanding of the part played in love by the woman, a role
> no longer of the virgin, forever promised to the third person, God, but
> that of a real woman whose essentially polymorphic sexuality will
> sooner or later have to deal with a man, a woman, or a child? ... It is
> unfortunately the case that some feminists insist in adopting sulking,
> and even obscurantist attitudes: those, for example, who demand a
> separate language for women, one made of silence, cries or touch,
> which has cut all ties with the language of so-called phallic communi-
> cation; or those who attack logic, the sign, currency, and the very
> principle of exchange on the grounds that women function as objects
> of exchange in the constitution of the patriarchal social order. ... the

time has come for each and every woman, *in whatever way we can*, to confront the controversial values once held to be universal truths by our culture, and to subject them to an interminable analysis. In a sense this may be a theoretical task; it is above all a matter of ethics. (115–17, my emphasis)

Kristeva cannot conceive of a 'feminine language', an *écriture féminine*, or a *parler-femme* (see below, Chapters 6 and 7 on the works of Irigaray and Cixous), and certainly does not believe that such a language, were it possible, would dissolve the sexed inequalities of human existence. The system has to be dealt with in its own terms. One has to analyse so-called universal truths to show that they are neither universal nor true, and that analysis has to take place in a process that both uses and questions the terms that already exist. Nonetheless, although she resists the idea of feminine language, she focuses on female bodies, and their relationships with language and institutions. She is interested not in Woman as a philosophical, explicable, totalising category, but in *a* real woman, who has relationships with men, with other women, and with children, relationships which are not the same as every other woman's relationships, though they may share something in common, too. Her appeal is individualistic rather than the traditionally communal position of liberal feminism, since her focus is on the individual speaking subject. The language that appeals to the communal, the universal (all women, Woman) explains the speaking subject away, and leaves no space for her in the system. Indeed, even when it has good intentions, it may just end up replicating in a different order the very system it was supposed to displace.

In her 1974 book, *Revolution in Poetic Language*, Kristeva developed her most influential ideas. The book bears the traces of both her linguistic training and her more recent training as a Lacanian analyst. Her writing is not a simple application of Lacan's ideas, but a modification and rewriting of them. The book is split into two parts. In the first she expounds her ideas of language and 'literariness' in ways that register both her formalist linguistic training and her analytic practice. In the second part of the book, she provides readings of a number of nineteenth- and twentieth-century *avant-garde* writers (Mallarmé, Lautréamont, Joyce), in order to demonstrate the ways in which the speaking subject in the literary text has changed because of a 'revolution' in the conceptual frameworks that language provides for the world from the nineteenth century onwards.[4] The title's allusion to 'poetic language' as opposed to 'literary language' is certainly derived from the Russian formalist linguistics. Kristeva refuses the term 'literature' because it implies a kind of writing that is beyond the reach of analysis because of the values attached to it, untouchable because perfect, a position she wishes to resist because of its implication in ideological formations which enact power relations. She chooses poetic language as the subject of her study to evade those power relations.

But whilst the term derives from formalist concerns, Kristeva is also anxious to avoid the idea that poetic language might simply function as a kind of sub-cultural code within dominant versions of language. For her, as Roudiez notes: 'it stands for the infinite possibilities of language' (Roudiez 1984, 2); and it is revolutionary because it is 'an exploration and discovery of the possibilities of language; ... an activity that liberates the subject from a number of linguistic, psychic, and social networks; ... a dynamism that breaks up the inertia of language habits'. As such, it 'grants linguists the unique possibility of studying the *becoming* of the signification of signs' (2–3).[5] It is not that our reading/speaking poetic language will lead us to man (woman?) the barricades. Rather, poetic language stretches our conceptual frameworks and liberates our thinking. It is language distinct from that ordinary language used for communication, the language of everyday speech, though it is recognisable within the terms of such ordinary communication. But it is also a language which draws attention to itself *as* language, a language of materiality, rather than the apparent transparency of ordinary speech in which the reader/hearer is encouraged to forget the words and to move straight to the world to which the words are supposed to refer. Poetic language advertises the writer/speaker's efforts to encase concepts or objects in sounds and rhythms. The recipient of such a language is therefore encouraged to notice language in use, rather than moving directly to the 'reality' or the abstraction to which the words are supposed to refer. Poetic language includes the works of 'literature', especially avant-garde literature: it includes Shakespeare, Racine, Mallarmé; it includes the Marquis de Sade and the works of Antonin Artaud; and it also includes the language of psychosis and might include the babble of a child who is learning to speak.

The key terms that Kristeva elaborates in the opening chapters of *Revolution* certainly bear the traces of their formalist linguistic origins. But they are also marked by a serious attempt to theorise the speaking subject within language, an attempt which requires psychoanalytic insight. For Kristeva, following Lacan, the speaking subject is always a split subject, divided between unconscious and conscious motivations, inhabiting both nature and culture since the physiological processes of speaking (the breath we have to take, the way tongues move around teeth, the way we sit, stand or hold a pen in order to speak or write) are derived from the body, but speech itself is also constrained by culture. Her insistence is that we must take both the conscious and the unconscious, both the mind and the body, both the cultural and the natural, seriously as being absolutely necessary to the process of forming meaning. In making connections between linguistics and psychoanalysis, between systems and individual speakers within those systems, Kristeva's concept of the split speaking subject maps onto her insight that any text is polyvalent, polylogical, plural, unfixed. It is the obligation of the analyst (whether in literary criticism or in psychoanalytic practice) to read the pluralities of both text and speaking subject.

Like the text, then, the subject cannot be fixed. The subject is not only split, but is also a 'subject in process', in French *sujet en procès*. The French word *procès* contains the double ideas of process and trial. The subject is always in process in that s/he is not fixed, but always developing. But also, the subject is always in process because s/he is always on trial, being tested against the various contexts in which s/he has his/her being. The idea of processive subjectivity is attractive to feminist thinkers because of its inherent resistance of the fixity of sexual or gendered identity which can trap women in the feminine mode. In Oscar Wilde's *The Importance of Being Earnest* (1895), Gwendolen Fairfax announces to Jack Worthing after he has told that she is quite perfect: 'Oh! I hope I am not that. It would leave no room for developments, and I intend to develop in many directions' (Wilde 1994, 364). Her words are a joke, but they make a serious point. Perfection is fixed. One might as well be dead. To be a subject in process, even if it means being often sorely tried, also means that one can develop.

In *Revolution in Poetic Language*, Kristeva accounts for the split of the speaking subject in terms that derive from, but which also modify, Lacanian analysis. She suggests that there are two kinds of signifying process at work in the making of meaning, and the two modes are locked together. She names the two modes the Symbolic and the Semiotic. The concept of the Symbolic mode of communication is an adaptation from Lacan's writings. It is the language of transparency, power and conformity, and, as such, is aligned with patriarchal functions in culture – *le non/nom du père* – which signals the father's name and the father's prohibitions in social and psychic formations. The Symbolic content of language is what is manifest or obvious, the language of content, the language from which general principles can be abstracted, the language which is open to paraphrase. It is traditionally the language of scientific discourses, of newspapers and history, the language into which authority is written. In Kristeva's model, as in Lacan's, the developing child comes to subjectivity in relation to the Symbolic functions of language. The child inserts him/herself into culture by submitting to the father's 'no', by conforming to the linguistic rules of grammar, syntax and propriety in vocabulary, and this process is related to the child's insertion into social rules. Since the social world is a patriarchal world, to learn the language of that world is necessarily to learn the language of the father. The process is instigated by the child's separation from the mother, his/her recognition that s/he is separate and different from the mother. The learning of symbolic language, therefore, necessitates a submission to masculine functions and a farewell to the feminised pre-Oedipal space of the mother–child bond.

Only, no speaker ever speaks entirely in the Symbolic language of patriarchy, which is where Kristeva's concept of the Semiotic comes in. Her use of this word is itself a kind of revolution, since semiotics is usually understood as the 'science' of signs, and it is usually therefore aligned with the Symbolic since it seeks to analyse meaning functions into a totalised system. When Kristeva uses the phrase 'the Semiotic', however, she is signalling a realm of meaning that resists any such systematisation. The process of learning to speak may well be a process that has as its goal the complete insertion of the speaking subject into the Symbolic function. A child's language, however, is a language of babble, incoherence, rhythm and sound, which are not exactly meaningless, but which are not susceptible to rationalistic systematic analysis. A child's babble cannot be paraphrased. This prelinguistic language, which will eventually be more or less successfully repressed by Symbolic functions, is what Kristeva terms 'the Semiotic'. She identifies it not only in children's developing language skills, but also in 'poetic' language, and in the language of psychosis, all of which are languages where the relationships between words and concepts privileged by the Symbolic, are significantly disrupted. They are languages of materiality; they each draw attention to themselves rather than inscribing an easy, transparent relationship between words and the world.

The concepts of the Symbolic and the Semiotic are not, however, to be simply understood as masculine and feminine relations with language and culture. The Symbolic may indeed be a function of patriarchy, but most women nonetheless successfully internalise its rules and learn to speak and function within its structures. Moreover, men as poets or mad men, can make use of semiotic pulsations against the rules of the Symbolic. These realms within the signifying process define potentially shifting relations to culture, not biological positions that cannot be altered. Kristeva sees these two concepts as interdependent, as absolutely inseparable, in the making of meaning. Even the most symbolically inflected authoritative language (such as the language of a scientific treatise, for example), bears the traces of the Semiotic: the words used even in such a context are still materialised, and the speaker/writer still has obligations to form as well as to content. Kristeva writes:

> These two modalities [the Symbolic and the Semiotic] are inseparable within the *signifying process* that constitutes language, and the dialectic between them determines the type of discourse (narrative, metalanguage, theory, poetry, etc.) involved; in other words, so-called 'natural' language allows for different modes of articulation of the semiotic and the symbolic. On the other hand, there are nonverbal signifying systems that are constructed exclusively on the basis of the semiotic (music, for example). But ... this exclusivity is relative, precisely because of the necessary dialectic between the two modalities of the signifying process, which is constitutive of the subject. Because the subject is always *both* symbolic *and* semiotic, no signifying system he produces can be either 'exclusively' semiotic or 'exclusively' symbolic, and is instead necessarily marked by an indebtedness to both. (Kristeva 1984, 24)

This is a restatement in psychoanalytic terms of the Bahktinian idea of the dialogic, with the emphasis shifted from text to speaking subject. The language the subject speaks is not fixed; and since language 'constitutes' the subject, the subject is not fixed either. Meaning, like the subject, is always *en procès*, in process, on trial.

The Symbolic and the Semiotic, then, are not quite binary oppositions at different ends of a rigid scale. Rather they are part of a continuum in the process of making meaning. They flow into each other, and as such they resist easy analysis. Central to Kristeva's notion of a continuum between the apparently meaningless babble of the Semiotic and the alleged transparency of the Symbolic in language is her concept of the *chora*. The word *chora* is derived from Plato's *Timaeus* where it has several possible meanings, including womb, enclosed space, nurse, receptacle and mother. As Jacques Derrida has shown, it is a figure of multiple contradictions, which has so many meanings that it threatens to collapse into utter unintelligibility because it refuses to be fixed:

> what Plato in the *Timaeus* designates by the name of *khora* seems to defy that 'logic of noncontradiction' ... that logic 'of binarity, of yes or no'. ... The *khora*, which is neither 'sensible' nor 'intelligible', belongs to a 'third genus'. One cannot even say of it that is *neither* this *nor* that or that it is *both* this *and* that. (Derrida, in Wolfreys ed. 1998, 231)

It is a word that refuses definition, and resists translation and abstraction; and yet *chora* is a real word that functions within Symbolic language formations, whilst at the same time enacting the Semiotic disruptions of those self-same formations. As Julian Wolfreys argues in his introduction to Derrida's text, 'Formulations of the sort "*khora* is/is not ..." miss the point and are neither true nor false inasmuch as *khora* is not determinable according to the conceptual framework which posits such questions in the first place' (Wolfreys 1998, 39).

We are anxious about words that we cannot define because they threaten the illusory stability of our linguistic universe. Inasmuch as the *chora* 'is' anything, it is a metaphor and a rhetorical device which expresses the idea that meaning may exist in places where it cannot be defined or abstracted. In a helpful commentary on Kristeva's concept, Michael Payne returns to the Platonic text, to show that Plato uses the word in a range of ways: it means receptacle, nurse, mother, space. Kristeva, Payne argues, 'seems determined to retain both Plato's maternal image and his more abstract formulation' of the term:

This is a remarkable rhetorical decision because when Kristeva writes about the body, unlike Lacan and Derrida, she gives it a sense of having bone and flesh and hormones. For her the body both is and is not external to language. (Payne 1993, 168)

Payne connects the *chora* to the Aristotelian concept of 'chorion', the membrane that encloses a foetus in a womb, and thus signals the codependent limits of the mother's and the foetus's bodies. It is a limit which expands and contracts with the movement and growth of each of the two bodies, enacting both their separation and their interdependence. Like language itself, it is a doubled structure, which 'defines the semiotic space of the other within the mother, and within its double structure, the first communication between the fetus and (m)other occurs' (169).

A question that might help in figuring out the concept of *chora* is: is your body nature or culture? The question establishes a binary opposition – an 'either/or' formulation which presupposes that bodies must belong to one realm or the other. The classic answer to the question, an answer derived from Enlightenment thought, is that bodies belong to the realm of nature: it is the mind or the soul or the intellect that is cultured. But it is precisely this kind of binarism that Kristeva's thought unsettles. In two essays that meditate on maternity, 'Motherhood according to Giovanni Bellini' and 'Stabat Mater', Kristeva shows that you cannot divide the world into opposing categories, indeed, that such categories are merely theoretical. She opens her Bellini essay with the following remarks:

> Cells fuse, split and proliferate; volumes grow, tissues stretch, and body fluids change rhythm, speeding up or slowing down. Within the body, growing as a graft, indomitable, there is an other. And no one is present within that simultaneously dual and alien space, to signify what is going on. 'It happens, but I'm not there.' 'I cannot realize it, but it goes on.' Motherhood's impossible syllogism. (Kristeva 1980, 237)

The word syllogism refers to a subtle rhetorical argument, usually made up of two propositions and the conclusion that necessarily follows on from them in the terms of philosophical logic. The logic that Kristeva proposes here, in her evocation of the early stages of pregnancy, is that the maternal body does certain things in order to support its foetus; the pregnant woman knows these things are happening inside her, but her knowledge is not susceptible to the rational analysis available in Symbolic language. The pregnant woman is the site of a particularly acute realisation of the inadequacy of Symbolic knowledge, which categorises by opposition, to represent Semiotic experience. There is almost a sense in which pregnancy is unspeakable in the language of Symbolic authority.[6] She goes on to suggest that the discourses of both science and established religion fail to account for the collapse of the nature/culture binary opposition in the figure of the pregnant woman. And she sees such a woman as 'a thoroughfare, a threshold where "nature" confronts "culture"' (238). As such, the pregnant woman might be understood as one of many possible images for the metaphor of the *chora*. She represents the site of continuation between apparent oppositions (a thoroughfare, a threshold), not their absolute separation. Symbolic and Semiotic coexist in her.

In the slightly later essay, 'Stabat Mater', Kristeva picks up on this same image of pregnancy and maternity, and expands its force and range. Her underlying argument is that Love, whatever form it takes, is a disruptive force in culture – a force that both shores up and undermines the institutions of culture: it is necessary, for example, to Western conceptions of the family; and yet it can also unsettle family life by authorising illicit activities such as adultery, or marrying out of the group of which the family approves. In 'Stabat Mater', we see Kristeva reflecting on the idea of mother love. The essay's title comes from a Roman Catholic hymn and prayer, 'Stabat mater dolorosa' [stood the mother, full of sorrows] in which the Virgin Mary is described sorrowing over the dead body of the body of Christ, her son. If the most common image of the Virgin in religious iconography is the image of her nursing the infant Christ-child, the second most common image is the *pieta*, the image of her cradling his dead body after the Crucifixion. The hymn takes the *pieta* image as its focus, and is thus an expression of the pain of love rather than of its wonders or pleasures. Kristeva's meditation on maternity dramatises the split subject of language. On the right hand side of the page is a learned discourse on the cult of the Virgin Mary, that most cultural of mothers, the acceptable face of maternity in Western Christian societies.[7] On the left-hand side of the page is a discontinuous narrative of Kristeva's own experience of maternity – a narrative that speaks poetically and evocatively (not logically or analytically) of love, pain, horror, delight, and which radically calls into question the 'authorized version' of motherhood. The typographical practice of the essay destabilises the Symbolic order which speaks of woman as a category rather than of *a* woman as a speaking individual. The co-existing and opposing discourses of the piece – Symbolic, authoritative historical narrative and Semiotic poetic musings – dramatise the idea that language is made up of meaning in process, particularly because there is a kind of leakage or contamination between the two types of writing, where history becomes personal, and personal experience is placed in the context of history. The writing subject here is most definitely a split subject, and also a subject in process. Kristeva, the philosopher and academic does not cease to exist in Kristeva, the maternal figure, and vice versa. Nature and culture, and all other two-term oppositions, are exposed as fictions. And there is power in this exposure. Thinking through the *chora*-body of the mother means over-turning the taxonomies that hold meaning into fixed categories. The *chora* offers a different model for conceptualising the world and our place in it.

Kristeva's importance for feminist literary criticism comes from several strands in her work. The combination of politics, linguistics and psychoanalysis is especially powerful. The idea that the speaking subject is always 'in process', developing, changing, tried and tested, is also a helpful intervention for the feminist reader. She is also an attractive figure because, for all the theoretical difficulty of her work, she is also genuinely interested in real people. For her, the ethics of reading and writing are finally about relationships in the realm of the real. Thus, as Payne argues, although she is rigorous in dismantling inadequate ideas of what is meant by the human derived from the Enlightenment, she is not anti-humanistic (Payne 1993, 195). All her writing returns to people in the end; and the people she refers to have a solid materiality – flesh, blood and bone, hormones, cells, skin and hair – such as we recognise in our own bodily lives, but from which we often turn away in our so-called intellectual pursuits.

Reading with mother?

How might such ideas be used? There is a danger with offering readings influenced by certain thinkers, that they encourage slavish imitation of inadequate models. The examples presented here and in subsequent

chapters are in no sense definitive. They are to be read as possible ways
in to thinking, not as the last word in how to 'do' a Kristevan reading.

There are many things that one might choose to say about D. H.
Lawrence's novel, *Women in Love* (1920), and it is indeed a novel
about which feminist critics have been very vocal. This is no surprise
since the novel is largely about mapping possible and even ideal (for
Lawrence) relationships between men and women. Lawrence's views
are idiosyncratic, and can certainly be read as masculist and destructive for women in terms of the ways in which he positions them materially in the world, as well as in his readings of female psychic and
cultural development. Feminist readings of Lawrence, therefore, have
tended to concentrate on issues of representation, and of the politics
implied by that representation. He has been much attacked.

   Both Simone de Beauvoir and Kate Millett have something to say
about the text. In de Beauvoir's reading, Lawrence's works preach a
message of self-abnegation, a self-denial that both men and women
undertake in order to come together in mutual (sexual) fulfilment.
She sees the relationship between the central characters, Birkin and
Ursula, as a kind of ideal: 'the sexual act is, without annexing, without
surrender of either partner, a marvellous fulfilment of each one by the
other. ... Having access to each other in the generous extortion of
passion, two lovers have access to the Other, the All' (de Beauvoir
1997, 246). This supposed ideal of sexual equality – or rather, of equality in sexual encounters – is, however, undercut in Lawrence's work
because of the physical, psychical and social inequalities of the
couple. She summarises his position thus:

> Not only does man play the role in the sexual life, but he is active also
> in going beyond it; woman remains shut up in it. Thought and action
> have their roots in the phallus; lacking the phallus, woman has not
> rights in either the one or the other: she can play a man's role, and
> even brilliantly, but it is just a game ... For woman 'the deepest
> consciousness in the loins and the belly'. If this is perverted and her
> flow of energy is upwards to the breast and head, woman may
> become clever, noble, efficient, brilliant, competent in the manly
> world; but, according to Lawrence, she soon has enough of it, every-
> thing collapses, and she returns to sex, 'which is her business at the
> present moment'. (248)[8]

As de Beauvoir goes on to say, Lawrence may appear to be saying radical things about sexual practice, but he is also reinscribing the bourgeois ideal of the separate spheres (male – active and external, female – passive and domestic), and there is no material gain for women from his thinking. Woman remains fixed as Other to the Lawrentian male ego.

Millett's reading is, as might be expected, powerfully polemical and angry. For her, the trajectory of *Women in Love* is Ursula's retreat into passivity, docility and virtual nothingness. The decline is a result of her relationship with Birkin, who uses 'psychological warfare' against her in a very modern battle of the sexes (Millett 1977, 263). Millett notes that Birkin tries to establish his relationship with Ursula as an ideal of modern sexual relations, but comments that his wish to produce a perfect equilibrium between them 'is betrayed over and over by the obvious contradictions between preachment and practice' (262). In particular she objects to the assumption that the balancing act depends on 'a denial of personality in the woman', on Ursula becoming 'more and more her husband's creature' (264), as she resigns her job and becomes Birkin's disciple in her marriage.

There is no correspondence between these content-based readings, however important they might be, and how a reading inflected by Kristeva's thinking might approach the Lawrence's text. Her technique in readings, arising from her training in linguistics, would tend to approach texts far more closely, and to submit shorter passages to rigorous analysis rather than drawing large conclusions from generalised readings. Her interest in the novel-genre's multivocality, and in the relationships between abstractable content and the material forms of language, make close textual study a more appropriate route into critical practice. Moreover, large generalisations cannot be the aim of a theoretical perspective that is constituted precisely to resist the totalising critical gesture.

In general terms, *Women in Love* is certainly open to readings refracted through Kristeva. In particular there is a marked tension throughout the text between the will towards expression and the narrative's pained realisation of the inadequacy of words to do the work of expression. Passage after passage is constructed through sentences whose syntax is on the verge of collapse, and whose content directly contradicts what is said immediately before and immediately after. The pressure of the Semiotic pulses against the Symbolic order throughout the prose. Lawrence also reuses words against the grain of their conventional meanings: for example, a word like 'perfect' is a term of disapproval since perfection is fixed and undeveloping. He undercuts conventional semantics and enacts his own revolution (albeit probably a conservative revolution) in the poetic languages of his texts. What follows is a discussion of a short passage from the text, chosen deliberately partly because both Millett and de Beauvoir also mention it, and partly because its content also allows me to reflect on Kristeva's concept of the *chora* and on her thinking about the maternal body as a critical site for the interrogation of the norms that structure Western thought.

In Chapter 7 of *Women in Love*, 'Totem', Gerald Crich, the Midlands industrialist, a conventional and mechanistic man of whom the novel disapproves, has found himself in the bohemian milieu of a group of London artists, friends of Rupert Birkin. He spends the night at the flat of a man named Halliday, and sleeps with an artist's model called Pussum.[9] When Gerald gets up in the morning, he is already out of his depth, feeling threatened by the unconventional behaviour and attitudes of the group, who are, for example, uninhibited about nakedness, and perfectly prepared to wander about the house with no clothes as the sign of their scorn for social norms. The nudity of the other men disturbs him, seeming 'to detract from his own dignity' and to reduce his sense of the importance of his humanity (Lawrence 1982, 132). Their bodies in their 'natural state' undermine Gerald's sense of his own cultured humanity. The totem of the chapter's title is an African carved figure which represents a woman in parturition. Gerald does not understand this image, and asks Birkin to explain it to him:

> Birkin, white and strangely present, went over to the carved figure of the negro woman in labour. Her nude, protuberant body crouched in a strange clutching posture, her hands gripping at the ends of the band, above her breast.
>
> 'It is art,' said Birkin. ... Strangely elated, Gerald ... lifted his eyes to the face of the wooden figure. And his heart contracted.
>
> He saw vividly with his spirit the grey, forward-stretching face of the negro woman, African and tense, abstracted in utter physical stress. It was a terrible face, void, peaked, abstracted almost into meaninglessness by the weight of sensation beneath. He saw the Pussum in it. As in a dream, he knew her.
>
> 'Why is it art? Gerald asked, shocked, resentful.

'It conveys a complete truth,' said Birkin. 'It contains the whole truth of that state, whatever you feel about it.'
'But you can't call it *high* art,' said Gerald.
'High! There are centuries and hundreds of centuries of development in a straight line, behind that carving; it is an awful pitch of culture, of a definite sort.'
'What culture?' Gerald asked, in opposition. He hated the sheer African thing.
'Pure culture in sensation, culture in the *physical* consciousness, mindless, utterly sensual. It is so sensual as to be final, supreme.'
But Gerald resented it. He wanted to keep certain illusions, certain ideas like clothing. (133, emphasis in original)

This object is strangely out of place in 'an ordinary London sitting-room in a flat, evidently taken furnished, rather common and ugly' (127). It does not belong there, and when Gerald first sees it, he wonders if it is 'obscene', and is shocked when Birkin pronounces that it is 'art'. As Lynda Nead has suggested, 'obscene' is a word of obscure etymological origins, but it is possible that it is derived from the Latin word 'scena', thus meaning 'what is off, or to one side of the stage, beyond presentation ... the art/obscenity pairing represents the distinction between that which can be seen and that which is just beyond representation' (Nead 1992, 25). The staging of the totem figure in a suburban London flat is a context that alters its possible readings. An African context would render the totem as an object of veneration, as a symbol of something more than itself, and as a focus for worship. When Birkin describes it as 'art' he places it as a fetish or totem of a different kind: he displaces the original purpose of worship from an African culture and claims it for a westernised aesthetic that robs it of its original power.

One of the interesting things about this passage, then, is the extent to which both men are somehow 'wrong' in their response to the object. Gerald's disgust is explicitly set up as a poor response to the artefact; Birkin's position is more ambiguous, since in naming the statue as art, he is at least giving it a kind of value that can be understood by himself and his European friends. But the naming of an object as 'art' (like the naming of a text as 'literature') renders it untouchable, unsusceptible to analysis. Birkin's comment that the statue 'conveys a complete truth', that it 'contains the whole truth of that state whatever you feel about it' is intensely problematic. The idea of complete or whole truth fixes the figure into a single state. He goes on to say that the statue expresses 'really ultimate *physical* consciousness, mindless, utterly sensual. It is so sensual as to be final, supreme.' But would a woman examining this figure feel the same? It is, after all, the representation of a *process*. Neither parturition nor the birth itself are final. They are, as it were, beginnings of something other than themselves – the outset of maternity for the woman, the beginning of life for her child. Thus, although Birkin's naming of this figure as 'art' values it, he is also submitting the figure to something that orders and fixes it into the Symbolic realm. The message he abstracts from the statue's text is not quite true to what the statue-text itself represents as a process (*procès*), both an ongoing motion and a trial.

Moreover, both men in their different responses to the statue insist on its inarticulacy, its speechlessness or meaninglessness or mind-lessness. The woman lacks language – or rather, they are incapable of hearing or reading her message. For although the figure represents 'utter physical stress', an animality that appears to undermine her humanity, it is also a figure of culture, created out of a culture that values the image of the childbearing woman as an object of power. It is an object that has a specific form which, in the context of an ugly London flat, draws attention to itself; it is a material object that is out of place. But it is also an object that has meaning, even if that meaning cannot be clearly articulated, as Lawrence's description of Gerald's reaction, with its accumulated and contradictory adjectives, suggests. Like the figure of the Kristevan *chora*, the totem contains oppositions and thereby undoes the oppositional structure of either/or which is how both Birkin and Gerald understand their world. Birkin's symbolic pronouncement, 'it is art', cannot in the end fix the figure into a Symbolic structure that absolutely contains it. His struggle to 'explain' the figure to Gerald ends in failure since Gerald wants 'to keep certain illusions, certain ideas like clothing'. The syntax of that sentence with its confusion of whether 'ideas like clothing' is a simile comparing ideas to clothing (ideas shrouding the nakedness of natural man and rendering him human and cultured), or whether it means that Gerald more literally prefers to keep his clothes on (in the context of a scene full of naked men) implies in language the polylogi-cal realm in which form and content collapse into each other.

For Kate Millett, the totem figure is 'a rebuke to the dangerous personal and artistic aspirations' represented by Ursula's sister,

Gudrun, in the novel. The statuette reduces woman 'to the level of a suffering animal, her face "transfixed and rudimentary"'. Birkin 'lectures on her meaning, proving that in the "savage woman" one sees the perfection of female function' (Millett 1977, 268). And Simone de Beauvoir reads the statue as Lawrence's emblem of perfected female self-abnegation: 'Nothing could be more beautiful than that little statue of a woman in labour', since she signifies Lawrence's view that 'it is not by asserting his singularity, but by fulfilling his generality as intensely as possible that the [male or female] individual can be saved' (de Beauvoir 1997, 245). Both of these readings, for all their differences, focus their attention on a content they can abstract from the text; and both also regard the text, and Birkin's position in it, as representative of Lawrence's own views. A closer attention to the tensions in the writing gives a different perspective. And if one follows Ursula's relationship with Birkin to its end in the novel, it is clear that Birkin's views are modified by his contact with his wife: he may have the novel's last words, but they are not necessarily triumphant or assertive. What Millett sees as his Symbolic authority, his phallic pride, is always under pressure from the pulsations of Ursula's opposition. A reading inflected by Kristeva's ideas of the contemporaneous existence of Symbolic and Semiotic utterance, and by her sense of speaking and writing as a process rather than a fixed position, allows us to reread Lawrence's book for the unconscious motivations that unsettle his supposedly entrenched masculist position and make fissures in his prose.

I have chosen my second example because Kristeva's own work on 'poetic' texts has concentrated its attention on *avant-garde* or modernist writing, on texts that are inherently 'difficult' because of their refusal of transparency. Kate Atkinson's 1995 novel, *Behind the Scenes at the Museum*, perhaps feels like an odd choice here, since it is not a difficult book, indeed has enjoyed a great deal of popular acclaim, and was on the best-seller lists in Britain for several weeks after its paperback publication in 1996. What I want to suggest here is that Kristeva's thinking has something to say to us even in relation to texts that do not advertise an explicitly *avant-garde* impetus.

Behind the Scenes at the Museum is the story of Ruby Lennox from her conception (with which the novel opens) to her mature reflections on life after her mother's death some forty-five years later. Alongside the focus on Ruby's story as she grows to maturity, there is a second narrative strand, chapters which are titled throughout as footnotes. The footnote chapters tell Ruby's family history on her mother's side, starting with an errant great-grandmother named Alice who ran away with an itinerant French photographer with devastating results on the children she left behind; there is the story of the woman who replaced Alice in the family as a stepmother; there are the stories of Alice's surviving children, Lillian and Nell (who will eventually be Ruby's grandmother) and their brothers; and finally, there is the story of Bunty, Ruby's mother. The status of the footnotes is difficult to gauge. The narrator's voice throughout the novel is Ruby's voice. It is clear that the story of the past is supposed to be seen as informing the present. And yet Ruby tells us things that logically she cannot know – the secret responses of various ancestors to particular events are reconstructed and then presented as fact by an uncannily omniscient narrator, who nonetheless does not know about the most important event of her own life (the death of her twin sister) until near the end of the text, thus calling into question her knowledge of all the other things she describes. The footnotes also deal with personal responses to official history. They chart, for example, the two world wars and their effects on the life of the family. Ruby's life is similarly punctuated by large events. Her early memories include a family gathering around the television to see the Coronation in 1953. Later, she is bridesmaid at a wedding that takes place unfortuitously on the same day as England's victory in the 1966 World Cup, an event during which her father dies of a heart attack in a farcical illicit coupling with a waitress at the wedding reception. Small lives and big events are juxtaposed, registering the ways in which people's lives are experienced both as personal and individual and as mediated by allegiances to larger groups. The experience of selfhood is very much presented as a both a process and a trial; tragedy and farce coexist and inform each other, neither taking precedence in the narrative's structure.

A second point about the footnotes is that they impose a partial patterning on events as the past leaks into the present. It is hinted, for example, though never stated, that 'Auntie Doreen', Ruby's father's 'bit on the side' in the 1950s is the same girl who slept with her cousin, over from Canada during the war, left pregnant and bereft by his death when he is shot down in a plane in a bombing raid over Germany. The pattern is there, but it is only half-glimpsed, making the narrative of history – even personal history combined with official history – only a very partial explanation of the past. *Behind the Scenes* is, in other words, a novel in part about the limitations of story-telling, the inability of narrative to tell all. Similarly, the recurrent pattern of twins in the family seems to be significant but its precise significance is never brought to the surface: it is just there as a pressure on the seamless present, appearing sometimes as comedy, sometimes as tragedy.

The tensions between knowing and being – the tension of the speaking subject in process – are present from the outset with Ruby's appearance on the scene as an incongruously knowing embryo at conception:

> I exist! I am conceived to the chimes of midnight on the clock on the mantelpiece in the room across the hall. The clock once belonged to my great-grandmother (a woman called Alice) and its tired chime counts me into the world. I'm begun on the first stroke and finished on the last when my father rolls off my mother and is plunged into a dreamless sleep, thanks to the five pints of John Smith's Best Bitter he has drunk in the Punch Bowl with his friends, Walter and Bernard Belling. At the moment at which I moved from nothingness into being my mother was pretending to be asleep – as she often does at such moments. My father, however, is made of stern stuff and he didn't let that put him off.
>
> My father's name is George and he is a good ten years older than my mother, who is now snoring into the next pillow. My mother's name is Berenice but everyone has always called her Bunty.
>
> 'Bunty' doesn't seem like a very grown-up name to me – would I be better off with a mother with a different name? A plain Jane, a mater- nal Mary? Or something romantic, something that doesn't sound quite so much like a girl's comic – an Aurora, a Camille? Too late now. Bunty's name will be 'Mummy' for a few years yet, of course, but after a while there won't be a single maternal noun (mummy, mum, mam, ma, mama, mom, marmee) that seems appropriate and I more or less give up calling her anything. Poor Bunty! (Atkinson 1996, 9)

In that passage, we can see the glorious illogicality and exuberance with which the text as a whole is written. It is a novel that overspills boundaries and thus exemplifies the function of the *chora* established by Kristeva as a realm which refuses the logic non-contradiction, of either/or by inhabiting the spaces of and/both. It is clearly impossible for the embryo who will become Ruby to proclaim her own existence.

It is even more impossible – if degrees of impossibility are imaginable
– for Ruby to situate that existence in the terms of literary beginnings,
in her reference to the chimes of the tired clock. Like both Tristram
Shandy and David Copperfield, the clock is essential to her beginning.
But her ability to know the clock rather suggests that the time is out of
joint.

Alongside these references to the 'high' cultural form of literature,
Ruby is also situated by the low cultural references of her individual
family circumstances: the five pints of John Smith's Best Bitter, her
mother's sexual indifference and her father's sexual persistence, all of
which will recur as themes through the novel, are always already
constitutive of her world and her place in it. While the text is illogical
in terms of its structuring of time and knowledge according to
common-sense versions of reality and to conventional linear narrative of time, it is also a version of polylogic. Ruby cannot know these
things now. But she can know them retrospectively through the imaginative reconstruction of her parents' marriage, and through the
process of education that she undergoes as a growing child. Indeed
they are the circumstances that have formed her. Like James Joyce's
Stephen Daedalus in *A Portrait of the Artist as a Young Man*, naming
things and people is a significant part of the process of development.[10] The world one names is the world one knows. Ruby's careful
naming of her father and mother in the second paragraph, and her
concern over how she ceases to name her mother because no name
for her seems to fit Bunty's rather morose reality, at once demonstrate
the necessity of language and its contingency. The failure of words
that name the maternal function registers a theme that will be
returned to throughout the novel, that Bunty is an inadequate
mother, and that her inadequacies have to do with her inarticulacy –
what Ruby will later call her 'autistic mothering' (374); Ruby cannot
name her mother because she cannot reconcile Bunty with the
cultural images of maternity that she has grown to expect.

Even that earliest of words – the word that names a parent as
'mummy' or 'daddy' – registers the doubled presence of both
Symbolic and Semiotic in language because it names both a demand
on the parent (a call for a physical need to be met), and articulates a
social relationship. Ruby's chain of possible mother-words are each
socially and historically inflected. When she calls her mother
'mummy' for a few years, as well as signalling the mother's maternity,
she also articulates her own dependence – mummy is a small child's

word in contemporary English culture.[11] The contractions 'mum', 'mam' and 'ma' dramatise the contraction of the mother's role in the life of the growing child. 'Mama' exists in her vocabulary as a literary allusion to nineteenth-century novels she may have read; 'mom' signals an exposure to American culture, and 'marmee', the name given to Mrs March by her daughters in *Little Women*, combines the literary and the American. Bunty's reality, for all that she imagines herself as a latter-day Deanna Durbin or Vivien Leigh, simply will not match up to any of the words that encase the concept of mother. Their materiality does not suit her version of maternity.

Kristeva's work is complex and difficult, but it is also rewarding. It has the potential to liberate the feminist critic from repeated gestures of critical disapproval of literary representation. Her sense that language is polyvalent, and that the speaking subject is always speaking 'in process', opens up textual spaces in which readers can see and analyse the contradictions and fissures inherent in all textual practices. Her combination of linguistic, political and psychoanalytic discourses is a major contribution to feminist thinking. And whilst it may be neither possible nor desirable to reproduce an accurate textual impersonation of her readings of poetic language, it is both possible and desirable to make use of her insights in forming readings of our own.

Notes

1. Poetic language is Kristeva's preferred term for what most people might call literature. For an explanation of the term, see below.
2. The details for the interview are: Jean Paul Enthoven, Interviewer, 'Julia Kristeva: à quoi servent les intellectuels?', *Le Nouvel Observateur*, June 20, 1977.
3. For a clear exposition of Kristeva's intellectual history see: Leon S. Roudiez's Introduction to Julia Kristeva. *Desire in Language: A Semiotic Approach to Literature and Art* Oxford: Basil Blackwell, 1981, pp. 1–20; Toril Moi, *Sexual/Textual Politics: Feminist Literary Theory*, London: Methuen, 1985, pp. 150–73; Toril Moi, Introduction to *The Kristeva Reader*, (Oxford: Basil Blackwell, 1986, pp. 1–22.
4. The English language translation of *Revolution in Poetic Language*, by

Margaret Waller (New York: Columbia University Press, 1984), is in fact only a partial translation. It reproduces Kristeva's theoretical framework which constitutes the first half of the book; but it omits her specific readings of such nineteenth-century *avant-garde* writers as Stéphane Mallarmé.

5. Roudiez is here quoting Kristeva's own words, from *Recherches pour une sémanalyse*, Paris: Seuil, 1969, pp. 178–9.

6. Adrienne Rich's book, *Of Woman Born: Motherhood as Experience and Institution* (London: Virago, 1977) makes a similar point in different terms. Rich's argument is that female experiences of maternity are invalidated by the social formations (the institutions of the title) that appear to celebrate maternity, but which often undermine it.

7. Kristeva acknowledges her debt to Marina Warner's book, *Alone of All Her Sex: The Myth and Cult of the Virgin Mary* (London: Picador [1976], 1990), for the treatise that occupies the right-hand side of her essay. Warner's book is significant here because of her insistence that Mary, far from being an embodiment of the 'eternal feminine' is in fact a figure who takes on the attributes of each historical period in which she appears. That focus in Warner's writing supports Kristeva's contention throughout her writing that all images are culturally and historically specific rather than universals. That the cult of the Virgin Mary has a *history* is significant for any feminist reappropriation of her myth because it shows her as a changing dynamic figure, not as a fixed, perfected image of femininity to which all women must aspire and to which no woman may ever attain.

8. De Beauvoir is quoting Lawrence's book, *Fantasia of the Unconscious* (London: Heinemann, 1961 [1923]) in this passage.

9. Pussum's name is, of course, an obvious sexual pun, and there is indeed a sense in the novel that her role is to act as available 'pussy' for a number of male characters.

10. In the early part of Joyce's novel, the young Stephen is obsessed with naming the world, and with working out how he fits into it. Joyce's point is that we can only conceptualise what we can name; our language constitutes our notion of reality. The making of the real in language, however, is an inexact science. As time goes on, we discover the extent to which words do not fit our world: there are ugly sounds for beautiful things and vice versa. Language is therefore merely contingent in his novel. It makes but does not fix reality.

11. In other parts of the British Isles, and in other parts of the English-speaking world, this is not necessarily the case; but in England, the shift from 'mummy' to 'mum' marks a process of maturation, a growing away from childish things and words which begins around the

time that a child goes to school. In Scotland and Ireland, however, 'mummy' does not have the same implications and can be used by people of any age.

6 'Mirror, Mirror ...': Luce Irigaray and Reflections of and on the Feminine

Luce Irigaray was born in 1930 in Belgium, though she is now a French national. As Margaret Whitford has noted, however, she strongly resists the tendency of criticism to focus on biography, fearing the kinds of *ad feminam* critiques that operate by 'neutralizing a woman thinker whose work is radically challenging [by reducing her] to her biography' (Whitford 1991, 1–2). Her work is in the fields of philosophy, linguistics and psychoanalysis, and she is also a regular contributor to Communist newspapers, especially in Italy. Although she rarely writes specifically about literary texts, she does have important things to say to feminist literary theory – those realms of oppression, repression and expression identified by Showalter as the foci of feminist thinking.

Her earliest book, *Le Langage des déments* (1973, The Language of the Demented), was an investigation into the linguistic collapse suffered by patients with senile dementia. Her focus was on the kinds of subjectivity that can exist for those whose language ceases to be a transparently expressive medium. She concluded that the dementia sufferer was disabled from speaking for himself, and was forced to repeat pre-existing language structures: the demented figure was denied a place from which to speak by the process of his disease, and ended by 'being spoken' by a language over which he had no control, which did not reflect any conscious intention, and which therefore undermined the very notion of subjectivity itself. It was a psycholinguistic study, heavily inflected by the training in Lacanian psychoanalysis that Irigaray had undertaken from the mid-1960s onwards. That interest in the subject as a speaking and spoken being is certainly derived from Lacan's view that subjectivity occurs in and through language. On the face of it, this does not look like a feminist intervention. But, as Toril Moi has argued, 'this passive, imitative or mimetic relationship to the structures of language [in sufferers from dementia] is strikingly similar to the ways in which ... women relate to phallocratic discourse' (Moi 1985, 127). The book in which Irigaray began to speak of the place of women in relation to the patriarchal languages of philosophy and psychoanalysis was *Speculum of the Other Woman*, published first in 1974, which was also Irigaray's doctoral thesis. Although this book, too, was heavily indebted to Lacan, Irigaray's main focus in *Speculum* was on the 'mastering' discourse of philosophy.

There was a personal cost to this second text. Immediately it was published, Irigaray was expelled from the École freudiennne at Vincennes, a research institution then under the directorship of Jacques Lacan himself, and was sacked from her University post there. Lacan was notorious for disapproving of theoretical deviations from his own point of view. Presumably, he recognised the implicit attack on his own position that *Speculum* represented. In fact, though, Lacan is not named in the book, which is a wide-ranging meditation on the writings of Freud and the Western philosophical tradition, from Plato onwards. Its structure, though, belies the very idea of linear history; it begins with Freud and ends with Plato, and it sets out to undo monological traditions of theory and philosophy that suggest that there is only one way to think or be. Indeed, its very method as well as its anti-chronological ordering attacks the position of monologic. As Jane Gallop writes:

> [The] encounter between Irigaray's feminist critique and Freud's final text on woman is an important training ground for a new kind of battle, a feminine seduction/disarming/unsettling of the positions of phallocratic ideology. Irigaray's tactic is a kind of reading: close reading which separates the text into fragments of varying size, quotes it, and then comments with various questions and associations. She never sums up the meaning of Freud's text, nor binds all her commentaries, questions, associations into a unified representation, a coherent interpretation. Her commentaries are full of loose ends and unanswered questions. As a result, the reader does not easily lose sight of the incoherency and inconsistency of the text. (Gallop 1982, 56)

In other words, Irigaray's critique in no way establishes itself as a master-narrative, a paraphrase that masters (mistresses?) the founding texts of psychoanalysis, whether by Freud or by Lacan. Instead, she mimics the psychoanalytic session in her writing: her written relationship with Freud (and later with Plato) is a dialogue of questions and occasional answers, in which neither she nor Freud has the last word. Indeed, it might well be this sense of the dialogic in psychoanalysis that attracts Irigaray to it; while she very often criticises the content of Freud's writings, she has successfully appropriated his form as the context in which her critique can take place.

So, although Irigaray was very distressed by her exile from the psychoanalytic community (she herself called it a 'quarantine' [Whitford 1991, 5], implying that the psychoanalytic academy saw her as infecting agent), she continues to use the insights of psychoanalytic theory even as she also provides a radical critique of its 'blind spots'.[1] But as Margaret Whitford has noted, her most recent work demonstrates a concern with having an effect on society, with changing social norms and values. Her attitudes, however, are not straightforwardly materialist, even when she discusses material conditions. As she writes in the Preface to the collection of essays, *Sexes and Genealogies*:

> Today it is all too clear that there is no equality of wealth, and claims of equal rights to culture have blown up in our faces. All those who advocate equality need to come to terms with the fact that their claims produce a greater and greater split between the so-called equal units ... Any woman who is seeking equality (with whom? with what?) needs to give this problem serious consideration. It is understandable that women should wish for equal pay, equal career opportunities. But what is their real goal? ... salaries and social recognition have to be negotiated on the basis of identity – not equality. Without women there is no society. Women have to proclaim this message loud and clear and demand a justice that fits their identity instead of some temporary rights befitting justice for men. To achieve this goal, women must learn how they relate both to gender and to kinship.
> (Irigaray 1993, vi)

In other words, the liberal feminist claim to equal rights within existing social structures is not the answer. When women seek an abstract equality ('with what?', 'with whom?' are both the pertinent and impertinent questions that Irigaray asks of liberal feminism), they risk becoming pseudo-men, and merely insert themselves into a social structure that has always already proven disabling, competitive and inequitable. Equal rights feminism is not the answer, says Irigaray. The answers (the plural is important) lie rather in identity.

Identity is, however, a complex thing. In Charlotte Brontë's *Villette*, Ginevra Fanshawe asks the 'heroine', Lucy Snowe: 'Who *are* you Miss Snowe?'

> 'You used to call yourself a nursery-governess; when you first came here you really had the care of the children in this house; I have seen you carry little Georgette in your arms like a bonne – few governesses would have condescended so far – and now Madame Beck treats you with more courtesy than she treats the Parisienne, St. Pierre; and that proud chit, my cousin, makes you her bosom friend!'
>
> 'Wonderful!' I agreed, much amused at her mystification. 'Who am I indeed? Perhaps a personage in disguise. Pity I don't look the character.' (Brontë 1979, 392)

It is a jokey response to what is, in the context, an impertinent question. But it raises the difficulties of knowing identity with which Irigaray is concerned. Ginevra, as it is in her character to do, tries to define Lucy in terms of her social and economic position, but finds that her ostensible occupations as nursery-governess or *bonne* (nursemaid) do not coincide with the social respect that she has earned from her employer, Mme Beck, or with the friendship Lucy has established with the aristocratic figure of Polly Home. Lucy's statement that she is a 'personage in disguise' aligns her with the fictionality of the literary text; but she is not so immediately readable, and does not 'look the part'. Her identity is withheld, kept back so that it is not available to scrutiny, not there to be seen.

In thinking about identity, Irigaray's writings suggest that who women are is similarly illegible or invisible, unrepresentable and unspeakable. For her, identity draws together the disparate discourses of explanation to be found in psychoanalysis, linguistics, philosophy, politics, history (including the family history of genealogy) and the body. Who we are depends on the complicated intersections of all these different kinds of explanatory narratives. And since all these discourses are 'man-made', a feminist politics of identity and representation needs to make use of, and to modify, all of them.[2]

Looking again: images of femininity, Irigaray and psychoanalysis

Nothing separates female experience from male experience more sharply and more early in life, than the compulsion to visualise the self.

Ellen Moers, *Literary Women*

There is an interesting contrast between the behaviour of the sexes. In the analogous situation, when a little boy first catches sight of a girl's genital region, he begins by showing irresolution and lack of interest; he sees nothing or disavows what he has seen ... It is not until later, when some threat of castration has obtained a hold on him, that the observation becomes important to him: if he then recollects or repeats it, it arouses a terrible storm of emotion in him and forces him to believe in the reality of the threat he has hitherto laughed at. This combination of circumstances leads to two reactions, which may become fixed and will in that case, whether separately or together or in conjunction with other factors, permanently determine the boy's relations to women: horror of the mutilated creature or triumphant contempt for her ...
A little girl behaves differently. She makes her judgement and her decision in a flash. She has seen it and knows that she is without it and wants to have it.

Sigmund Freud, 'Some Psychical Consequences of the
Anatomical Distinction Between the Sexes'

In Lacan's mirror stage the infant is fixed, constrained in a representation which the infant believes to be the Other's, the mother's image of her [or him?]. The representation freezes the nameless flow ... Yet without representation there is only infantile passivity, powerlessness, anxiety. The only way to move is to exercise power *and* criticize it, not let it gel into a rigid representation.

Jane Gallop, *Feminism and Psychoanalysis:*
The Daughter's Seduction

In the scene Freud describes where the boy-child sees the girl-child's genitals, the emphasis is on his 'seeing', with all the emphasis that implies on distance, perspective, objectivity and mastery. For Freud seeing eventually becomes believing. For the boy-child, what he first sees is unthreatening absence in the girl; later he sees a significant and dangerous lack in her that appears to threaten his own masculine identity with castration. What he sees and the way he sees it determine his subsequent response to the idea of femininity: it is either monstrous or contemptible because it is different from what he sees in his own body, one of the sites of his own subjectivity. In this scene the boy-child has alternative responses: indifference, horror, triumph. The girl-child has only one response: desire for the apparently missing penis. Freud cannot imagine other ways of responding to the sight of the male genitals that might include laughter, horror, disgust, curiosity – and, importantly, indifference to the boy's possession. His writing of this scene, that is, is constructed from a space of masculine privilege that assumes that sexed identity is necessarily male.

For Irigaray, this is one of the blind spots of psychoanalysis, which begins by inscribing inequality in sexuate identity. The blind spot derives from Freud's failure to imagine a female desire that is not penis-oriented, not directed at this one object of absolute sexual potency. In *This Sex Which is Not One* (1977), her critique is in part directed against the monological construction of sexuality as inherently masculine. She argues that 'Female sexuality has always been conceptualised on the basis of masculine parameters'; Freud has 'nothing to say' about woman and her pleasure because her sex is an absence, a nothing-to-be-seen (Irigaray 1985a, 23). This is a failing in Freudian analysis, but it is also an understandable failing that does not undo the importance of psychoanalysis. Freud was a man of his time, influenced not only by the mores of the late-nineteenth and early-twentieth centuries, but also by the entire philosophy of Western Europe, which was also a significant part of his training. In Irigaray's terms, what Freud describes is in no sense a naturally occurring development of sexuality and gendered identity in men and women, but the result of a whole history of philosophy that was structured on similar assumptions. If 'Woman ... is only a more or less obliging prop for the enactment of man's fantasies' in the sexual imaginary of the present, this is because of the effects of her disappearance from subjective identity that are, in turn, the consequence of her disappearance from social, civic, economic, philosophical and religious importance.

> As Freud admits, the beginnings of the sexual life of a girl child are so 'obscure', so 'faded with time', that one would have to dig down very deep indeed to discover beneath the traces of this civilization, this history, the vestiges of a more archaic civilization that might give

some clue to women's sexuality. That extremely ancient civilisation would undoubtedly have a different alphabet, a different language. (25)

In that different language, female sexuality might be representable, might be allowed a linguistic and thence a social existence – might become presence rather than absence.

For Irigaray, it is the emphasis on seeing and believing – and on telling what one has seen – that is responsible for disappearance of female sexuality, for the elision of differences in sexualities, and for the inscription of that monological sexual identity that depends entirely on the possession of the penis. She argues that women are less likely than men to be aroused by seeing an erotic image; and that they are also less likely to be turned off by seeing too:

> the predominance of the visual, and of the discrimination of form, is particularly foreign to female eroticism. Woman takes pleasure more from touching than from looking, and her entry into a dominant scopic economy signifies, again, her consignment to passivity: she is to be the beautiful object of contemplation. While her body finds itself thus eroticized, and called to a double movement of exhibition and of chaste retreat in order to stimulate the drives of the [male] 'subject', her sexual organ represents *the horror of nothing to see*. A defect in this systematics of representation and desire. A 'hole' in its scoptophilic lens. It is already evident in Greek statuary that this nothing-to-see has to be excluded, rejected, from such a scene of representation. Woman's genitals are simply absent, masked, sewn back up inside their 'crack'. (25–6)

For Western culture, says Irigaray, seeing is the place of privilege. What you can't see – or what you can't see easily – can't be there: 'So woman does not have a sex organ?' (28). And if she has no sex organ, how can she have, express, write or live a sexuality of her own? The problem, says Irigaray, is not with woman, but with the systems of representation which focus on sight, and which render women as the objects of other people's (men's) appraising and appropriative gazes.

In this critique of seeing, Irigaray also criticises and modifies Lacan's construction of the mirror phase in the infant. In his seminar 'Le Stade du miroir' (usually translated as 'The Mirror Stage'), Lacan had argued that one of the formative moments of a child's development is when he (sic) catches sight of himself in a mirror. *Seeing* his own reflected image allows the child to hypothesise his own identity, and to view that identity as coherent and stable, as particular, individual and at one with itself. Lacan, however, had read the founding works of structuralism by Ferdinand de Saussure; when he suggests that the image the child sees is *not* himself, but rather an *image* of himself, and that therefore the child's recognition of himself is in fact a *mis*recognition, Lacan was appealing to the Saussurean concepts of signifier and signified, which are the connected, but not the self-identical, constituents of words. For Lacan, this misrecognition is a kind of necessary fiction, for as Gallop puts it, 'without representation there is only infantile passivity, powerlessness, anxiety'. Possessing a single, coherent image, even if the image is a kind of lie, is a necessary stage in the formation of subjectivity.

For Irigaray, it is necessary to rewrite this paradigm of one-ness and coherence. She concentrates on the idea that the mirror image is a signifier, and is therefore part of a system of representation as opposed to an unmediated reality. It is the system of representation based on sight, not reality itself, that replicates sameness, that insists on the identification of image and self as the same. She argues that all the major representations of Western thought, based as they are on the seeing male I/eye, have constructed a logic of the same which she calls '*hommosexual*'. There is a pun here in French, as in English, deriving from the etymology of two words that sound the same: 'homo', Greek for same, and 'homo', Latin for man. In the logic of the same, male identity is sexed identity, and sexuality is therefore always the same thing, always *one* thing: a masculine thing. The feminist task, Irigaray argues, is to break up this logic, to pose alternative systems of representation than those based on the 'seeing–believing' model, and to find new languages in which women can render themselves speakable, representable and, importantly, in which women's sexuality can be understood not as *one* thing, the lacking Other of male sexuality, but as *many* positive presences.

This is the force of the two titles of her best-known works, *Speculum of the Other Woman* and *This Sex which is not One*. A speculum is a concave mirror, like the internal surface of a spoon. The image it reflects in its surface is therefore upside-down. The speculum, as opposed to the flat mirrored surface in which the Lacanian child presumably constructs his self-image, radically demonstrates that image and self, signifier and signified, are not the same, are not *as one.* In addition, the speculum is the kind of mirror used to examine the cavities of the body: in particular, dentists use specular mirrors to examine teeth; and gynaecologists use speculums to examine the vagina during internal examinations on female patients. The speculum is absolutely not, then, a mirror that frames visual experience with distance and perspective. It is, as it were, an intimate mirror; a mirror that helps one to see, but which also touches the objects it examines, denying the alleged mastery of distance. A physicist might call it a distorting mirror: but for Irigaray, its importance is precisely that it illustrates the extent to which the flat 'realist' mirror of patriarchal systems of representation is also a distorting mirror, refusing to reflect female sexuality on a woman's own terms. Irigaray sees that realist mirror as a frozen mirror, a mirror that fixes images into one version and that enforces distance: 'the mirror is a frozen – and polemical – weapon to keep us apart. ... The mirror, and indeed the gaze, are frequently used as tools that ward off touching and hold back fluidity, even the liquid embrace of the gaze' (Irigaray 1993a, 65). She proposes the speculum as an alternative mirror of intimate embrace with many meanings.

This Sex which is not One, like the 'homo–homo' of 'hommosexuality', is a pun. Puns, of course, disrupt the logic of the same, since they depend on two or more possible meanings for the 'same' words. Irigaray's title draws on the subversive potential of punning: it means both 'this sex which is not a sex' – since woman has no sexuality of her own; and 'this sex which is not single, unified, coherent, this sex which is not one sex'. Her aim in *Speculum* and *This Sex* is to rewrite the term 'sexuality' so that it means not one thing, but many: so that 'hommosexuality' can become multisexualities. In order to do this, Irigaray returns to the female body as the site of feminine sexualities that are multiple, since her pleasures are not focused on one organ like the male penis, but on lots different erogenous zones. First, her genitalia are already doubled: 'Woman "touches herself" all the time, and moreover no one can forbid her to do so, for her genitals are formed of two lips in continuous contact. Thus, within herself, she is already two ... that caress each other' (Irigaray 1985a, 24). More than that, in fact: '*woman has sex organs more or less everywhere.* She finds pleasure almost anywhere' (28). Erotic zones, that is, need not be limited to the genital area – a limitation that serves male fantasy rather than female pleasure. All parts of the a woman's body can partake of her sexuality, so long as she has found a system of representation that permits the articulation of her multiple pleasures. The body and the languages in which it is understood are interrelated in Irigaray's thought. Women have to learn a new speech in order to develop a sexuate identity of their own, since sexuate identity, like all modes of subjectivity, depends on the use of language.

Speech is never neuter/neutral

It is perhaps in her writing about speech and language use that Irigaray's writings are most approachable from the point of view of *literary* theory. In this context, again, she both makes use of and modifies Lacanian psychoanalysis. From Lacan she takes the insight that subjectivity is linguistically constructed: to become the subject of a sentence or a verb is the prerequisite of identity – the speaker becomes what s/he says or what s/he can imagine saying. The relationship between identity and language is foundational. Implicitly, though, Irigaray's writings are also a critique of Lacan's emphasis on the Symbolic order, on the languages of mastery, power, objectivity – of, in the end, masculinity. As I've already suggested, the very structure of *Speculum of the Other Woman* undermines the Symbolic order through a kind of creative disorder. And individual essays further mimic that disruption in their refusals of totalising narratives or complete answers to their many rhetorical questions. What Irigaray proposes, both in her practice and in her content, is the need to develop alternative linguistic systems, alternative modes of representation; she seeks to rewrite the Symbolic order in such a way that it would allow women a space to speak from, and which would also permit women to hear their own speech as valuable. She calls this women's speech '*parler-femme*', a phrase that means 'speaking woman', 'speaking about woman' and 'woman speaking *to* women'.

Like Hélène Cixous's *écriture féminine* (see above, and Chapter 7), *parler-femme* refuses the logic of the 'self-same' discourses of masculine power, and is thus connected to the multiplicity of feminine sexuality. *Parler-femme* refuses to talk 'straight', refuses the limitations of coherence and stability that are to be found in the Realist, phallocratic modes of writing that make up the Symbolic order. It is a metonymic language practice rather than a metaphoric one: that is, it depends on connections made by contiguity, which are often 'illogical', rather than on connections made on the basis of similarity or sameness, which are supposed to be understood as making logical sense. Women's words, writes Irigaray:

> are contradictory words, somewhat mad from the standpoint of reason, inaudible, for whoever listens with ready-made grids, with a fully elaborated code in hand. For in what she says too, at least when she dares, woman is constantly touching herself. She steps ever so slightly aside from herself with a murmur, an exclamation, a whisper, a sentence left unfinished. ... When she returns, it is to set off again from elsewhere. [...] One would have to listen with another ear, as if hearing an 'other meaning' always in the process of weaving itself, of embracing itself with words, but also of getting rid of words in order not to become fixed, congealed in them. (29, emphasis and first ellipsis in original)

Parler-femme is a language between women that requires sympathetic female auditors who listen with 'another ear'. This other ear discerns the subtexts and alternative patterns in women's speech. It is necessary, Irigaray argues, because without it, 'if we go on speaking the same language together, we're going to reproduce the same history' (205). But not speaking is not an option. Silence is death, since subjectivity requires language. At the end of *This Sex which is not One*, then, Irigaray, writes:

> Speak, all the same. It's our good fortune that your language isn't formed of a single thread, a single strand or pattern. It comes from everywhere at once. You touch me all over at the same time. In all senses. Why only one song, one speech, one text at a time? To seduce, to satisfy, to fill one of my 'holes'? ... We are not lacks, voids, awaiting sustenance, plenitude, fulfilment from the other. By our lips we are women: this does not mean that we are focused on consuming, consummation, fulfilment. (209–10)

She draws here on the structuralist linguistics that also influenced Lacan. Language itself is multiple. The Symbolic order is not the only route by which the speaker can make herself understood. Speech comes from the body: you have to take breath to speak, move the tongue and the teeth, use also perhaps the languages of gesture.[3] The whole body is in play, and the woman's body can become the subject of language, can satisfy herself, and can satisfactorily represent herself, so long as she is not written out of the equation as a subject of speech.

All of which sounds like a very Utopian project. But Irigaray's interest in psycholinguistics also leads her to make very practical analyses of the power of language, particularly in master-narratives like science, history and philosophy. The title of her 1985 book *Parler n'est jamais neutre* translates as both 'Speech is never neuter' and 'Speech is never neutral'. The point is that privileged language is gendered as masculine even when it claims to be neutral/neuter/natural. In her essay 'The Three Genders',[4] Irigaray pursues the implications of non-neutrality in speech. She argues that the languages of privilege – especially science in this context – appears to aspire to a kind of neutrality: 'man today is committed to keeping himself out of language, no longer saying *I* or *you* or *we*'. That is, the language of science seeks to appear as impartial, neutral, objective rather than subjective. The point of disguising subjectivity in science is that words are surrendered 'to some agent that is supposedly more worthy to articulate our truth' (Irigaray 1993, 170). Neutered (impersonal) discourse is apparently a matter of nature. Phrases such as 'it is raining, it is snowing' take place in a neutered voice. Irigaray suggests that the attempt by powerful discourses to appropriate the neutered position is in fact an attempt to claim for man-made discourses the power of nature. The sexed being who says 'I' is displaced by an apparently extra-human unsexed power that says 'it is so', and this is a powerful tool because there is a sense in which saying that something is so appears to 'make it so'. The responsibility of the critic, Irigaray argues, is to 'analyse very rigorously the forms that authorise ... content' (172), the ways in which certain kinds of speech make meaning more powerfully than other kinds.

What Irigaray notes about the power of the neuter voice is that it has, in fact, been appropriated by masculinity, so that even apparently neutral phrases are really masculine in everyday grammar:

> in French, the masculine gender always carries the day syntactically: a crowd of a thousand persons, nine-hundred and ninety-nine women and one man will be referred to as a masculine plural; a couple composed of a man and a woman will be referred to as a masculine plural; a woman telling the story of her love affair with a man will have to use the supposedly neutral masculine plural form in her agreement of past participles when she says 'we fell in love' (*nous*

nous sommes aimés), etc. In other places the neuter is expressed by the same pronoun as the masculine: *il tonne* ('it is thundering') and *il faut* ('it is necessary'), not *elle* tonne or *elle* faut. These laws of syntax in French reveal the power wielded by one sex over another. (173)

It's for these kinds of reason that Irigaray sees a *parler-femme* as necessary to break down the surface neutrality and 'hommosexuality' of powerful discourses. If subjectivity depends on language, it is a function of the ability to say 'I'. Powerful discourses, in their masculine appropriation of the neuter/neutral/natural, leave no space for femininity, no words in which *her* subjectivity can be powerfully expressed, can be expressed as having power. Irigaray's writing here constitutes a powerful rebuke to people like me. As a university lecturer, I spend a lot of my life crossing out phrases like 'I think', 'I believe' from student's essays, because I know that the apparently objective statement that something 'is so', is far more powerful than any statement that depends on my own thought or belief. *Parler-femme* helps to construct an impertinent feminine 'I' that pokes wholes in the 'I-less' subjectivity of neutered language.

Politics and French feminism

It is a very common criticism of the kinds of writing produced by Irigaray, as by Kristeva, indeed of what is now called 'French Feminism', that they ignore political, materialist and historicist concerns. A glance at Marks and de Courtivron's collection *New French Feminisms* (1981), or at Toril Moi's *French Feminist Thought* (1987) shows that this is a rather skewed view of feminist movements in francophone traditions. Amongst the essays on psychoanalysis and philosophy, there are Marxist, materialist and liberal feminist traditions alive and well in France represented by this collections, traditions that coexist with the more obviously theoretical reflections of Irigaray and Kristeva. For both writers, nonetheless, formal 'party' politics have been part of their training and experience. As I suggested in writing of Kristeva, her early life in Bulgaria was profoundly influenced by the political thinking of a Communist regime. And Irigaray continues to work in dialogue with Italian Communists. For both writers, though, there are limitations to what political understanding can do to analyse and alter the position of women. The social and the economic are not adequate explanations for women's interpellation into systems that radically disadvantage them. Moreover, the view that theory is not political is also problematic. Irigaray's appropriations and rewritings of Freud and Lacan demonstrate the political power that psychoanalysis has claimed for itself – the power to pronounce on pathology and normality. Her rewritings are therefore political interventions in discourse of mastery that unsettle the master-narratives. Implicitly, she argues that we cannot change the world without changing the way that we look at the world.

Her work, though, does not deal with historical specificities. Because the master-narratives against which Irigaray pits herself set themselves up as universal and eternal, her responses are similarly slippery customers that posit alternative possible truths. She writes in grand gestures not in terms of locally-determined, historical specific differences. Her essay 'Women on the Market', collected in *This Sex*, does engage with the politics of women's positions in societies around the world; but it draws large general, not small particular, conclusions. The essay begins with the insight from Claude Lévi-Strauss's structuralist anthropology that all cultures appear to be based on the exchange of women. Women are exchanged, says Lévi-Strauss, because they are scarce, though this 'scarcity' is not an absolute value, as Irigaray points out: birth rates of male and female children are roughly equal. The scarcity comes about because of a 'deep polygamous tendency' among men which renders women scarce because there are never quite enough of them to satisfy men's multiple desires. Lévi-Strauss was recording what he believed he had observed. Irigaray looks differently at the issue, wondering to herself whether women might have polygamous desires, whether it is possible to imagine a society in which men's bodies were objects of exchange between women, whether male bodies are as desirable to women as women's bodies appear to be to men.

These are, again, impertinent questions; and Irigaray does not quite answer them. She suggests instead that under the patriarchal organisation of society, it is not possible to imagine women as promiscuous, polygamous figures with polymorphous desires for many different men. It is not just psychoanalysis or psycholinguistics that can explain the unrepresentability of female desire. There are material reasons that have psychic effects for women, and which construct their subordinate position in patriarchal cultures:

all the systems of exchange that organize patriarchal cultures and all the modalities of productive work that are recognized, valued and rewarded in these societies, are men's business. The production of women, signs, and commodities is always referred back to men (when a man buys a girl, he 'pays' the father or the brother, not the mother ...), and they always pass from one man to another, from one group of men to another. The work force is thus always assumed to be masculine, and 'products' are objects to used, objects of transaction among men alone. (Irigaray 1985a, 171)

Women are commodities, she suggests. In an analysis that owes much to her readings in Karl Marx, they have a use value (that is, they labour in both senses of that word: they go into labour and they do work) and they have an exchange value as objects that pass between men. In the context of the other essays of *This Sex*, Irigaray's arguments suggests that female commodification in social structures intersects with visualisation of their psychic and physical 'lack' in psychoanalytic structures. She proposes no formal political programme to combat these structures. Instead, her argument appears to be that women must make an identity for themselves which will enable them to re-imagine their social and psychic positions. The process of identifying themselves anew is the prerequisite of social change.

It is, perhaps, a chicken-and-egg argument. If social structures conspire to deny female subjectivity, how can such a subjectivity come into existence without changing the social structures? But, on the other hand, unless the impertinent questions are asked, how can women even know the terms of their own oppression and repression? And how can they express themselves unless they know they need to learn to do so?

Reading with Irigaray: three Gothic reflections[5]

In Bram Stoker's 1897 novel *Dracula*, the young English lawyer, Jonathan Harker begins to discover the absolute strangeness of the Transylvanian count when he finds that Dracula has no reflection in a mirror:

> I had hung my shaving-glass by the window, and was just beginning to shave. Suddenly I felt a hand on my shoulder, and heard the

Count's voice saying to me, 'Good morning.' I started, for it amazed me that I had not seen him, since the reflection of the glass covered the whole room behind me. ... Having answered the Count's salutation, I turned to the glass again to see how I had been mistaken. This time there could be no error, for the man was close to me, and I could see him over my shoulder. But there was no reflection of him in the mirror! (Stoker 1984, 37)

Dracula, realising what Harker has seen – or rather, not seen – takes the mirror and throws it out of the window, pronouncing it a 'wretched thing ... a foul bauble of man's vanity', leaving the lawyer feeling very annoyed, 'for I do not see how I am to shave' without it (38).

Dracula's lack of a reflection in the novel stands as a sign of his supernatural status. It alerts Harker to his strangeness and his danger. More significantly, though, it is also a powerful disruption of the world-view that Harker inhabits. The mirror is traditionally a metaphor for Realism, those conventions and systems of representation that are supposed to reproduce the world as it really is in art and literature. The realist world is a specular world: seeing is believing, what is not seen cannot be there, hence the uncanny effect of Dracula's unmarked entrance into Harker's room. Despite his apparent corporeal solidity, he looks like a trick of the light. Now although Dracula is gendered as masculine, his position in the text, and in relation to the views of its narrators who are nothing if not realists, signalled by their professional and social status (two doctors, a lawyer, an aristocrat, a teacher and an American man of adventure), is feminised. He is an Eastern European, not a Westerner inhabiting the traditions of Western rationalist thought. As Judith Halberstram has noted, he has the racialised characteristics of the Wandering Jew, who is, like woman, a dispossessed figure in western patriarchal Christian cultures (Halberstram in Ledger and McCracken 1995, 248–9). He has, Dr Van Helsing says, a 'child-brain' not a 'man-brain', a common view of the difference between men and women. And in his grotesque assault on Mina Harker (an attack that no 'real man' would have mounted, since it goes against all the rules of gentle-manliness to attack a woman at all), he makes her drink blood from his breast in a perversely monstrous maternal gesture.

Like a woman, Dracula is a figure who evades the representation of the patriarchal glass, and yet who refuses not to exist. At the end of the novel, he is defeated, beheaded and staked – and there is nothing particularly subversive about that ending. On the other hand, the manner of his defeat has required a paradigm shift in the world-views of the heroes of masculine rationality, whose belief systems are overturned by Dracula's very existence. As Dr Van Helsing comments to Dr Seward:

> you reason well, and your wit is bold; but you are too prejudiced. You do not let your eyes see nor your ears hear, and that which is outside your daily life is not of account to you. Do you not think that there are things which you cannot understand, and yet which are; that some people see things that others cannot? But there are things old and new which must not be contemplate [*sic*] by men's eyes, because they know – or think they know – some things that other men have told them. Ah, *it is the fault of our science that it wants to explain all; and if it explain not, then it says there is nothing to explain.* (Stoker 1984, 229, my emphasis)

In other words, what Irigaray might call a 'ready-made grid ... a fully elaborated code' (Irigaray 1985a, 29) for comprehension constructed by science cannot account for everything. The scientists and lawyers of *Dracula* have to learn to see things anew, and to put aside their codes of knowledge and ethics. They do not defeat Dracula by applying the systems they explicitly acknowledge; rather they defeat him by superstition (garlic, crosses, stakes and the communion host), by forgery (of Lucy Westernra's death certificate), by bribery (of eastern port officials): in short, they defeat him by believing in him – a belief that goes against everything they stand for. Their science cannot help them, as evidenced by their application of the new science of blood transfusions, that do not save Lucy's life. Dracula may be male; but he is also 'feminine'. His powerful femininity produces fissures in the facade of patriarchal knowledge.

In a different kind of Gothic mirror, the speaker of Mary Elizabeth Coleridge's 'The Other Side of the Mirror' (1908) is indeed reflected; but the image that she sees is monstrous: 'The vision of a woman, wild/With more than womanly despair'.

> Her hair stood back on either side
>   A face bereft of loveliness.
> It had no envy now to hide

What once no man on earth could guess.
It formed the thorny aureole
Of hard unsanctified distress.

Her lips were open – not a sound
Came through the parted lines of red.
Whate'er it was, the hideous wound
In silence and in secret bled.
No sigh relieved her speechless woe,
She had no voice to speak her dread.

And in her lurid eyes there shone
The dying flame of life's desire,
Made mad because its hope was gone,
And kindled at the leaping fire
Of jealousy, and fierce revenge,
And strength that could not change nor tire ...

Coleridge, 'The Other Side of the Mirror' 1908, 8–9

The horror of the image is in the whispered recognition that '"I am she!"' When Gilbert and Gubar read this poem in *The Madwoman in the Attic*, they saw it as a metaphor for female creativity, which, though bounded by social and psychological limitations, is still able to express 'an invincible sense of [the speaker's] own autonomy, her own interiority' (Gilbert and Gubar 1979, 16).[6] They argue that the female imagination 'has perceived itself, as it were, through a glass darkly: until quite recently the woman writer has had (if only unconsciously) to define herself as a mysterious creature who resides behind the angel or monster ... image' of conventional femininity. The speaker is 'an enraged prisoner' (15) of the patriarchal glass.

That is an important and interesting commentary. But a reading inflected through Irigaray's ideas about mirroring might have other things to say. For one thing, any identification of the mirror's image with the reflecting self is a misrecognition, a misidentification. The monstrous ghost in the glass is *not* the self, just as the 'aspects glad and gay/That erst were found reflected' in the glass were not the self either. Neither image has anything very much to do with a 'real' female identity. As Irigaray writes in her essay 'Divine Women':

Female beauty is always considered a *garment* ultimately designed to attract the other into the self. ... We look at ourselves in the mirror *to*

> *please someone*, rarely to interrogate the state of our body or our
> spirit, rarely for ourselves and in search of our own becoming. The
> mirror almost always serves to reduce us to a pure exteriority ... The
> mirror signifies the constitution of a fabricated (female) other that I
> shall put forward as an instrument of seduction in my place. (Irigaray
> 1993, 65)

The speaker of Coleridge's poem speaks of the silence of the reflected
monstrous image. She can *see* its despair figured in its bleeding lips
and thorny halo of hair, but the image is inarticulate. The lips in
particular are a figure of the pain of femininity – the lips of the mouth
denied speech, the lips of the genitals denied existence *as* sexuality.
But those red lips and that wild hair could easily be rewritten as the
fetishised female body parts that are supposed to attract male desire:
lips, hair and eyes are the staple points of emphasis in male-authored
love poetry and in pornographic images. The silence of those red lips
is eloquent despite its wordlessness. Irigaray argues that there is no
language in which women can speak their own desires, their own
sexuate identities. In patriarchal libidinal economies, women are
objects of sexual desire, not desiring subjects. Coleridge's speaker,
then, might be said to misrecognise the image in the mirror as one of
terror, rather than one of desire because she is forced by phallocracy
to represent that desire in relation to male models that insistently
construct female desire as monstrous.

It is nonetheless important that Coleridge has spoken in her poem.
She may be speaking a language shot through by the Symbolic order;
but her *parler-femme*, because it speaks *to* women who might listen
with 'other ears', as well as *about* women, and because it is spoken *by*
a woman, it resists the freezing monologic of the patriarchal mirror.
Because language 'isn't formed of a single thread, a single strand or
pattern', it is a creative writing of female identity that can be read
creatively to help us re-imagine female identities of our own. Gilbert
and Gubar offered one kind of reading; Irigaray's ideas give us
another strand.

One last, and very famous example, is the reflection that Jane
Eyre sees in the Red Room episode of her narrative. Jane is imprisoned in the Red Room, in a child's version of a Gothic confinement,
following her violent outburst against John Reed's treatment of her.
She is unstrung, nervous, and upset in the aftermath of these events,
all of which are 'realist' explanations for her subsequent apparently

non-realist experiences. Left alone in the room, she observes the mirror:

> I had to cross before the looking-glass; my fascinated glance involuntarily explored the depth it revealed. All looked colder and darker in that visionary hollow than in reality: and the strange little figure there gazing at me, with a white face and arms specking the gloom, and glittering eyes of fear moving where all else was still, had the effect of a real spirit: I thought it like one of the tiny phantoms, half fairy, half imp, Bessie's evening stories represented as coming out lone, ferny dells in moors, and appearing before the eyes of belated travellers.
> (Brontë 1996, 21–2)

Indeed, a few pages later, the reader encounters one of Bessie's (the nursemaid's) songs, telling of the hard life of the poor orphan child who haunts the deserted byways of the moors (29–30). What Jane sees in the mirror is, presumably, herself; but unlike Coleridge's speaker, she does not whisper 'I am she'. Instead, the reflection appears as quite alien, as supernatural even – a spirit, a phantom, a fairy, an imp – figures who are not at home in houses like Gateshead, indeed who are not at home anywhere. (And of course, when Freud defined the Uncanny, in his essay 'The Unheimlich', it was in relation to the word's etymology – *unheimlich* means unhomely, not at home.[7])

The child, however, is not frightened by the image in the mirror. She understands its strangeness but is not afraid of it. She remains instead preoccupied with the causes of her incarceration, and with a meditation on her place in Mrs Reed's house. The phantom in the mirror, in other words, does not provoke irrational superstition, but rational analysis of her situation, and slightly less rational ideas about how she is to escape from that situation. She wonders why she could never please at Gateshead: 'I dared commit no fault: I strove to fulfil every duty; and I was termed naughty and tiresome, sullen and sneaking, from morning to noon, and from noon to night.' All she can make of these facts is that they are:

> 'Unjust! – unjust!' said my reason, forced by the agonising stimulus into precocious though transitory power; and Resolve, equally wrought up, instigated some strange expedient to achieve escape from insupportable oppression – as running away; or, if that could

not be effected, never eating or drinking more, and letting myself die. (22)

That childlike and unfulfilled resolve leads to a meditation on Jane's dead uncle, in whose room she is now incarcerated with an aching and bloodied head, and an overwrought frame of mind. As the room grows darker and the afternoon fades to evening, she thinks about how he would have treated her had he been alive, and wishes that he would rise from his grave to punish her aunt and her cousins. That image, no sooner conjured, seems to be fulfilled by a light shining and moving along the wall of the room. In Jane's already emotional state, she screams; but Mrs Reed refuses to free her from the Red Room, and Jane faints from terror.

What interests me here is the juxtaposition of a Gothic image – the ghost in the mirror – with Jane's first serious attempt to analyse her own situation. The mirror image whom Jane does not identify explicitly as herself, but which must be her signifier, provides the spur to reason and resolve: the illogical image provides the conditions for an alternative logical diagnosis of Jane's position. She is not 'really' 'naughty, tiresome, sullen and sneaking', as the powers-that-be would have it. Her deliberate misrecognition of the image that is imposed on her from outside is the spur to power. At ten years of age, the power does not last very long and ends in a fainting fit and utter defeat. But the beginning of this power of logical analysis stems from the illogical phantom of the Red Room mirror, that allows Jane to see with other eyes, to hear the criticisms of her 'with other ears'. It is a small moment, but it is foundational in Jane's development into a grown woman with a sexuate, desiring identity of her own.

Notes

1. One of the chapters in *Speculum of the Other Woman* is entitled 'The Blindspot of an Old Dream of Symmetry'. It refers to Freud's 1933 essay on 'Femininity', and Irigaray shows in her chapter how Freud remained captivated by a pseudo-symmetrical theory of male and female sexuality, despite the obvious asymmetries between them.
2. It could obviously be argued that bodies are not 'man-made'. But the ways that bodies are represented and understood clearly are man-

made, and it is representation, and the ways in which we inhabit representation, that are at stake in Irigaray's theoretical interventions.

3. One of the essays in the collection *Sexes and Genealogies*, 'Psychoanalysis and Gesture', is particularly concerned with reading the gestures of the psychoanalytic session, with the patient objectified on the couch before the mastering subjectivity of the seated analyst. See Luce Irigaray, *Sexes and Genealogies*, trans. Gillian C. Gill, New York: Columbia University Press, 1993, 89–104.

4. 'Genders' in this title translates the word 'Genres'. The word 'genre' in French has a number of meanings. It can mean type or kind, it can mean genre of literary text; and it can mean gender. Biology, sociology and literature are all compressed into the possible, multiple references for this signifier.

5. I think I should repeat here my warning for my readings through a Kristevan lens. These readings are not intended as the last word; they are just possible ways of thinking about how Irigaray's writings might be applied to literary texts.

6. I should, perhaps, note here, that I would not have come across Coleridge's poem had it not been for Gilbert and Gubar's discussion of it in *The Madwoman in the Attic*.

7. See Freud's essay 'The Uncanny' in *The Penguin Freud Library*, Volume 15, *Art and Literature*. Harmondsworth: Penguin, 1990, 335–76.

7 Cixous: Laughing at the Oppositions

In English-speaking countries, Hélène Cixous is primarily known as a theorist of language and literature, and one whose works focus in particular on the sexual differences inherent in language. This is an especially pressing issue for a writer/speaker in the French language, since French is heavily gender-inflected, and any adjective attached to a speaking subject immediately alerts the reader/hearer to the issue of gender. Her project is Utopian: her writing seeks what she calls an *écriture féminine* (feminine/female writing), a writing that could adequately represent female/feminine positions in relation to culture.[1] There has been a concentration on her interest in the body and writing, which she sees as linked because of the gender inflections of French, and this has led in turn to much criticism of her work because it sometimes appears to be dangerously essentialist, mixing up culture (language) and nature (bodies).

The accusation of essentialism arises in part because of the vagaries of the French language, a fact that enacts one of Cixous's most central points: she suggests that language thinks us, and that a revolution in language practice is a first stage in a revolution in subjectivity. She wrote her doctoral thesis on the writings of James Joyce, a writer who was particularly concerned by the idea that language is at once the medium of thought, and a limitation on thought – one can only think in language, and yet one cannot think what one has no vocabulary for. One of the problems of the French language for conceptualising feminisms is the difficulty in distinguishing between female and feminine. There is a French word *femelle*, which is similar in derivation to 'female'. But it is a word that cannot properly be used to describe a human female, being used exclusively to describe the female of animal species. Thus the word *féminin* has to do double service for female and feminine, making it difficult sometimes to distinguish whether

Cixous's usage is one derived from biology or one derived from acculturation.

This linguistic fact is important in Cixous's work, though it does cause problems for readers of her writing in translation. Her writing suggests (rather than states) that the ambiguities of language are both a trap and a potential space of liberation since ambiguity can produce fissures and disjunctions in a totalising version of the world. Since totalisation has tended to suppress women in general, finding the holes in the arguments can be part of the process of breaking open the structures (in language and elsewhere) which oppress them.

Her fundamental arguments are based on the premise that the Enlightenment tradition of Western philosophy, with its emphasis on gendered binary oppositions, has profoundly influenced the ways in which knowledge can circulate in the world, and by extension, has limited the possible meanings of woman who is particularly disadvantaged by the closed system of binary logic. She suggests that any system of binary logic constructed by our society is always a hierarchical opposition – one term is more privileged, accorded more status, more power, and more desirability than the other, is defined at the expense of the other in an economy of the word which then has real effects. In addition, the less favoured term is always feminine and Other – so that the feminine is always conceived of as a negative proposition. Patriarchy shores up its own position of power by developing a whole series of characteristics which it labels 'feminine' – characteristics such as sweetness, subservience, irrationality – and it then elides any distinction between these culturally derived characteristics and the female body. Patriarchy argues that if you are born a woman, if you have a female body, you will necessarily and naturally exhibit these characteristics. Not to exhibit them (in case anyone would dare), is to risk being labelled monstrous, unnatural, antisocial, deviant, mad. Her attack on patriarchy, then, is that it is patriarchy itself that is essentialist and biologist; it bestows feminine virtues on all the female bodies that it is prepared to tolerate.

In themselves, these arguments are not new. Even an early feminist such as Mary Wollstonecraft went this far in analysing the social structures of patriarchal oppression. But materialist feminists, while they might accept the analysis, are concerned that Cixous appears to propose no activist agenda to go with it. That is, she tells us about the nature of the problem, but not what we should do politically to combat it. Her relationship to the feminist movement is a complex one. Cixous did participate in the women's liberation debates in the 1970s, but she is not a card-carrying member of any party. Her reasons are that she is wary of aligning herself with what she sees as masculist political procedures. Hers is not a liberal feminism, based on the bourgeois woman's will to material or political equality with bourgeois man. She would prefer a more radical shift in power relations in culture as a whole, as part of her own ideal revolution. In other words, she fears merely replicating the system as it currently exists if she engages in fighting it only with its own weapons and on its own terms. She does not want a mere reversal of the site of privilege within binary logic. And rather than activist politics, she emphasises writing itself as the site of the revolutionary expression which will eventually overthrow both women's material oppression and their psychic repression.

Her procedure, therefore, is to mount a profound critique of the principle of the binary oppositions that structure Western thought. In 'Sorties', her contribution to the work which has found her widest English audience, *The Newly-Born Woman*, co-authored with Catherine Clément, and published in French in 1974, she argues that violence and death are at the heart of patriarchal thought. Under the heading 'Where is she?', she provides the by now infamous list of binary oppositions:

Where is she?

Activity/Passivity
Sun/Moon
Culture/Nature
Day/Night

Father/Mother
Head/Heart
Intelligible/Sensitive
Logos/Pathos ...

(Cixous 1986, 63, ellipsis in original)

All these oppositions, she argues, are structured on the underlying opposition of 'Man/Woman'. Because these oppositions take place in language, and because language forms what it is possible for us to think, these relative positions of mastery and subordination are

inescapable in language and thought as they are currently constituted. In this schema, woman is defined by passivity, and rendered
non-existent as a subject, since subjects (in grammar as in life) are
participators in action: 'Either the woman is passive or she doesn't
exist. What is left is unthinkable, unthought of' (64). Cixous reads the
oppositions as violent and death-dealing because for one of the terms
to inhabit meaning and presence, it must destroy the other term into
meaninglessness and absence. Binary thought is a war zone in which
a struggle for mastery is ceaselessly played out. For this reason, Cixous
does not propose a simple equality within the existing system. Indeed,
it is her contention that such an equality is impossible in the existing
system, which is why she is not an activist, since contemporary politics is so implicated in the system of oppression. Instead, she
proposes that we must rewrite the system in such a way that the
conflict between two terms could be replaced by something else.

The argument takes place both as a theory and as a practice of
writing. It is dramatised, that is, in the forms in which Cixous chooses
to write, as well as in her content. Her writing enacts a resistance to a
closed system of duality, through a mode of writing which is rhetorical, excessive and poetic rather than logical, ordered and prosaic.
Although she does not cite Lacan, owing a more self-evident allegiance to the works of Jacques Derrida, her writing establishes a space
between the Symbolic and the Imaginary, analysing the rules, and
disrupting them through overflowing linguistic practice. In this practice, then, meaning comes not from the closed relationship of two,
but from an endless stream of differentiations: not one, not two, but
many, an idea which derives from, and partly rewrites in the terms of
gender, Derrida's concept of *différance*. In French, *différance* puns on
two meanings; difference and deferral. Derrida argues that all
meaning takes place within the realm of *différance*; words mean in
terms of their differences to other words, rather than having meanings fixed within them, and therefore meaning is always deferred, put
off, never present (see Wolfreys 1998a, for more information). The
binary relationship that appears to affirm the presence and meaning
collapses, not into meaninglessness, but into a different and deferred
set of possibilities that is not foreclosed (already decided and fixed). It
is this practice that Cixous calls '*écriture féminine*'.

Like Derrida's word 'deconstruction', *écriture féminine* 'is not a
method and cannot be transformed into one' (Derrida, ed. Kamuf
1991, 273). The whole problem of the limitations imposed by defini-

tion is precisely what the terms seek to evade, since definition operates by the same exclusions as binary thought in general – if man is defined by what woman is not, then feminine writing would be the negative position in relation to masculine writing. So, writes Cixous:

> It is impossible to *define* a feminine practice of writing, and this is an impossibility that will remain, for this practice can never be theorized, enclosed, encoded – which doesn't mean that it doesn't exist. But it will always surpass the discourse that regulates the phallocentric system; it does and will take place in areas other than those subordinated to philosophico-theoretical domination. It will be conceived of only by subjects who are breakers of automatisms, by peripheral figures that no authority can ever subjugate. (Cixous in Marks and de Courtivron 1981, 253)

In 'The Laugh of the Medusa' (from which the above extract is taken), as well as in 'Sorties' and almost all her critical writing, Cixous uses a language which simply does not read like traditional essay-language. She refuses the stance of impersonality or objectivity associated with academic writing. She eschews linearly logical formations. Her language is poetic, making use of a logic of conflation and juxtaposition in which the reader is invited to make her own connections. This is a politicised writing, because it is a radical attempt to subvert the prevailing order in writing, the order which has insidiously presented itself as natural writing. Its rhetoric appeals to the logic of the voice, where a direct and urgent tone can be as persuasive as argument. It is an erotic, fluid language, built up around puns, poetic images, and ellipses (fill in the gaps for yourself). It has none of the conventional reserve or poise of objectivity of academic writing. The reader is supposed to be involved completely, in body as well as in mind, not merely in parts as has been the case with a masculine mode of writing which admits only the mouth and the phallus (sex in the head, mealy-mouthed academic-speak, in which sexuality is limited to genital function in the service of masculinity, not of female/feminine overflowing excessive desire) (251).

The relationship between writing and the body is appealed to in many different ways through Cixous's texts. The most obvious place is in the autobiographical stance she takes up and the performance of an autobiographical critique of both literature and philosophy. Experience, says Cixous, is what has taught her to want to think in a non-linear and non-binary way. She was born, as she sees it, by historical accident in Algeria. This does not quite make her an Algerian though. Rather she was an Algerian French girl (Cixous 1986, 70) whose multiple national, racial and gendered identities (her ancestors Christians and Jews, who came from Spain, Morocco, Austria, Hungary, Czechoslovakia, Germany; and as a woman she can claim none of these identities for herself (71)) placed her as a person in between oppositions. As a French national, she was taught official French history: 'The routine, "our ancestors, the Gauls" was pulled on me' (71). But as a French Algerian, she sees also the other side of the coin, the master–slave relationship on which the French occupation of Algeria was predicated. The accident of where a body happens to have been born, perhaps especially a Jewish body, especially in the twentieth century, makes a lot of difference in how that body views the world. From a different subject position (whether the difference is constituted in terms of gender, race, nationhood, class), one sees a different world, or rather, Cixous suggests, one sees multiply different worlds proliferating beyond the capacity of Western thought to order them.

Meaning, then, is carried in and through the body. The body of the text is related to the bodies of its writers and readers, who choose their reading and their writing routes through the texts on the basis of where and how their bodies mean. And although bodies are biological entities, Cixous is much more interested in their cultural meanings than in the apparently simple facts of sex or race. Thus, for her, femininity is not a matter of sex; rather it describes a position in relation to culture which is not dependent on biology, though she concedes that women are more likely to occupy this position than men are in society as it is currently constituted. Both women and men are capable of feminine writing, it's just that women are more likely than men to want to engage in it, because they have less invested in the discursive status quo. Cixous concedes that it might have been better to choose other words than masculine and feminine, but 'because we are born into language, and I cannot do otherwise than find myself before words ... there is nothing to be done except to shake them like apple trees, all the time' (Cixous 1994, 133). Elsewhere she writes, 'Great care must be taken in working on feminine writing not to get trapped by names: to be signed by a woman doesn't necessarily make a piece of writing feminine. It could quite well be masculine writing, and conversely, the fact that a piece of writing is by a man does not in itself exclude its femininity' ('Castration or Decapitation', quoted in Moi 1985, 108). Biology, therefore, is not the only determinant of femininity or masculinity: it's a question of attitude, of cultural positioning.

The route for collapsing the structure of binary opposition in gender in Cixous's argument is the route of bisexuality. In both 'Sorties' and 'The Laugh of the Medusa', she argues that the classic conception of bisexuality is a concept of the neuter, neither one sex nor the other, a kind of nothingness. It has been defined in this way, she suggests, because men fear bisexuality. In part their fear arises from its possible suggestion of castration – the male body becomes neuter only when it is mutilated. More importantly, perhaps, they also fear the loss power and mastery to which binary thought entitles them. Opposing this neutered, unsexed, unsexy bisexuality, Cixous argues for what she calls 'an other bisexuality', a variable and ever-changing sexuality that consists of 'non-exclusion either of the difference, or of one sex'. This other bisexuality works rather by 'the multiplication of the effects of the inscription of desire, over all parts of my body, and the other body, indeed this other bisexuality doesn't annul differences, but stirs them up, pursues them, increases them' (Cixous in Marks and de Courtivron 1981, 254). She goes on to argue that in the present state of history and culture, women's writing is more likely than men's to be bisexual and/or feminine because women have a different material, psychic and social stake in that culture. Men seek to repress their fear of femininity by oppressing real women, and they have a vested interest in keeping the status quo. Occasionally, some exceptional men might break through the culture of monosexualism and achieve that 'other bisexuality'. Her point is not that men cannot be feminine or bisexual, but that they will generally choose not to be, because it would require a sacrifice of their mastery.

Is this a political analysis? It depends, of course, on one's definition of the political. Marxist/Socialist feminisms might object to the idealism and impracticality of a political agenda based on language without action. Cixous's response to this kind of criticism is to seek a rewriting of the terms of politics and activism. She is resolutely not interested in dismantling old structures merely to clear space for new (and probably similar) structures to be re-erected. Rather, she wants to call the very notion of structure into question, wherever it resides. In writing, this means committing linguistic outrages on systematic beliefs and logical grammatical forms. It means using this language terrorism to attack the mythic structures of subordination, amongst which she counts psychoanalysis. Her critique of Freud is based on her sense that his system is woman-hating and woman-fearing, and that the system has real effects. Her activism takes place in words that undo structures. In 'The Laugh of the Medusa', she suggests that the anarchic activities of sex, laughter and writing can undo the edifices of patriarchy. In an explicit reference to Freud, who said that woman was 'the dark continent' of psychology, she says that *The Dark Continent is neither dark nor unexplorable. – It is still to be explored only because we've been made to believe that it was too dark to be explorable. And because they want to make us believe that what interests us is the white continent, with its monuments to Lack'* (255). She describes the figure of woman as a figure trapped between the myths of the monstrous Medusa and non-being of the Abyss which is the logical conclusion of a femininity defined by Lack. This placement of the feminine is stupid enough, unrealistic enough 'to set half the world laughing, except that it's still going on ... regenerating the old patterns, anchored in the dogma of castration'.

What is the way out of this impasse? Cixous suggests laughter. Her call is: 'Let the priests tremble, we're going to show them our sexts!' This call is based on a fundamental objection to the Freudian version of femininity which defines it as negative hole, or Lack. Men both fear and desire this lack: fear it because it suggests their own mutilation, desire it because it is the locus of their sexual fulfilment. Seeing the face of the Medusa or seeing a woman's genitals petrifies men, turns them to stone in terror, or turns them into stone by giving them a hard-on as their symptom of desire. Feminine writing plays around with the oppositions of desire and terror, hence the pun on 'sexts', a conflation of (women's cultural) texts and (women's biological) sex. What is signalled here is something that seldom happens: the woman writer as flasher. For a woman to show her genitals is somewhere between offensively outrageous and farcically funny, an act of aggression, but also something to snigger at in which laughter disperses the fears that keep current structures in place.

The borders of the body, as I have already suggested (see above, Chapter 5), are the location of obscenity, of what remains off the scene, what is unrepresentable. Laughing and flashing are actions in which those corporeal borders are transgressed. Laughter, like desire, is involuntary. It opens up the body to external scrutiny and the closed system (of the body, of the world) is attacked, which is why the body's borders should not be represented to patriarchal eyes. Cixous's laughing Medusa, and her play on sex and text are monstrous, the very things that the Enlightenment tradition posits as outside the limit. She, however, is suggesting an alternative economy of meaning in which the monstrous might be rewritten as also liberating, hilarious, pleasurable and erotic. Her procedure, as Derrida has commented, is 'to make language speak, down to the most familiar idiom, the place where it seems crawling with secrets which give way to thought. She knows how to make it say what it keeps in reserve, which, in the process also makes it come out of its reserve' (Derrida 1994, vii). Reserve here means the structures of patriarchy which impose reserve (good manners) and constraint on the subjects who live under its rule. The erotic flow of the language of the body mounts an attack on, poses a critique of, both the reserve of language and the reservations about the body. A flash of the genitals as it were sheds a least momentary light on the paradox of the 'dark continent' constructed out of Enlightenment, and supposedly enlightened, thought.

The point here is that this is a generous movement, a movement based on the gift. Along with her other descriptions of the binary masculine/feminine, Cixous argues that masculinity aligns itself with the realm of property and ownership, whilst femininity resides in the realm of the gift. In French the word *propriété* accumulates clustered meanings: property that is owned, that which is one's own, appropriate (proper) behaviour, clean and tidy. This etymological link between concepts of property and propriety dramatises a relationship between economics and psychology/behaviour. One's properties (characteristics) are what one is; they form the sense of self by exclusion and accumulation. What is not one's own is what one is not, what one is is what one owns. Where property matters, Cixous argues, there must be proper ordering, structures of knowledge that keep property in its proper place.

This view of the world cannot conceive of generosity. It gives only to receive more, in an economy of exchange (another word might be intercourse) that depends on the rigidity of the structure. But in the realm of the gift, woman is open to difference, and is willing to be traversed by the other. This realm is characterised by a generosity that flows out from the self, from the body even, rather than imposing limits on a rigidly defined set of bodily margins which must not be

transgressed because this threatens the fundamental binary oppositions of self/not-self, male/female:

> To love, to watch-think-seek the other in the other, to despecularize,
> to unhoard. Does this seem difficult? It's not impossible, and this is
> what nourishes life – a love that has no commerce with the apprehen-
> sive desire that provides against lack, and stultifies the strange: a love
> that rejoices in the exchange that multiplies. (Cixous in Marks and de
> Courtivron 1981, 264)

The source of this generosity is woman, who doesn't order what she
gives, count it out, profit from it. Her gifts destabilise 'all the old
concepts of management', and displace the necessity for presence to
be defined against absence, property to be defined against lack

Her metaphor for writing comes, therefore, from the maternal
body: the feminine text is written in white ink (251), mother's milk, a
gift given from the body to the body (before the process of differentiation between mother and child has been initiated), without hope or
expectation of return. It is a writing that does not depend on hierarchy, mastery or power. A Utopian project, perhaps, especially if the
revolution is supposed to occur only through language. But it does
offer new ways of thinking ourselves out of structures of oppression,
and into new possibilities for expression: and some day that might
make a difference.

Reading with Cixous

The difficulty in dealing with Cixous's ideas has to do with the extent
to which they depend as much on their formulation as on their
formulae. The extent to which discursive mastery is important in
Western culture is clearly signalled by the fact that the student who
writes her essay in her own version of *écriture féminine* might well
find that her grades drop. And my discussion of Cixous has not taken
place in the kind of writing she recommends. Indeed, in describing
her work, I am almost certainly doing violence to it, so caught up am I
in the system of language and thought she evokes and attacks. The
pretence that she works as a theorist whose ideas can be picked up at
will and applied to whatever one chooses, without her readers modifying their own discursive praxes probably will not do. It is important

to recall that Cixous is a writer of fiction as well as of criticism and theory, and that her mixing up of genres (fiction written in the mode of academic essay, a critique of Freud couched as a play, essays written in poetic prose) is an issue of politics as well as of style. It makes her hard to 'use' if we want to 'use' her honestly, and probably a certain damage is inevitable.

The temptation with Cixous's writings is to take the easiest concept – that of the hierarchised, gendered construction of binary opposition – and see it as a totalising concept that can explain everything, in a kind of 'vulgar Cixousism'. So, for example, a poem like D. H. Lawrence's 'Bei Hennef' could simply be read as replicating the structure she describes. The poem is a honeymoon piece, written to and for Frieda Lawrence, during their trip to Germany soon after their marriage. The poem opens with a description of 'almost bliss', placed in the context of a twilit river, with the world and its interruptions 'shut up and gone to sleep'. The peace of the scene allows the speaker to know the nature of his love for his wife, which, at this moment feels complete. He expresses this perfection or completion in a series of images of what he sees as complementarity:

> You are the call and I am the answer,
> You are the wish, and I the fulfilment,
> You are the night, and I the day.
>> What else? It is perfect enough.
>> It is perfectly complete,
>> You and I,
>> What more —?
>
> Strange, how we suffer in spite of this!
>> Lawrence, 'Bei Hennef', 1977, 203

Armed with Cixous's notion of gendered opposition, we can see the structure of gender at play in the oppositions, call/answer, wish/fulfilment, night/day, and we can see also that the second term of each opposition answers the lack of the first (feminised) term. The question 'what else?', with its answer 'it is perfect enough' closes down the possibility of alternative formulations: there is nothing else, and what is there is perfect. The perfection and completion named by Lawrence's speaker seek to articulate a system without disjunction, with no gaps in which to insert a difference of equality. The last line,

however, undermines the structure of the perfect. The couple continues to suffer despite perfection precisely because it is based on the
unwilled subordination of one term to the other. Perhaps for the
reader of Cixous, the suffering is not strange at all, but the obvious
consequence of the implied lack of the first term.

All of which is interesting in its way, but it tends to risk making the
reading of the poem into a mechanical procedure which ignores the
specific structure of the poem as well as making Cixous's opening
remarks in one essay into the be-all and end-all of her critique. A
theoretical reading indebted to Cixous must pay more careful attention. For example, the phrase 'perfect enough' is surely oxymoronic,
since perfection, by definition takes no qualifiers. That's one of the
places in which the structure which seems at first to be impenetrable
breaks down. A second place might be in the word 'suffer'. Its most
obvious meaning is that of 'undergoing pain'. It also means to endure,
meaning 'to put up with, tolerate', but also 'to last'. It contains within
it other possibilities, the ghosts of other words, including 'sustain', the
meaning of its Latin root word *sufferre*; and it is also the word that
defines passion (which signals suffering as well as anger and desire).
The strangeness the poem identifies may actually have to do with the
ways in which words, for all their apparently structuring functions, do
not actually fix meaning at all. And this is compounded by the context
of the poem as a whole whose title 'Bei Hennef' means *poste restante*
or temporary address in the town of Hennef am Rhein. The structure
of call/answer, wish/fulfilment etc. is not necessarily, in this context,
the catch-all that it first appears. It is a temporary frame, something
that holds good just for this moment and in this place. In other words,
the gaps in the structure can be found. For the theoretical reader, it is
never enough just to notice that the structure exists by passively
applying a pre-existing model. She must also be an active reader,
searching for a plurality and contradiction, even when the discourse
seems closed.

Similarly, it is difficult to exemplify *écriture féminine* without fixing it
into defining limitations. What follows in the following brief reading
of Angela Carter's novel *Nights at the Circus* first published in 1984,
therefore, should be taken merely as examples of what such a writing
might look like, rather than a final definition of what it always is. *Écriture féminine* is about disrupting oppressive structures of signification

from the macro level of, say, genre, to readings and writings of a given text's content, right down to the micro-level of the sentence. What I propose here therefore is to think through the lens of the idea of *écriture féminine*, rather than try to impose a Cixousian reading on Carter's text.

The first thing that becomes apparent in reading the novel is that this is a textual world in which reality and fantasy are inseparable. In part, this is a function of the novel's setting in the world of popular entertainment, the music-halls and circuses of the end of the nineteenth century, spaces in which illusion plays a significant part, and yet spaces which are also inhabited by 'real' people. The central figure of the novel, Fevvers, dramatises the paralysis of binary thought in the face of anything that questions its logic. She is a real woman, with real wings, a biological impossibility who is also a logical absurdity. 'Is she fact or fiction?' asks her own publicity material, playing on the binary logic of either/or – but the answer to the question is 'yes': she is both. Fevvers's very existence, albeit in a fictional text, throws into doubt a number of apparently certain facts of epistemology and ontology. Her appearance, as a larger than life woman, with life-like wings, undoes any theory that implies that one can unproblematically believe what one sees. Common sense and its related discourse of Realism tell us that Fevvers is impossible, a point made in the novel by the journalist Walser who uses both his common sense and his knowledge of biology to make the point that she cannot exist: 'what about her *belly button*? Hasn't she just this minute told me she was hatched from an egg, not gestated *in utero*? The oviparous species are not, by definition, nourished by the placenta; therefore they feel no need of the umbilical cord ... and therefore don't bear the scar of its loss. Why isn't the whole of London asking: does Fevvers have a belly button?' (Carter 1984, 17–18). The question, a realist's question, is posed but not answered: and this is a function of the novel's genre, which might be termed that of Magic Realism.

The term itself is a paradox. Realism is precisely that mode of writing that eschews magic. It is the writing that represents the status quo, and as such, it has increasingly been read as a conservative and reactionary mode (Belsey 1980, 67–84). Not only does it attempt to reproduce the world as it is currently constituted as natural, it also produces a version of the reader who is constituted, like the realist character, as stable, coherent, knowable: to go against such a mode of representation is to use form in a political way, by writing alternatives.

The addition of magic to reality unsettles reality. This is especially powerful in the novel in its effects on Walser, a supremely realist character who is drawn into the web of Fevvers's narrative as well as her world, and loses his stable sense of self in the process. He is reduced through the process of the novel to a man who wears make-up as part of his disguise as a clown, rendering his gender status uncertain; he dresses as a chicken in the Russian circus, losing his species identity too; and for part of the novel, he wanders the Siberian waste land, having lost his memory, shouting 'cockle-doodle-dooski' (a rough approximation of a Russian chicken's language), signalling his loss of language itself, as well as his tenuous grip on his own humanity. In the battle between magic and reality in the context of the novel, neither wins. Both are necessary for survival, though there is always some sacrifice of each in its relation with the other. This genre of magic realism makes the hierarchical organisation of discourses impossible. Fevvers's chaotic autobiographical oral narrative, with which the novel opens, has more authority than Walser's impassive, objective journalism, even if we cannot believe a word she says.

In its representation of male and female, moreover, the novel continues its subversive process, since it undercuts what Cixous saw as the gendered hierarchical binaries that organise thought. As Margaret Atwood has argued, using a Cixousian model derived from Blake's poem 'The Tyger', with its (gendered) opposition of tiger and lamb:

> It is Carter's contention that a certain amount of tigerishness may be necessary if women are to achieve an independent as opposed to a dependent existence; if they are to avoid – at the extreme end of passivity – becoming meat. ... although society may slant things so that women appear to be better candidates for meathood than men and men better candidates for meat-eating, the nature of men is not fixed by Carter as inevitably predatory with females as their 'natural' prey. Lambhood and tigerishness may be found in either gender, and in the same individual at different times. (Atwood in Sage 1994, 121–2)

Now the novel clearly shows 'lambhood', and what happens to the passive is very disturbing. The role of woman as dead meat is taken to its logical conclusion in Madame Schreck's Museum of Horrors in the figure of Sleeping Beauty, who sleeps for a living and is gawped at by voyeuristic punters. Her sleeping is her livelihood, but it will also be the death of her. But the novel also shows that 'tigerishness' is not the preserve of masculinity. Fevvers, for example, is physically voracious: she eats like a horse, drinks like a fish – is greedy for all kinds of physical experience. Even so, she has nearly become a human sacrifice on a number of occasions. And Walser's pose as very manly man, the war correspondent and man of action, a tiger if ever we saw one, is belied by his treatment of the poor girl, Mignon, whom he chooses not to exploit. Mignon herself, a classic victim, becomes a happy person in the arms of the Abyssinian princess who keeps tigers. The brutal Strong Man even finds his gentle side. Oppositions inhabit the same bodies, whatever their gender, and nowhere is this more the case than with Fevvers herself.

Fevvers represents both a stifling femininity (corsets, dyed hair and feathers, overwhelming perfume and make-up laid on with a trowel), and its liberation. She inhabits the divide between culture and nature. In material terms she is very successful; she is the mistress of her own destiny; she makes her own contracts with her employers and is clearly a powerful player in the apparently masculine world of capitalistic commerce. She holds her place there by the maintenance of a powerful illusion of femininity which must *appear* natural, but which is, in fact, entirely faked. Her body, even in corsets, does not conform to the supposed standards of feminine delicacy: she takes after her father the swan in the shoulder parts, for example; her voice is like dust-bin lids, never 'gentle, soft and low'; she is well over six feet tall ('she was a *big* girl'), and her height is emphasised by big hair. She also claims to be a virgin (though the claim is open to some doubt), not for reasons of morality, but explicitly for reasons of commerce – the mystery makes her more marketable. Her status as a commodity breaks down some of the negative assumptions that might go with that label. For after all, Fevvers made herself, and controls the terms under which she is bought and sold. She is always contradictory: at once a high culture Valkyrie and a low culture 'bird in a gilded cage'; at once woman and symbol, subject and object. She inhabits the oppositions and undoes their logic. The contradiction of magic realism is played out in the representation of her contradictory physique – woman and bird.

Alongside genre and representation as aspects of a possible *écriture féminine*, Carter's writing style in the novel partakes of excess. She makes reference to every area of cultural life, from the highest to the lowest, and mixes them up to such an extent that it is virtually impossible to reinscribe the hierarchy that the words high and low most usually represent. The writing itself subverts order, and defuses its categorisations into anarchic laughter. In Cixous's writing laughter functions as both mockery and sheer pleasure. Fevvers's laughter, with which *Nights at the Circus* ends, is a similarly subversive force which undermines the force of binary thought. As Cixous recommends, Fevvers laughs at the oppositions:

> The spiralling tornado of Fevvers' laughter began to twist and shudder across the entire globe, as if a spontaneous response to the giant comedy that endlessly unfolded beneath it, until everything that lived and breathed, everywhere, was laughing. (Carter 1984, 295)

Notes

1. In a recent interview with Hélène Cixous in the collection *Rootprints*, Mireille Calle-Gruber notes that English-speaking criticism has tended to assume that Cixous is primarily a critic, and that this blindness to other aspects of Cixous's writing (her plays and novels, for example) is a kind of 'amputation' of her work, a reduction and a reification of an oeuvre which is 'plural; overflowing; which incessantly questions what it draws' (Cixous and Calle-Gruber, London: Routledge, 1997, 5). This is a timely warning, but unfortunately it is an amputation that this book will tend to replicate since its own subject is feminist theory. Moreover, much of Cixous' creative work in fiction and drama remains to be translated.

Part III

Differences

8 Differences of View and Viewing the Differences: Challenging Female Traditions

Ain't I a woman?

Ain't I a Woman? Black Women and Feminism is the title of bell hooks's 1981 exploration of the position of Black women in relation to feminist thinking. The title comes from a speech delivered in 1852 at an Ohio women's rights convention by Sojourner Truth. Sojourner Truth was a Black-American woman, born into slavery in 1797, who campaigned actively for Abolition, and for the rights of Black women. The speech was a powerful rebuke not only to white men who sought to deny women (Black and white) the vote, but also to white feminist suffrage campaigners who failed to see the Black woman as a woman like themselves. Sojourner Truth said, in response to a male delegate who had argued that women could not have equal rights because they could not participate equally in manual labour being physically weaker:

> Dat man ober dar say dat women needs to be helped into carriages, and lifted ober ditches, and to have de best places ... and ain't I a woman? Look at me! Look at my arm! ... I have plowed and planted, and gathered into barns, and no man could head me – and ain't I a woman? I could work as much and eat as much as a man (when I could get it) and bear de lash as well – and ain't I a woman? I have borne five children and seen 'em mos all sold into slavery, and when I cried out with my mother's grief, none but Jesus hear – and ain't I a woman? (Sojourner Truth, quoted in hooks 1982, 160)

The rebuke was necessary because for most of her audience, the defi-

nition of 'a woman' was derived from a white middle-class perspective on feminine propriety. A Black woman who could work as hard as
a man, and who could eat like a man, who could be punished like a
man, might not have seemed much like a woman in those terms. But
the evidence of Truth's life is undeniable: she *is* a woman, and she
displays her body to prove it; she has borne five children, and has
wept for them just as any white mother might. She claims the right to
be defined as a woman, though she does not match all the criteria of
femininity (of the upper-class white privileges of attenuated appetite,
and the incapacity for physical work) that framed upper-class white
women of the time. As hooks comments, 'Unlike most white women's
rights advocates, Sojourner Truth could refer to her own personal life
experience as evidence of women's ability to function as a parent; to
be the work equal of man; to undergo persecution, physical abuse,
rape torture; and to not only survive but emerge triumphant' (160).

When hooks took Truth's battle cry as her title, 130 years later, she
signalled the extent to which the Black woman remained an absence
from woman-centred thinking. The Civil Rights movement that had
emerged in the 1960s to overturn the colour bar, and to lobby for
equal-rights legislation for Black and white first in the United States,
then in Britain, had done little for Black women. For hooks, Black
women were silenced by the oppressive assumptions of white women
and white men, and also very powerfully by the sexism of Black men.
The women's liberation movements of the early 1970s seemed to say
nothing to Black women, because they operated within discourses
that separated sex from race and from class, and were established by
white women for whom race was invisible as a structure of sexist
oppression. Sojourner Truth's speech might have been electrifying in
1852: but even in the late 1970s, Black women still needed to claim the
womanhood that she had made her clarion call. In a later speech,
delivered in 1867 to the first annual meeting of the American Equal
Rights Association, Truth had said: 'I am above eighty years old; it is
about time for me to be going. I have been forty years a slave and forty
years free, and would be here forty years more to have equal rights for
all' (Truth in Lauter 1998, 2052). Subsequent history has shown her
prediction to be wildly optimistic, in particular in relation to the
struggle for equality of Black women both in white-dominated
Western societies and in Black societies.

The emphasis in this book so far has been on the modes of feminist
criticism that have become most widely accepted in the British and

American academies. Quite apart from the socio-economic grouping that such an emphasis implies (on women who are already sufficiently economically and socially privileged to form part of the academy) such a focus also disguises the differences between women inside the academy: Black feminist criticism has scarcely had its say; lesbian-feminist criticism has not yet been mentioned. I am extremely aware of the ways in which the structure of *Literary Feminisms* potentially reproduces the exclusions of which working-class, Black and lesbian women complain when they are confronted by a feminist criticism and theory that claims to speak as, to and for all women, in utopian projects like *parler-femme* and *écriture féminine*, and yet which cannot imagine speaking for or to them, and which does not hear their voices. As Elizabeth V. Spelman has argued in her important book *Inessential Woman: Problems of Exclusion in Feminist Thought* (first published in 1988), unthinking exclusion is the single most significant problem in the kinds of feminist theories that have become, as it were, the 'respectable', academic face of feminism. In fact, far from being respectable, exclusion is the scandal of feminist theory. Spelman castigates feminist thinkers such as Simone de Beauvoir and Nancy Chodorow (in particular her book *The Reproduction of Mothering*, 1978) for forgetting that their views about 'woman' mean only a certain kind of woman in a particular society:

> If gender identity were isolatable from class and race identity, if sexism were isolatable from classism and racism, we could talk about relations between men and women and never have to worry about whether their race or class were the same or different. ... If gender were isolatable from other forms identity, if sexism were isolatable from other kinds of oppression, then what would be true about the relation between any man and woman would be true about the relation between any other man and any other woman. (Spelman 1990, 81)

But catch-all explanations about man/woman relations (or about woman/woman relations) are not true. The totalising gestures of feminism – those times when feminist thought seeks to speak for all women, and to create a sisterly solidarity between all women – disguise differences between women that actually matter a great deal.

These differences have historically been one of the major blind spots of academic feminism, and various explanations have been put forward for the failure to view the differences between women. For Barbara Smith, the reason for the excision of Black lesbian voices from the authorised version of feminist theory is simply the racism that comes when white critics (female and male) know no Black women, professionally and personally, a not-knowing that renders them unable to imagine and value a Black woman's identity, and unable even to imagine a lesbian identity that is other than white. White feminist critics, she suggests, take their own situation as the paradigm of women's position. They interrogate neither their whiteness nor their (hetero)sexuality as political institutions that cushion them against the worst effects of racist and sexist violence. They fear the surrender of their heterosexual and white privileges. Nor do they value Black women's writing as 'literary' since they are blind to the social/economic circumstances that condition a Black woman's choices of image, metaphor and plot (Smith in Showalter 1986, 168–185). For bell hooks, the reasons have to do with the silencing of Black women's voices by the sexism and racism of whites (whether this is registered either as overt hostility, or whether it is registered as indifference), and by the sexism of Black men. As Smith argues elsewhere, in an address to a Women's Studies conference, racism is an issue that feminism has to confront because of what feminism is supposed to mean: 'Feminism is the political theory and practice that struggles to free *all* women: women of color, working-class women, poor women, disabled women, lesbians, old women – as well as white, economically privileged, heterosexual women. Anything less than this vision of total freedom is not feminism, but merely feminist self-aggrandisement' (Smith in Hull *et al.* 1982, 49). Her speech and her writings elsewhere constitute an important rebuke to a white Western feminism that never examines its own criteria properly, and which proceeds on the basis that the problems of the white woman are the problems of all women.

The origins of Black feminist literary criticism, as they are established in Smith's 1977 path-breaking essay, 'Towards a Black Feminist Criticism', are always far more politically grounded than the liberal womanist[1] origins of white feminist critiques. Ellen Moers and Patricia Mayer Spacks, after all, both refused even to use the word 'feminist' in describing their own projects, as we have already seen. Moreover, theirs is writing that does not even *see* the differences between women of different races and classes and sexual choices, let alone make those differences the object of their view. They establish a view of women which is collective – women's experiences are essentially the same across time, space, economic and material circumstance. Well – they would say that, wouldn't they? Their examples make precisely that point, since they are drawn from privileged white circles, and are chosen because of pre-existing standards of literary value, standards that their works leave unquestioned.

Black feminist criticism therefore has had to restage many of the battles of white feminist criticism within the terms of both feminist and anti-racist activism. Only, where the white woman fought mostly against white patriarchal privilege, the Black woman had to fight on many fronts: against white patriarchy, against white women's racism, and against the sexism of Black men. It had to begin by establishing that Black women actually have histories and experiences that are specific to them, which it did by starting the process of uncovering the words of Black women about their own experiences, and by criticising histories of Black people that assumed that Black experience was male. Erlene Stetson's essay, 'Studying Slavery: Some Literary and Pedagogical Considerations on the Black Female Slave', describes a college course she began to teach in the late 1970s. The fundamental problem of such a course is that the written materials in which women's experiences are expressed in their own words are 'hidden or submerged': they exist in the forms of 'narratives, letters, diaries, and unpublished documents, court transcripts, and sometimes bills of sale' (Stetson in Hull *et al.* 1982, 61). To read and interpret these documents, they first have to be found. There is no ready-made Great Tradition of Black slave-women's writings that is already published and easily available. Once the materials had been found, the class Stetson taught had to begin to establish a methodology for reading them. Stetson began with what might be called the 'authorised' version of slave history, studying contemporary and then twentieth-century histories of slavery in the United States. This study established the racism of many of the so-called 'objective' histories of slavery; but it also established that the lives of slave-women had not been objects of study at all – the slave-woman's narrative was a lacuna, an absence at the centre of the story. Stetson also noted how difficult her students found it to read against the grains of these authoritative studies: how they were blinded by the wealth of statistics and the apparently objective voices in which so many of the studies were written.

She sought to help her students to unpick the supposed logic of histories of slavery through the appeal to Black slave-women's own narratives of their own experiences. The monologic of traditional history was modified by the polylogicality of hearing the different voices, the different genres and versions of slave experience from a Black woman's point of view. Stetson argues that Black feminist perspectives have to develop alternative reading strategies because:

> Black women's slave narratives contained some problems unique to themselves. For one thing, there is the question of genre: what are the most useful ways to study female slave narratives? Is there a generic way of describing them as literary-historical documents? Should slave narratives be studies as fiction (literary document), as history (anti-slavery documents), as autobiography (the slaves' own story)? ... the Black female slave narratives were the most exciting, perhaps because they seemed closer to literature than to history. (68)

The class eventually decided that genre was a limiting category – that the slave narratives of Black women were history, literature and auto-biography all at once. To privilege one signifiying discourse over another was to belie the force of the narratives. And in making this decision, Stetson and her students were creatively disrupting the boundaries between the narrative modes, showing that autobio-graphical writing can have both the force of historical evidence and the potency of literary value: they authorised personal experience as valid in both history and literature. Reading these neglected texts was a re-vision of that powerful matrix that makes meanings in a binary mode: as either one thing or another. These readings and rereadings, that is, were subversive in the very fact that they took Black women's voices seriously as emanating from people who had valuable, impor-tant things to say, and who were themselves valuable and important. Their narratives were open to analyses that showed how oppression and expression had to be read together, just as sexism and racism should also be read together.

Stetson's critique and analysis of the apparently objective voice of 'history' is also a significant part of the development of Black feminist criticism, which does not want to disguise itself as writing by white men in order to get its point across. As Luce Irigaray argues, speech is never neuter. The adoption of an objectivist discourse that excises the speaking 'I' from the critical text plays white men at their own game. The game is a game that Black women have been trained to lose through poor education and social deprivation. More importantly, it is a game whose rules Black feminist criticism disputes. After all, that objective voice that said 'there shall be only one version of truth' is precisely the voice that excluded them in the first place. And white women's mimicry of the objectivist stance is not much help either. Stetson's article is at least implicitly autobiographical, making her own experience of teaching the focus of her argument. Other Black feminist interventions, notably Alice Walker's *In Search of Our Mothers' Gardens* (1983), perform the writing of theory as a creative, as well as a critical, performance, writing dialogues, imaginary conversations, and including apparently non-academic materials (cooking, sewing, folklore) as the structures of the argument. As Gloria T. Hull puts it, describing her approach to the works of the Black woman poet Alice Dunbar-Nelson:

> It goes without saying that I approached her as an important writer and her work as genuine literature. Probably as an (over?)reaction to the condescending, witty but empty, British urbanity of tone which is the hallmark of traditional white male literary scholarship (and which I dislike intensely), I usually discuss Dunbar-Nelson with level high seriousness – and always with caring. Related to this are my slowly-evolving efforts at being so far unfettered by conventional style as to write creatively, even poetically, if that is the way the feeling flows ... the question of audience is key. (Hull in Hull *et al* 1982, 194)

The title of Hull's essay is 'Researching Alice Dunbar-Nelson: a personal and literary perspective'. The point she makes is that the personal and the literary (and the literary-critical) can be found together. She is trying to find a voice that suits the material, and a voice that suits the politics of interpreting that material. There is more than one audience, and there are more ways than one of writing Black feminist criticism to address the different audiences.

Given that Black women have been – and continue to be – the most disprivileged groups within both white and Black societies, the development of a feminist literary theory may not seem to be their most pressing need. Where people are hungry, one assumes, they do not need to analyse their hunger and its causes: they want to be fed. But as Barbara Smith persuasively argues, political theories are a vehicle for raising the consciousness of oppressed groups; knowing the terms of one's oppression is the prerequisite for changing it. Moreover, because literature is itself one of the terms of privilege, claiming the status of literariness for Black women's texts is a highly charged political act that helps to claim value for the Black women's lives that Black women's writing most usually represents. In Black feminist criticism, aesthetics and politics are inseparable terms. Barbara Smith, Alice Walker or bell hooks would never distance themselves from the explicit feminist politics of a woman-centred approach, as Moers and Spacks, as Showalter and Gilbert and Gubar, did.

Once a tradition of Black women's writing has been established, then Black feminist criticism sought to read it differently and to rewrite the meaning of literary value so that Black women writers were shown to have it. Instead of being viewed as merely a minority interest group, Black feminist criticism focused its attention on the content of Black women's writing, on its (mediated) reflections of experience, but also on the forms, images, metaphors and plots that this writing expressed. This emphasis involves viewing Black women's writing in the context of Black women's writing, rather than measuring it against some apparently universal standard, or reading it as a mere adjunct to the writing of Black men or of white women. Having a tradition of their own and fostering a familiarity of that tradition, would, argues Barbara Smith, allow Black feminist critics to see that 'thematically, stylistically, aesthetically, and conceptually, Black women writers manifest common approaches to the act of creating literature as a direct result of the political, social, and economic experience they have been obliged to share'. In the works of Zora Neale Hurston, Margaret Walker, Toni Morrison and Alice Walker, for example, one would find repeated references to the domestic skills of Black women, but also to their powerful folk memories, their use of herbal medicines, their relationships with magic, their knowledge of midwifery, their cooperation with each other, their potent female friendships and love. One would also find a 'specifically Black female language' to express their experiences, and an emphasis on oral traditions which are brought into the realm of the literary. In the nurturing readings of a Black female literary tradition, these forms and themes can be celebrated rather than criticised (Smith in Showalter 1986, 174). In turn, Black female languages find their way into the discourses of criticism.

One theme that such a criticism might examine is that of the trope of maternity. Motherhood is, of course, a function that is universally female. Moreover, in most societies, the care of pre-school and/or pre-adolescent children, whether male or female, is socially constructed as the role of women. For many early white feminist theorists, maternity was one of the major problems that feminism had to address, since maternity and economic independence were constructed as incompatible. In Simone de Beauvoir's meditation on motherhood, conception is usually the result of failed contraception, pregnancy is a time of morbid pathologies, birth is traumatic, and the child itself is abandoned to the care of a neurotic woman who has so many social and psychic frustrations that 'one is frightened at the thought that defenceless infants are abandoned to her care' (de Beauvoir 1997, 529). And for Shulamith Firestone, individual mother-hood would ideally be replaced by artificial wombs and centralised child-are, to alleviate women from the pain and disgust of pregnancy and social deprivations involved in prolonged child-rearing (Firestone 1972).

Black feminist criticism exposes the ways in which such views are the product of white feminism and privileged experience, and do not accurately map Black female experiences at all. For Black women, so often placed in situations of serious economic need, there has very often been no choice between work and childbearing. Indeed, in slave times the two kinds of labour went together, with female slaves often being forced to bear children from systematised rape by Black slaves and/or white slave-owners. Where explicit systems of slavery are not the issue, as in certain Third World countries, work and children are not oppositions, and they are seldom matters of choice. It is only in the sphere of the privileged woman, usually a white woman, that childbirth and work are separated; the disgust expressed by de Beauvoir and Firestone depend on a particular narrow version of what is meant by femininity. As Alice Walker quietly comments in one essay, ('One Child of One's Own' [1978]): 'Our Mother thought, cradling her baby with one hand, while grading student papers with the other (she found teaching extremely compatible with childcare)' (Walker in Hull et al. 1982, 39). The comment might almost pass without notice, in its muted parenthesis. But presumably the point is that university teaching, a privileged kind of labour after all, makes caring for children much easier than working in low-paid, low-status jobs, with awkward hours and no autonomy over conditions of work. Similarly, the Nigerian-born novelist Buchi Emecheta dedicates her novel *Second-Class Citizen* (1974) 'To my dear children, Florence, Sylvester, Jake, Christy and Alice, without whose sweet background noises this book would not have been written'. The dedication gives the lie to the commonly held view that creativity and mothering do not mix, a view perpetuated by Elaine Showalter in *A Literature of their Own*, who noted that the majority of the women writers she discussed were childless. Emecheta's book shows Adah, her protagonist, writing around the needs of her family; she sees no personal conflict between childbearing and training and work, except the conflict imposed on her by her white employers in Nigeria and then in London. These are very small examples, but they do suggest that there are different views of female experience. Sojourner Truth appealed to her maternity as the sign of her womanhood. It was a different appeal from one that might have been made by upper-class white women in her time: but the differences should not imply inequalities.

The phrase Black feminism is itself, of course, a term that disguises differences within Black communities, and across varieties of geographical locations. The experiences of Black women in the US or Britain may have much in common with the experiences of women in Africa, the Middle East or Asia; but an element of shared experience is not the same thing as saying that all women are treated in the same way, perceive themselves in the same way, or that one can easily extrapolate from that shared experience a theoretical model that applies to all Black women. Black and white represents precisely the kind of binary opposition that seeks to totalise experience, and that feminist theories have so urgently tried to dismantle. Blackness and whiteness are much more complicated relations than a binary opposition implies. Where, in that oppostion, are the women who inherit Chinese or Indian ethnicities, or are Puerto Rican, Latina or Chicana? Where are the women who inhabit multiple combinations of identity in relation to race, class, culture, nationality, religion and sexuality? As Black (and sometimes white) feminisms have developed, they have increasingly tried to ensure that complex identities are not erased in the process of seeking to make large statements about the position of all women in the world.

What feminisms have to negotiate is the relationships between structures of systematic oppressions and individualised, localised experiences of them. Global capitalism is a system that has to be analysed; but how I experience it, living in relative privilege in the West, is different from the ways in which a low-paid Korean worker in Silicon Valley, California experiences it; and both of our experiences are different again from middle-class women in Egypt and from peasant workers in India. As Chandra Talpade Mohanty eloquently demonstrates, phrases like Black women, women of colour, Third-World women, have a tendency to disguise important differences. In her essay 'Under Western Eyes: Feminist Scholarship and Colonial Discourses', she analyses the ways in which generally well-meaning Western feminists belie their own good intentions in their critical practices. Their analyses, she suggests, take place within what Inigaray would call ready-made grids derived from pre-existing Western models.

These analyses find what they seek, rather than what is there, and tend to reproduce Third-World women as a uniformly oppressed category, rather than seeking their subjectivities and valuing their own culturally specific strategies of survival and resistance:

> What is problematical about [the] use of 'women' as a group, as a stable category of analysis, is that it assumes ahistorical, universal unity between women based on a generalized notion of their subordination. Instead of analytically *demonstrating* the production of women as socioeconomic political groups within particular local contexts, this analytical move limits the female subject to gender identity, completely bypassing social class and ethnic identities ... women are thus constituted as a coherent group, sexual difference becomes coterminous with female subordination, and power is automatically read in binary terms: people who have it (read: men), and people who do not (read: women) ... Such simplistic formulations are historically reductive; they are also ineffectual in designing strategies to combat oppressions. All they do is reinforce binary divisions between men and women. (Mohanty 1991, 64)

If the phrase 'the personal *is* political' is more than a convenient slogan, it means that there is an obligation on us to understand that the systems of oppression do not impinge on us all equally, and to recognise the specificity of different women's experiences, and the validity of their own views about them. Seeing the world in terms of Black and white disguises all those other colours in the spectra of women's lives.

These complexities are at the heart of edited collections of critical and autobiographical writings by US feminists of colour such as Cherríe Moraga and Gloria Anzaldúa. The first of these, *This Bridge Called My Back: Writings by Radical Women of Color*, originally published in 1981, opens up discursive spaces for some of the women who are rendered invisible by terms like Black and white. 'Here are women of every shade of color', writes Moraga:

> We were born into colored homes. We grew up inside the inherent contradictions in the color spectrum right inside those homes: the lighter sister, the mixed-blood cousin, being the darkest one in the family. It doesn't take many years to realize the privileges, or lack thereof, attached to a particular shade of skin or texture of hair. It is this experience that moves light-skinned or 'passable' Thirld World women to put ourselves on the line for our darker sisters. We are all family. From those families we were on the one had encouraged to leave, to climb up white. And with the other hand, the reins were held tight on us, our parents understanding the danger that bordered our homes. We learned to live with these contradictions. This is the root of our radicalism. (Moraga and Anzaldúa, 1983, 5)

The word 'passable' refers to the idea of women of colour 'passing for white' because of the race disprivilege of Blackness. The very idea of 'passing' radically dismantles the binary opposition of Black and white: one cannot always tell race/ethnicity merely by looking. But 'passing' also depends on a version of the world in which Blackness/colour cannot be conceived as positive identities. The collection of poems, letters, autobiographical essays and fragments, and interviews that makes up *This Bridge Called My Back* both drama-tises the reasons why it is sometimes safer to 'pass', and challenges the idea of needing to 'pass' by fostering strong, attractive images of women of colour. The book is written by Black American women, by Latinas and Chicanas, by Native American women, by Asian American and Chinese American women. This proliferation belies the simplicity of Black and white. Moreover, these identities are not exactly precise or secure. Rosario Morales writes of being US American, but also of being Cuban, Puerto Rican, Jewish and Catholic, and of speaking each of the possible languages that go with each of those identities (Moraga and Anzaldúa 1983, 14–15). For Gloria Anzaldúa, the inheritance is German and Spanish and Mexican Indian as well as US American. No single identity holds up: identity is multiplied and fragmented. But that does not mean that these identities have no valid existence, nor that it is permissible to render them invisible. Specificity must never be disguised by generalisation.

The writings of women of colour and of Third-World women are very various. They do not propose a totalising theoretical model, nor a unified critical practice. They do, however, demand that white Western feminists take the real conditions of their oppression and repression seriously, and they express the grounds of their own pains and pleasures in strikingly creative ways. White women, it becomes clear, in reading the writings of Spivak, Mohanty, Moraga and Anzaldúa, are part of the problem for women of colour. White women seldom see their own race as an issue at all, since they live with the privileges of whiteness that blind them to the systemic oppressions of race. Feminisms must wear coats of many colours. The different colours can speak to each other, but that requires that white feminists in particular learn to hear the real differences that colours make, and in the words of Gloria Anzaldúa, 'acknowledge that they [are] agents of oppression', and stop seeking 'reassurance, acceptance and validation from *mujeres-de-color* [women of colour]' (Anzaldúa 1990, xx). Women of colour have their own battles to fight; it would be better if they didn't have to fight them with white feminists.

Ghosts, traces and sexual 'Others': lesbian feminist theories

It is neither an accident nor a mistake that lesbian feminist theory appears here in the immediate context of Black feminist theory. For all kinds of reasons these two forms of thinking have much in common, not least the emphasis that Barbara Smith placed on the Black lesbian woman in 'Toward a Black Feminist Criticism' in her reading of Toni Morrison's novel *Sula* (1974). Smith describes hearing a definition of lesbian textuality at a conference in 1976:

> Bertha Harris suggested that if in a woman writer's work a sentence refuses to do what it is supposed to do, if there are strong images of women and if there is a refusal to be linear, the result is innately lesbian literature. As usual, I immediately wanted to see if these ideas might be applied to Black women writers that I know and quickly realised that many of their works were, in Harris's sense, lesbian. Not because women are 'lovers', but because they are the central figures, are positively portrayed and have pivotal relationships with one another. The form and language of these works are also nothing like

what white patriarchal culture requires or expects. (Smith in
Showalter 1986, 175)

For Smith, this way of thinking offered a new of way of approaching
Black women's writing. The term 'lesbian' in literature did not
need to mean a particular sexual object choice; it could mean
experimental forms in sentences and plots. The text had to be
woman-centred, but it did not have be filled with the kinds of
woman–woman love scenes that are a staple of male-authored and
male-consumed pornography. She was attracted to this mode particularly because it helped to relieve Black feminist criticism from any
kind of male dependency. Because Black women suffer the double
oppression of white sexism and racism and Black male sexism, positive images of female friendship break the mould and enable a Black
feminist discourse that is autonomous from most of its sources of
oppression.[2]

This very positive view of the lesbian in literature is not of course
how the word 'lesbian' is always used. It is often hurled as a term of
abuse in my experience in British playgrounds and pubs: it can be a
frightening word, filled with the threat of violence. In other words, it is
a contested word. As Joseph Bristow suggests in his book *Sexuality*,
the word 'lesbian' began to emerge in the early twentieth century to
describe women whose primary sexual object-choices were other
women (Bristow 1997, 50–1). It emerged in the context of the pseudo-
science of sexology, and it was viewed as a more or less pathological
condition, which could either be treated and normalised, or which
was 'incurable' and would ruin the 'sufferer's' life. In this kind of
context which has been more or less apparent for most of the twentieth century, it has often been very hard for a woman-identified
woman to claim a lesbian identity as her own, and to claim such an
identity positively. As Adrienne Rich argued in her important essay
'Compulsory Heterosexuality and Lesbian Existence' (1980) 'lesbian
experience is perceived on a scale ranging from deviant to abhorrent
or simply rendered invisible' through the biases of compulsory
heterosexuality (Rich 1987, 26). It provokes either hostility or disbelief.
Why, then, would anyone want to claim it?

Because any word used to so aggressively clearly expresses power.
What Rich calls 'compulsory heterosexuality' seeks to disarm the
subversive potential of lesbian existence. Heterosexuality and patriarchy are both threatened by women who love women. What Luce

Irigaray called 'hommosexuality', the masculine logic of the same, is undone if women turn away from a sexuality that depends on the male: 'men fear ... that women could be indifferent to them altogether, that men could be allowed sexual and emotional – therefore economic – access to women *only* on women's terms, otherwise being left on the periphery of the matrix' (43). Hence, argues Rich, the enormous forces that are deployed to keep women heterosexually compliant in patriarchal cultures. Her list of patriarchal strategies against women is massive, but it includes social and economic deprivations, sexual subordination, denial of female sexuality (through everything from clitoridectomy to the death sentence for heterosexual adultery or lesbian relationships), rape, control of women's labour, control of their children, erasure of women from history and cultural achievement, inadequate education and objectification. Women confront a 'pervasive cluster of forces, ranging from physical brutality to control of consciousness'. The energy that goes into this repression 'suggests that an enormous potential counterforce is having to be restrained' (39). On the whole, it is likely that women who identify themselves as heterosexual believe either that their heterosexuality is 'natural' (they were born that way) or that it was freely chosen. In other words, heterosexuality, like whiteness, takes itself as the norm and the ideal: as such it does not need to theorise itself. It those who are Others – those who are not white, not straight, who have to do the thinking in the first place.

As Rich argues, this will not do. Just as Smith castigated white feminism for its inherent racism based on ignorance, hostility and failure to interrogate whiteness as an identity, Rich wants to castigate straight feminism for its heterosexist assumptions:

> The assumption that 'most women are innately heterosexual' stands as a theoretical and political stumbling block for feminism. It remains a tenable assumption partly because lesbian existence has been written out of history or catalogued under disease, partly because it has been treated as exceptional rather than intrinsic, partly because to acknowledge that for women heterosexuality many not be a 'preference' at all but something that has had to be imposed, managed, organized, propagandized, and maintained by force is an immense step to take if you consider yourself freely and 'innately' heterosexual. Yet the failure to examine heterosexuality as an institution is like failing to admit that the economic system called capitalism or the

caste system of racism is maintained by a variety of forces, including both physical violence and false consciousness. (50–1)

Implicitly, Rich suggests that if we allow 'lesbian' to continue to be used as a term of insult, and if we refuse to see it as a positive choice, we help to perpetuate the heterosexism that underpins patriarchy. Feminism has to have lesbianism at its heart, and in its heart. It wouldn't be much of a feminist revolution if it left out women who love women.

Rich therefore identifies two ways of thinking about the lesbian in feminist theory. She uses the terms *lesbian existence* and *lesbian continuum* to evade the 'clinical and limiting ring' of the word *lesbianism*, a term imposed by sexology and psychoanalysis to describe a sickness, a word that regulates a constrictive normality on femininity:

> *Lesbian existence* suggests both the fact of the historical presence of lesbians and our continuing creation of the meaning of that existence. I mean the term *lesbian continuum* to include a range – through each woman's life and throughout history – of woman-identified experience, not simply the fact that a woman has had or consciously desired genital sexual experience with another woman. (51)

These two ways of using the word lesbian are not oppositions, erecting a firm fence between heterosexual and lesbian women. Rather, they are to be understood as allowing both women who love women and all other women access to their woman-to-woman experience in contexts where the word 'lesbian' is not being used as an insult or a diagnosis. Lesbian existence is part of the lesbian continuum; but the lesbian continuum also consists of mother–daughter relationships, sisterly relationships, women's groups of many different kinds, female friendships *and* female love affairs. Rich asks us to consider the possibility that all women, from the suckling female child, to the mother who gives her milk, to the women who share professional commitments and workspaces, to the woman who dies in old age nursed by other women, all exist on a lesbian continuum which they move in and out of at different times (54). The lesbian is not just a sexualised being. She partakes of all areas of female life; and all women could fruitfully rethink their relationships with other women as a resistance to their sexualisation by patriarchal culture. Texts that celebrate female relationships, whether sexual or not, are part of the continuum, and can be read as attempts to re-articulate relationships between love and power.

The first explicitly lesbian–feminist critiques, however, did not quite behave in this way. Like all kinds of feminist criticism, they began by finding images, and then moved on to describing a tradition. A case in point is the 'founding' text of lesbian critique, Jane Rule's *Lesbian Images* (1975). The book is an 'images of women' critique with a lesbian gynocritical basis. It takes lesbian writers such as Gertrude Stein and Ivy Compton-Burnett and reads their images in an analysis that is a lesbian-inflected version of liberal humanist criticism. In itself, that was of course a radical attack on the unspoken assumptions of humanism – humanism had no place for the lesbian, after all. Rule did, however, implicitly and explicitly, go further than that. Her introduction, for example, is an autobiographical exploration of her own 'coming-out' story – she uses her own experience to validate the claim that lesbian criticism is necessary. Moreover, she also undertakes historical surveys of sexual practices and mores in Ancient Greece and Rome, and in the Middle East, thereby establishing that the normative heterosexuality of the present is neither universal nor trans-historical. She shows the ways in which the powerful discourses of the law, religion and medicine conspire to construct the heterosexual world as 'natural'; and argues that the figure of the lesbian is the most significant victim of these discourses, since they conspire to erase her existence entirely. In her readings of individual writers, she traces a history of different kinds of lesbian image. This is, as it were, history as necessary fiction, by Rule's own admission. It is fiction because the structure of a narrative history tends to imply progress and teleology, features that may not be 'really there'; it is necessary because how else are lesbian readers and writers to rediscover themselves? The writing of this history exemplifies what Adrienne Rich called 're-vision' – 'the act of looking back, of seeing with fresh eyes, of entering an old text from a new critical direction.' Re-vision is 'an act of survival' for all women, and perhaps especially for lesbian women (Rich 1993, 177).

As Bonnie Zimmerman has noted, if Jane Rule's *Lesbian Images* was a founding text for a tradition of lesbian–feminist criticism, it was not exactly an overnight success. It took another five years for a second book-length study of women-identified women in literature

(Zimmerman in Showalter 1986). This book was Lillian Faderman's *Surpassing the Love of Men: Romantic Friendship and Love Between Women from the Renaissance to the Present* (1981). It is notable that the word 'lesbian' does not appear in the title of this work, presumably precisely because of the hostility that the word often generates. Nonetheless, in her Introduction, Faderman argues for an inclusive definition of lesbian existence, one which does not require a prurient interest in women's sexual activities and which does not insist on evidence of woman-to-woman genital activity for the word lesbian to be invoked. Faderman argues that the focus on sex acts is a twentieth-century preoccupation. Women in previous centuries were 'encouraged to force any sexual drive they might have to remain latent', with the consequence that passionate romantic attachments between women might have had no explicitly sexual content:

> in many other centuries, romantic love and sexual impulse were often considered unrelated. ... But the lack of overt sexual expression in these romantic friendships could not discount the seriousness or the intensity of women's passions toward each other – or the fact that if by 'lesbian' we mean an all-consuming emotional relationship in which two women are devoted to each other above anyone else, these ubiquitous sixteenth-, seventeenth-, eighteenth-, and nineteenth-century romantic friendships were 'lesbian'. (Faderman 1985, 19)

Faderman charts the social tolerance that romantic friendships between women enjoyed before the twentieth century; and remarks with pain that such friendships were increasingly policed in the light of the development of the discourse of sexology, which defined lesbianism as 'a medical problem'. Faderman, that is, uncovered a lesbian history that was resolutely not a history of progress. The twentieth century created the lesbian as an outlaw figure who had internalised the view of her sexuality as disease, and consequently suffered from it rather than celebrating it as earlier generations had been able to do. Only comparatively recently has lesbianism become a relatively more acceptable choice for women. For Faderman, although there are significant differences between lesbian choices in the late twentieth century and the choices of earlier women, it is important to register the continuity of lesbian experience, to affirm that it has existed and that it continues to exist: 'had the romantic friends of other eras lived today, many of them would have been lesbian-feminists; and had the lesbian-feminists of our day lived in other eras, most of them would have been romantic friends' (20)

What follows this introduction is a massive excavation of female friendships across five centuries, using the evidence of their letters and diaries as well as of their literary texts to uncover the patterns of female feelings. What she notes from this discussion is the fact that for very few women was it possible to invest all their emotional energy in romantic friendships. Their passions for other women largely took place in the contexts of heterosexual marriages and maternal duties. The distrust of romantic friendship arose not only with the patholo-gised discourse of sexology, but with the rise of the increasingly inde-pendent woman who did not marry or have children – the so-called Boston marriage of late-nineteenth-century America, and the rela-tionships of the New Women in both Britain and the United States. The overt independence of these women was a direct threat to male heterosexual privilege; patriarchy closed in over the lesbian. It created a vision of her as mannish, unfeminine, unattractive – the invert figure of the man trapped in a woman's body that is explored in Radclyffe Hall's 1928 novel *The Well of Loneliness*. It is this image that is so often invoked when the word lesbian is used as an insult. Only in the very recent past, Faderman argues, has it been possible to rescue the word from its hostile, aggressive usages. Its rewriting as a positive term describing woman-identified experience, including sexual expe-rience, becomes possible only in the wake of the sexual revolution of the 1960s and of the women's liberation movements. (Even then, the progress has not been, as it were, in a straight line: there has been hostility to lesbian women in the women's movements, too.) Faderman ends her book with the hope that lesbian-feminist women will be able one day to live as they choose, without the pain of exclu-sion, and without feeling that separatism is the only political choice if all women are to become free.

Faderman's work is monumental and important. But like the estab-lishment of other feminist traditions of writing, it has some significant limitations as a *literary*-theoretical account of lesbian writing. It tends to concentrate on content; and although Faderman examines the covertness of female affections – the coding that disguises desires deemed unpalatable by normative heterosexism – the focus is neces-sarily on the content of the texts as a reliable indication of the experi-ences of the writers. Uncovering a tradition is about seeing similarities of image, plot and language that validate the claim that lesbian existence has always existed. It is also necessarily a biographical approach since the experience of lesbian existence and identity is what one has to try to find.

More recently, then, lesbian feminist criticism has begun to seek out lesbian textualities as dramatising lesbian experience, rather than representing it. Indeed, where sex was not quite the issue for Faderman (at least in looking back at earlier centuries), the expression of the specificity of lesbian sexual desire has become highly significant for lesbian theory. Terry Castle's recent book, *The Apparitional Lesbian: Female Homosexuality and Modern Culture* (1993), argues that the lesbian has tended to be a ghostly figure who is seldom properly seen. Castle says that her project is 'to bring the lesbian back into focus ... in all her worldliness, comedy and humanity' (Castle 1993, 2). The words 'worldliness' and 'humanity' are very important here for the politics of Castle's project. Worldliness is a term she borrows from Edward Said; it means 'that humane and expansive faculty of mind which allows one to see things "in a global setting" – as part and parcel of a larger world of "formal articulations"' (15). Lesbians have to be understood in their multiple relations to themselves as sexed beings, and to other definitions of sexed identity. She is in profound disagreement with modes of lesbian and queer theory that owe allegiance to post-structuralist formations of identity as provisional and even irrelevant.[3] She is unwilling to pronounce the death of lesbian identity not least because the obituaries would reconstitute the lesbian as a ghost effect. One of the effects of lesbian ghosting is the denial of the sexual experiences of lesbian women, the loss of the lesbian body in discussions about and representations of sexuality.

The ghostliness of the lesbian seems to affect the ways in which lesbian writing might be defined. Castle hypothesises a number of possible ways of glossing the term 'lesbian fiction'. She rejects a definition that insists on the depiction of sex between women, not least because this has been a popular trope in the writings of many men, and in particular is a repeated figure in male-authored and male-consumed pornography. The formula that 'a lesbian novel is a novel written by a lesbian' does not quite work either: there are women writers who were lesbians whose fiction eschews lesbian identity. 'A novel written by a woman depicting sexual relations between women' is another formulation: but it relies 'too heavily on the opacities of biography and eros, and lacks a certain psychic and political specificity' (67). The problem, suggests Castle, is that lesbian writing is under-theorised as a category. And it needs a theory that will liberate it from invisibility, will put the bodies back as sexuate bodies, because only by elaborating theories of lesbian existence and self-expression can lesbian women hope to gain the freedom to walk the streets arm in arm without the threat of violence. As with all kinds of feminist theory, then, there is a commitment to seeing and making the connections between the theoretical realm and the real – life as it is lived by real lesbian women.

In order to work out what a lesbian fiction might look like, Castle turns to the model produced by Eve Kosofsky Sedgwick in her 1985 book *Between Men: English Literature and Male Homosocial Desire*. Sedgwick's book argues that what appear to be heterosexual relationships between men and women in literature (the marriage and courtship plots that are so central to fiction), are often, in fact, male–male homosocial relationships. A man's marriage to a woman can be read as cementing his relationship with the woman's brother, father or friend. Sedgwick elaborates this idea in the figure of the triangle: two men and one woman – the woman is the common term between the men. When Castle examines *Between Men*, she is distressed that there is apparently no place for the woman-identified woman in Sedgwick's analysis. Indeed, Sedgwick more or less abandons the lesbian as a desiring subject. Sedgwick in fact unwittingly shows up the limitations of Rich's lesbian continuum, as Castle points out: 'Lesbians, defined here, with telling vagueness, only as "women who love women", are really no different, Sedgwick seems to imply, from "women promoting the interests of other women"'. Castle is alarmed that the specificity of lesbian existence is 'lost to view' in the unthinking appropriation of the lesbian continuum model (Castle 1993, 71).

She turns instead to a model for lesbian fiction that rewrites the erotic male–male–female triangle at the heart of *Between Men*. She shows that this triangle is only secure so long as the female term has no female bonds of her own – so long, that is, as the woman in the triangle has no other female relationships. As this is unlikely, in life as in literature, the stability of the homosocial triangle is immediately threatened by the incursion of a fourth female term, which makes it possible to imagine an alternative triangular structure – female–female–male – a new erotic triangle in which female desire is paramount and the male term drops out of the equation as a functioning desiring subject. Such a model would be radically subversive of the male plots that patriarchy enforces on women. Castle argues that this model could be read as a model for a definition of lesbian fiction that is not biographical but textual. It is not a model that can be found in nineteenth-century or earlier texts since the ideological constraints of the marriage plot were much stronger then. But it can be found in a rereading of Sylvia Townsend Warner's novel *Summer Will Show* (1936), a novel set in the mid-nineteenth-century context of the European revolutions of 1848, which rewrites 'Victorian fiction itself' (Castle 1993, 80).

In examining this 'under read' text Castle undertakes a very traditional act of feminist recuperation. She takes a number of pages to summarise the novel's plot so that the unknown novel can become 'known' to the reader. She concentrates in particular on the developing relationship between the heroine, Sophia, and her husband's mistress, Minna, a relationship in which 'the male homosocial triangle reaches its point of maximum destabilisation', to the point of collapse. The novel replaces the male homosocial triangle with a female triangle in which women's erotic desires for each other are central, thus displacing the patriarchal plot. It does this in the context of a pastiche of Victorian novel-writing: a novel that appears to conform to the conventions of Realism in fact produces the traces of a 'counterplot' in the 'authorised' version. Castle argues from Warner's novel that a definition of lesbian fiction can be found in the textual performances of writing, and need not be excavated from unreliable biographical evidence. In this reading, lesbian fiction: 'resists any simple recuperation as "realistic". Even as it gestures back at a supposedly familiar world of human experience, it almost invariably stylises and estranges it – by presenting it parodistically, euphuistically, or in some other rhetorically heightened, distorted, fragmented or phantasmagoric way' (90). These effects come precisely from the effects that accrue because lesbian fiction refers insistently to the conventions of canonical texts with the purpose of unsettling them:

> by plotting against ... the 'plot of male homosociality', the archetypal lesbian fiction decanonizes, so to speak, the canonical structures of desire itself. Insofar as it documents a world in which men are 'between women' rather than vice versa, it is an insult to the conventional geometries of fictional eros. It dismantles the real, as it were, in a search for the not-yet-real, something unpredicted and unpredictable. It is an assault on the banal ... As a consequence, it often

looks odd, fantastical, implausible, 'not there' – utopian in aspiration if not design. It is, in a word, imaginative. This is why, perhaps, like lesbian desire itself, it is still difficult for us to acknowledge – even when (Queen Victoria notwithstanding)[4] it is so palpably, so plainly, there. (90–1)

Realism is the place where male homosocial bonds are validated. Lesbian fiction has to resist the plots that render the lesbian invisible, as Realism must tend to do. In its stylisation, parody, mockery and counterplotting, Castle argues, lesbian fiction has a political voice because it unsettles the idea that Realism provides a version of the real that holds true for everyone. This is a criticism that makes lesbian women visible to a culture that does not want to see them; close textual attention is combined with political commitment – aesthetics and politics are the necessarily juxtaposed in theorising the presence of the many lesbian 'others' in the face of the critical/creative/political indifference ('hommosexuality', the logic of the same) that erases them.

Queering the patch: Marjorie Garber, Judith Butler and the slippage of identity

> When you meet a human being, the first distinction you make is 'male or female?' and you are accustomed to make the distinction with unhesitating certainty.
>
> Sigmund Freud, 'Femininity'

> One is not born, but rather, becomes a woman.
>
> Simone de Beauvoir, *The Second Sex*

> What do I mean by masquerade? In particular, what Freud calls 'femininity'. The belief, for example, that it is necessary to *become* a woman, a 'normal' one at that, whereas a man is a man from the outset. He has only to effect his being-a-man, whereas a woman has to become a normal woman, that is has to enter into the *masquerade of femininity*.
>
> Luce Irigaray, *The Sex Which is Not One*

All the theories and ideas that we have dealt with so far have been thoroughly bound up in the idea of an identity that can be known.

Even where the emphasis has been on the multiply-possible ways of being a woman – a white woman, a Black woman, a straight woman, a lesbian woman, a working woman, an upper-class woman, and many, many more – the claim is still that we know what a woman is, what women are. And we claim further that women in all their many differences have some experiences in common. In other words, femaleness shares features across historical, geographical, economic and psychic boundaries. It is a kind of common-sense position: we all know what a woman is, what a man is, and we are 'accustomed' says Freud, to be able to tell the difference 'with unhesitating certainty'. But if de Beauvoir was right, and being a woman is not 'essence' but a learned configuration of gender, precisely *how* do we know? If gender identity is socially constructed, presumably we cannot tell just by looking. Gender can be a kind of clothing, a disguise – what Irigaray calls a masquerade, a performance, in which appearance masks 'reality' and one cannot tell clearly precisely what one has seen.

Recently, then, the assumptions of common identity between women have been shaken up by the interventions of a number of critics whose work is inflected by the discourses of new lesbian and gay-male critiques that are often designated by the term 'queer theory'. For example, the literary critic and social historian Marjorie Garber's book *Vested Interests: Cross Dressing and Cultural Anxiety* (1992) explores the ways in which 'clothing constructs (and deconstructs) gender' (Garber 1992, 3). The fact that biology (male or female?) and gender (masculine or feminine?) are articulations of a binary opposition troubles Garber because such thinking enforces an 'either/or' version of the world. Binary thinking, as Cixous argues, is always hierarchised with one term privileged over the other. It is an attempt to fix things – to fix everything from political systems to the proper way to be a woman; and it tries to suggest that the fixed position is natural, eternal and immutable. For Garber, transvestism (wearing the clothes of one sex when one is, 'in fact', the 'other' sex) introduces a destabilising third term into the system of binary opposition, a term that produces a crisis in such thought: 'Three puts into question the idea of one: of identity, self-sufficiency, self-knowledge' (11). The effects of this are felt strongly in the area of gendered identity, but they go beyond that too: the third term is 'the disruptive element that intervenes [and produces] not just a category crisis of male and female, but the crisis of category itself' (17). In a remarkably detailed and interesting series of examples, including everything from the Shakespearean stage to Elvis impersonators, Garber exposes the ways in which clothes have been seen as the markers of identity. But because clothes are provisional – you take them off as well as put them on, you wear different clothes for different occasions – the identity they mark, including the gender of that identity, is also provisional. The implications of this insight are very far-reaching and disturbing for traditional formations of feminist theory that are founded on knowing what a woman or a man is and claiming common cause on the basis of such knowledge. What can feminist theory do if it can no longer be sure of the grounds on which it speaks?

Vested Interests and Garber's later book, *Vice Versa: Bisexuality and the Eroticism of Everyday Life* (1995), may be disturbing in what they imply about identity (gender identity and sexuate identity) as unstable, but they are very readable accounts of why simplistic views of who we are can be both seductive and inadequate. More disquiet has been voiced (by, for example, Terry Castle 1993 and Nicole Ward-Jouve 1998) over the works of Judith Butler, whose style is very different, and who draws out the implications of her views with much more vigour. Butler's arguments are strongly influenced by postmodernist and post-structuralist theories of identity. For her, gendered identity is far more than a matter of clothes, though clothes play their part. Her arguments begin from the wish to disrupt the binary opposition of sex and gender – the opposition that is at the heart of feminist theory, and which is often rewritten as nature and culture. The problem of this binary opposition, Butler suggests, is that it privileges nature over culture, assumes that sex is the immutable, gender the mutable; gender is therefore to be understood as a copy – more or less 'accurate' – of the 'original' sex/nature. Nature, however, is not 'natural'. It is constructed through discursive practices. And if nature is not 'natural', then sex is not 'natural' either: sex is also a discursive formation, taking place in language, not simply existing in real bodies. Bodies do not intrinsically have sexes; sexes like genders are imposed upon them in language and culture because of the perceived necessity in language and culture to taxonomise – to put everything into categories.

You will notice here that I am not quoting Butler's own words. Her arguments are very densely written, as she herself admits (Butler 1993, 99), and are consequently difficult to extract in short quotation.

Nonetheless, a brief extract exemplifies her theoretical position, and dramatises her 'difficulty':

> The insistence on coherent identity as a point of departure presumes that what a 'subject' is is already known, already fixed, and that that ready-made subject might enter the world to renegotiate its place. But if that very subject produces its coherence at the cost of its own complexity, the crossings of identifications of which it is itself composed, then that subject forecloses the kinds of contestatory connections that might democratize the field of its own operation. (115).

Butler is here reading the idea of selfhood through the lens of Lacanian psychoanalysis which suggests that the self exists only in and through language, and is therefore provisional. Her writing takes this position absolutely seriously to posit that there is no identity that can be known as a stable coherent entity. Indeed, any such identity would be dangerously limited because 'already known, already fixed'. Moreover, stability comes at the cost of complexity. An identity that can be wholly known is a very simple thing. In order to change the world, the subject needs its complexity, even if the subject him/herself cannot fully comprehend it. If one agrees to be fixed in an identity, one agrees to the conditions in which that identity was formed.

Butler's particular points of interest are in the marginalised figures of gay men and lesbian women. But her discourse is not only talking to or about these groups. What she says about identity as performative and provisional has knock-on effects for everyone, and perhaps especially for theoretical discourses that rely on identity, such as feminist criticism, Black-feminist criticism, lesbian-feminist criticism. What price any feminism that cannot tell what a woman is? What of a Black criticism that cannot describe blackness, or of a lesbian criticism that doesn't quite know what lesbians are? Nicole Ward-Jouve's impassioned defence of a more humanist version of identity against Butler's deconstructive critique dramatises how unsettling these ideas are. Ward-Jouve writes, in the wake of Butler's first book, *Gender Trouble: Feminism and the Subversion of Identity*:

> The very term 'Woman', which had been a rallying call [for women's liberation movements] like 'workers of all countries unite' in the old

Internationale, came under attack: the job to do, it now seemed, was to unmoor women from that body that had always been the pretext for their suppression. The body had to be mastered, shown to be changeable, malleable [...] Identity had to be tactical, forever reinvented, a mask to put on, and cast off. Guerilla tactics became the order of the day [...] alliances with other oppressed groups, theoretical wizardry, deconstruction, imaginary geometries, transvestism, transsexuality, endless transformations of your body, your image ... [...] You had to be nimble. Question, and question again. You had to 'position yourself' before you talked. Swiftly slot into opposition. (Ward-Jouve 1998, 7, ellipses in square brackets mine)

The highly charged rhetoric here in a sense says it all. For Ward-Jouve there is a fundamental dishonesty in parading performance, and it appears to her as a dangerous thing to try entirely to suppress binary opposition as a tool for thinking. Collapsing the hard-fought distinctions between sex and gender risks collapsing the possibility of meaning, and of meaningful action, altogether. 'Without the much denounced so-called binaries,' she writes, 'male and female, masculine and feminine – there would be nothing: no generation (the root is the same as for gender). No meaning' (10).

The debates about *Gender Trouble* (1990) and *Bodies that Matter* (1993) rumble on. The last word has not been had. But these debates do register the ways in which gender remains a usefully contested term. Feminist literary theories, of whatever kind, have not finished yet, just as feminisms in the 'real world' have yet more things to do. Butler's work has at least the profoundly useful function of making us continue to question our own assumptions, and to keep differences – between women and even within individual women – in view.

Notes

1. 'Liberal womanist' is of course a rewriting of the term 'liberal humanist', used to describe traditional, untheorised, male-authored criticism. Moers and Spacks tried to put white women into the definiton of 'human'; they forgot – to put it at its kindest – to try to include Black women too.
2. I say 'most', not 'all' because although female friendship supports Black women in a nurturing environment in this view, what is missing from the equation is the economic oppression caused by capitalist econom-

ics. Black women may help each other, but they don't quite escape the networks of oppression even in their positive relationships.

3. In particular, she is concerned with the effects of discourses of 'provisional identity', such as those articulated by Judith Butler in her two recent books, *Gender Trouble* (1990) and *Bodies the Matter* (1993). For more information, see below.

4. The reference to Queen Victoria refers to a possibly apocryphal story that the Queen was so incapable of imagining female–female desire that she refused to sanction legislation that would outlaw it. 'The Queen Victoria principle of lesbian non-existence' is a recurring figure in Castle's text, used to demonstrate the ongoing invisibility of the lesbian as a person, and of lesbian desire as a possible object choice.

Part IV

Readings

9 Reading the Boys' Own Stories: *The Strange Case of Dr Jekyll and Mr Hyde, The Picture of Dorian Gray* and *Heart of Darkness*

I inscribe this book of adventure to my son, Arthur John Rider Haggard, in the hope that in days to come he, and many other boys whom I shall never know, may in the acts and thoughts of Allan Quatermain and his companions, as herein recorded, find something to help him and them to reach to what, with Sir Henry Curtis, I hold to be the highest rank whereto we can attain – the state and dignity of English gentlemen.

H. Rider Haggard, dedication to *Allan Quatermain*

My father is Lord Bracknell. You have never heard of papa, I suppose? ... Outside the family circle, papa, I am glad to say, is entirely unknown. I think that is quite as it should be. The home seems to me the proper sphere for the man. And, certainly once a man begins to neglect his domestic duties, he becomes painfully effeminate, does he not? And I don't like that. It makes men so very attractive.

Gwendolen Fairfax to Cecily Cardew, in Oscar Wilde, *The Importance of Being Earnest*

On the face of it, it would be difficult to imagine three texts, short of overtly pornographic writing, which are less attractive to feminist theorists than Stevenson's *The Strange Case of Dr Jekyll and Mr Hyde* (1886), Wilde's *The Picture of Dorian Gray* (1890, 1891) and Conrad's *Heart of Darkness* (1900). These fictions, all produced during the last fifteen years of the nineteenth century, give little obvious purchase to feminist readings. As Stephen Heath has written, quoting Henry

James's contemporary response to Stevenson's novella, the episode in which Hyde tramples a little girl on the street 'is one of the very few female references in a story that does ... "without the aid of the ladies"' (Heath in Pykett 1996, 65). Heath goes on to note that women are absolutely peripheral in *The Strange Case*, consisting only of servant girls and women in the streets of London (women who might also be thought of women *of* the streets of London):

> the brevity of their appearance goes along with the lowness of their class which itself in turn runs into their marginalisation in the given middle-class male story-world. James was more than right: there are indeed no *ladies*, no women who could enter the story, play a part. The female is shut out, a thing of the streets which then take on their femaleness. (66)

The world of *The Strange Case* is a world of cosy interiors, but they are distinctively not the domestic sphere of respectable femininity. These are the interiors of bachelordom, of male friendships and clubbishness from which women are excluded.

Much the same can be said of Wilde's *Dorian Gray*. The novel does have significant female figures: the actress, Sibyl Vane, who is the occasion of Dorian's first act of cruelty, Lord Henry's wife, the incidental duchesses and aristocrats who populate the drawing rooms which are his *mise-en-scène*, and the street girl who, like Sibyl, calls him Prince Charming, and alerts Sibyl's brother to his real identity (Wilde 1985, 225). But in terms of the action of the story, even the most significant of these female figures, Sibyl, is less important than the moral story being told about the male protagonist's decline and fall. And again, the world is one of interiors, but they are domestic spaces inhabited by men rather than by women. Indeed, the intimacy of the bachelors' rooms leaves no significant space for female figures to occupy, registered in Lord Henry Wotton's cynicism about his own marriage:

> the one charm of marriage is that it makes a life of deception absolutely necessary for both parties. I never know where my wife is, and my wife never knows what I am doing. When we meet – we do meet occasionally, when we dine out together or go down to the Duke's – we tell each other the most absurd stories with the most serious faces. My wife is very good at it – much better, in fact, than I

am. She never gets confused over her dates, and I always do. But when she does find me out, she makes no row at all. I sometimes wish she would; but she merely laughs at me. (26)

Lord Henry's own wife is merely incidental in his life, and is also merely incidental to the novel's action.

Similarly, *Heart of Darkness* has only incidental female characters. There is Marlow's aunt, who gets him the job on the Congo steamer; there are the two enigmatic female figures in the ante-room of the shipping office, who knit in black wool, and whom Marlow sees as 'uncanny and fateful' (Conrad 1983, 37); and there are the two women associated with Kurtz, his Intended back in Europe for whom and to whom Marlow lies, and his magnificent African mistress, who terrifies Marlow. Again, however, these figures are scarcely central. Their appearances are brief and symbolic rather than sustained and active within the plot. Moreover, although Conrad's novella belongs in part to the genre of male adventure fiction, it is recounted in a safe space that approximates domesticity: on board a ship named the *Nellie*, told by a man to a group of fellow men. It discourses on horror, and brings that horror 'home', to London, to the banks of the Thames, rendering home unhomely, or in Freud's terms, 'uncanny'.[1]

Apart from their historical proximity of production and publication in the *fin de siècle*, these three texts are united by their acute focus on the agonised male figure, whom they each present in a gothic world where all the usual certainties – the certainties associated with Realist modes of presentation and common-sense views of the world – have all been somehow undermined. They are stories about masculinity, and particularly about masculinity in crisis. Why, then, would a feminist theorist wish to read them at all? And what can a feminist theorist say about them which is useful to the political and cultural projects of feminisms?

Reading the stereotypes

From what I've already said, it should be clear that an 'images of women' approach to these texts would be difficult to maintain precisely because that kind of textual critique depends on a sustained representation of female characters, whereas the images we have in these texts are isolated and ephemeral. In comparison, say, to other

contemporary late-nineteenth century fictions by men, to Thomas
Hardy's *Tess of the D'Urbervilles* (1891) or *Jude the Obscure* (1895), or
to George Gissing's *The Odd Women* (1893), all of which make the
'problem' of femininity into a central plank of their plots and themes,
there appears to be very little to say. These fictions largely eschew the
female. They are perhaps misogynist texts, signalled by the exclusion
of the female, but once one has said so much, it could mean that
feminist literary theories have very little else to say to these fictions. It
would, however, be an impoverished theory that admitted defeat so
easily. There is a feminist critique to be made about these texts on the
grounds of their representation; and there is much to say about how
the texts present women and men, and why they do so. Thus, Heath's
insight that Stevenson's *Strange Case* contains no women who
'count', no ladies, no social, economic or cultural equals to the
middle-class white men in the tale, is not just an admission of female
exclusion from the male story world. It also tells us something about
the constitution of maleness, of masculinity, in a particular culture at
a specific historical period, as that constitution is what the story
represents.

The critique of stereotypical representations has to take place
within a context. Whilst stereotypes present themselves as unchanging, as constants no matter what the history and the geography, the
class and the culture, to take them at face value, as it were, is to render
them untouchable truths; it fixes them and places them beyond the
reach of a critique that demands change as part of its political agenda.
Stereotypes, feminist theories suggest, have to be *placed* in order to be
understood. They operate inside contexts, not outside them. To read
the stereotypes in Conrad, Stevenson and Wilde requires a historicist
intervention and contextual reconstructions.

The late nineteenth century, Elaine Showalter has argued, borrow-
ing the phrase with which she titles her book from George Gissing,
was a period of 'sexual anarchy' (Showalter 1991, 3), a period in which
gender definitions were acutely threatened by a variety of social
changes. Simple demographics was one major cause of gender confusion. The returns from the 1861 British census provided evidence that
there were far larger numbers of women than men living in the British
Isles. This fact produced enormous cultural anxieties in mid- to late
Victorian Britain. As Mary Poovey (1989) and Lynda Nead (1988) have
both demonstrated, the 1860s were also the high point of the ideology
of the separate spheres for men and women which had been develop-

ing since the mid-eighteenth century: the phrase describes the belief
that men were active, economically independent, competitive, striv-
ing creatures whilst women were passive, dependent, nurturing and
weak. If such were the 'natures' of male and female, it made social
sense to organise human life to reflect the capacities of each sex. As
Tennyson put it, possibly ironically, in *The Princess* (1847):

> Man for the field and woman for the hearth:
> Man for the sword and for the needle she:
> Man with head and woman with the heart:
> Man to command and woman to obey;
> All else confusion.

The separate spheres of man and woman, then, were respectively the
worlds of competitive work and domesticity; as an ideology it defined
men as active, women as passive, men as workers outside the domestic sphere, women as confined (for their own protection and for the
comfort of men) inside it. The binary oppositions structured all social
thinking about the relationships between the sexes: without them, 'all
else confusion'.

But, if there were significantly more women than men, then it was
clear that not all women could marry and take their places in the safe
domestic sphere to act as wives and mothers.[2] Economic necessity
dictated that many women from the middle orders had to work for a
living, despite the fact that their education had not fitted them for
work, and that they risked the loss of social status as middle-class
women (as 'ladies', as Henry James might have put it) if they left the
safety of the domestic sphere. On the back of these demographic and
economic facts, therefore, there had been a wave of serious agitation
for women's rights: for better education, for the opening up of the
universities and then the professions (legal and medical in particular)
to women, and for the vote. In tandem with these explicit political
demands, there was a general feeling that (middle-class) women were
becoming more socially assertive, more independent, less passive and
domesticated. As an 'Angry Old Buffer' put it in *Punch* in 1895 (27
April):[3]

> When Adam delved and Eve span
> No one need ask which was the man.
> Bicycling, footballing, scarce human,

All wonder now, 'Which is the woman?'
But a new fear my bosom vexes;
Tomorrow there may be no sexes!
Unless as end to all the pother,
Each one in fact becomes the other.

The message of the skit is clear. Uppity women are a direct cause of effeminate men, and androgyny is to be feared, not welcomed, since it undoes the binary opposition of gender that structured all contemporary thought. The crisis of late nineteenth-century masculinity is, then, a crisis caused by a shift in gender relations in general. The disruption of the binary opposition, of the separate spheres, rebounded on men as well as on women. If femininity was not what it was supposed to be, then masculinity was troubled as well. The pervasiveness of the separate spheres ideology is signalled in both the epigraphs to this chapter. Rider Haggard, dedicating his book to his son and to his son's school-friends, appeals to the values of masculinity, and wills their continuity – English gentlemanliness is the 'highest rank' for anyone to aspire to: his adventure stories articulate the testing of those values in the romantic space of imperial territory, a space which is resolutely male and undomestic. Gwendolen Fairfax, on the other hand, in Wilde's *The Importance of Being Earnest*, upends those selfsame assumptions. Domesticity is the male sphere and male effeminacy is dangerously seductive, views which overturn the normative values of masculinity and femininity for respectable Victorians. The ideology of separate spheres can be at once appealed to and parodied: confusion indeed.

This is not the only context in which Conrad, Stevenson and Wilde can be read, but it is perhaps the most significant context for a feminist appraisal of their texts which chart in their different ways the dismantling of long-cherished versions of gender relations, and a desperate attempt to reassert the values of masculinity. Showalter defines texts such as Conrad's and Stevenson's as 'male quest romances' – romantic quests for the elusive qualities of masculinity (Showalter 1991, 81), an interesting take on the genre of romance quests, whose usual object is the passive lady love of the active male protagonist. She argues that the removal of women from the plots of these texts is also a strategy for removing them from the readership of the texts: like Haggard's novels, they are addressed to 'all the big and little boys' who read them. And the homo-erotic tale of *Dorian Gray*

exists within this frame as well since the all-male worlds of the gentleman's club (*The Strange Case*) and the ship (*Heart of Darkness*) shade
very easily from homosocial to homosexual nuance.[4]

Despite the repression of female characters, therefore, these texts
have interesting perspectives to offer to feminist thinking. New
answers to the question: what does it mean to be a woman? require a
reappraisal of what it might mean to be a man. The analysis and re-
evaluation of one half of any binary opposition has repercussions for
the other half. The three fictions deal with those effects in different
ways and reach different but related conclusions.

Case-Notes: Stevenson's *Jekyll and Hyde*

> Men still have everything to say about their sexuality, and everything
> to write. For what they have said so far, for the most part, stems from
> the opposition activity/passivity from the power relation between a
> fantasisized obligatory virility meant to invade, to colonize, and the
> consequential phantasm of woman as a 'dark continent' to penetrate
> and 'pacify' ... Conquering her, they've made haste to depart from her
> borders, to get out of sight, out of body. The way man has of getting
> out of himself ... deprives him, he knows, of his own bodily territory.
> (Cixous in Marks and de Courtivron 1981, 247, n)

What exactly is the matter with Henry Jekyll? What makes him search
out the seamy side of his own nature through the process of quasi-
scientific experiment, and through the masculine discourse and practice of science? Because *The Strange Case* is a gothic text, the answers
it proposes to these questions are not clear cut, and are not scientific.
Rather they are symptoms which have to be read back to pathological
causes: but the route of cause and effect is a winding path, not a
straight one. One of the definitions of the gothic genre is that it
disrupts the common-sense discourses of Realism where explanations are readily forthcoming and explanation dissolves mystery. In
Freud's terms, the familiar comes back in an unfamiliar guise which is
the source of fear. The mystery must remain in some sense intact in a
gothic text: the symptoms are multiply-caused and invite multiple
diagnoses. One possible feminist diagnosis of Henry Jekyll's particular
pathology goes as follows.

At the end of the text, we read Jekyll's 'full statement of the case', which is both a scientific text describing what happened (a scientific case study), and a confession which eschews the objectivist stance of science and places itself in the personal, subjective voice of the man *in extremis*. The dual nature of Jekyll's narrative is a dramatisation of the duality he describes in his own personality: he is at once a scientist and a hedonist; a man of honour and a rake; a moral man and an amoral monster. That these oppositions inhabit the same body is the root of the problem. As Jekyll himself describes it in his statement:

> I was born in the year 18— to a large fortune, endowed besides with excellent parts, inclined by nature to industry, fond of the respect of the wise and good among my fellow men, and thus, as might have been supposed, with every guarantee of an honourable and distinguished future. And indeed, the worst of my faults was a certain impatient gaiety of disposition, such as has made the happiness of many, but such as I found it hard to reconcile with my imperious desire to carry my head high, and wear a more than commonly grave countenance before the public. Hence it came about that I concealed my pleasures; and that when I reached the years of reflection, and began to look round me and take stock of my progress and position in the world, I stood already committed to a profound duplicity of life. (Stevenson 1979, 81)

Much earlier in the century a certain Jane Austen had noted, probably ironically, but also appealing to cliché, that: 'It is a truth universally acknowledged, that a single man in possession of a good fortune, must be in want of a wife' (Austen 1972, 51). On the face of it, Henry Jekyll was just such a man: he had fortune, good looks, a disposition to hard work and will to be respected by his peers. An ideal man, and an eligible bachelor indeed, especially if his worst fault was to pretend to be more serious than he actually felt like being. The pleasures of which he partook, and yet disguised, appear to have been fairly innocuous – 'many a man would have even blazoned such irregularities as I was guilty of' (Stevenson 1979, 81). Jekyll, however, preferred to pretend. And although he led a double life even before he discovered the potion that produced his alter ego, Edward Hyde, he denies that he was a hypocrite: 'both sides of me were in dead earnest' (81). And despite his evident eligibility, he never marries. Indeed, the story contains no hint of any woman who could represent an eligible spinster for such a man.

The source of his trouble is traced in his own narrative to an idiosyncrasy of his own personality. He liked to look on himself as a fine upstanding figure; he liked to have the approval of his friends: but he also 'learned to dwell with pleasure, as a beloved daydream' (82) on the idea of self-indulgence, establishing a binary opposition between the prosaic world of everyday objectivity and the daydream world, almost a narcotic world, of subjective pleasure. On the one hand, then, he played the part of the picture of English gentlemanliness with all its implications of self-denial and self-restraint;[5] on the other, he played the unrestrained man, untouched by the fetters of civilisation. His is a story of 'going native', argues David Punter: and, 'it is precisely Jekyll's "high views" which produce morbidity in his *alter ego*' (Punter 1980, 241). Knowing how he should look and behave, knowing the rules of civilisation, produces a kind of 'reverse' knowledge of what breaking the rules might mean, a capacity to imagine the transgression of social values. What Jekyll suffers, therefore, is the split between nature and culture, inherent in all human beings, yet most usually figured in the female of the human species, for she most usually is understood as being both closer to nature, and the bearer of cultural significance. He recognises that his 'proper' masculinity is merely a performance. He likes the adulation it brings when he pretends to be working at the 'furtherance of knowledge or the relief of sorrow and suffering' (81); but he also enjoys those 'other' pleasures. He thinks that he is unusual, but he also extrapolates from his own experience to make a universal claim: 'man is not truly one, but truly two', and may indeed be multiple rather than merely double (Stevenson 1979, 82). His discovery is disturbing to his fellow professional men, the doctor (Lanyon) and the lawyer (Utterson) both because it threatens their own sense of upstanding masculinity, and because it contaminates masculinity with the threat of the feminine other within the supposedly indivisible male self – the word 'individual', valued in Victorian discourses, literally means that which is undivided.

When the lawyer Utterson breaks into Jekyll's private rooms and finds the body of Hyde, he is shocked by a number of other circumstances in the closet. One is a pious work that has been annotated, apparently by Jekyll, with dreadful blasphemies. But more significant is the mirror he finds in the rooms:

> the searchers came to the cheval-glass, into whose depth they looked
> with an involuntary horror. But it was so turned as to show them

> nothing but the rosy glow playing on the roof, the fire sparkling in a
> hundred repetitions along the glazed front of the presses, and their
> own pale and fearful countenances stooping to look in.
>   'This glass has seen some strange things, sir,' whispered Poole.
>   'And surely none stranger than itself,' echoed the lawyer, in the
> same tone. 'For what did Jekyll' – he caught himself up at the word
> with a start, and then conquering the weakness: 'what could Jekyll
> want with it?' he said. (71)

Mirrors have many meanings. They represent the scientific view of
the world, the objective image or representation on which science
might pride itself. In this guise, they are the metaphor of Realism.
What is seen in the mirror is what is 'really' there. And yet: mirrors
might also act as a metonym of femininity, frames in which both
culture and nature are inscribed. What one sees in a mirror is what is
'really' there, but it is also the space in which one sees the process of
the creation of oneself, the mask or persona of social performance.
Traditionally, it is women who gaze obsessively at their own images.
When a man does so, he partakes of the commodification and objectification of femininity. When Narcissus fell in love with his own image,
it destroyed him; when Jekyll obsessively observes his external
appearance, he is also destroyed. Utterson and Jekyll's butler, Poole,
are themselves unmanned by their reflections. They look into the
mirror with 'involuntary horror', and see themselves as pale ghosts of
themselves in the uncanny atmosphere of Jekyll's room. Jekyll's
effeminate self-consciousness is potentially catching, since all men
have the seeds of his disease.
    The consciousness that his gentlemanly identity is a performance
rather than an inherent essence produces Jekyll's horror which then
extends to his circle of friends. For if he merely performs manliness
rather than inhabiting its essence, then so do they. The absence of
women from the text signals that one need seek no further than one's
own (male) self for the disturbing 'other', the difference within the
same. Indeed the absence of women who 'count' within the confines
of the story world emphasises an uncomfortable duality in all the men
with whom Jekyll associates. And without that 'other' against which to
define a stable masculine identity, that identity is compromised,
because it cannot know its own borders, the defining limitations
which guarantee its existence. In this case, a world without women is
also a world in which 'real' men do not exist.

As pretty as a picture? Wilde's *Dorian Gray*

'My dear boy, no woman is a genius. Women are a decorative sex. They never have anything to say, but they say it charmingly. Women represent the triumph of matter over mind, just as men represent the triumph of mind over morals.'

Lord Henry Wotton to Dorian Gray

When Wilde's *Picture of Dorian Gray* appeared in 1890, in *Lippincott's Magazine*, it received some very hostile reviews. The anonymous reviewer in the *Scot's Observer* slated the novel in the following terms:

> Why go grubbing in muck heaps? ... Mr. Oscar Wilde has again been writing stuff that were better unwritten; and while *The Picture of Dorian Gray* ... is ingenious, interesting, full of cleverness, and plainly the work of a man of letters, it is false art – for its interest is medico-legal; it is false to human nature – for its hero is a devil; it is false to morality – for it is not made sufficiently clear that the writer does not prefer a course of unnatural iniquity to a life of cleanliness, health and sanity. The story – which deals with matters only fitted for the Criminal Investigation Department or a hearing *in camera* – is discreditable alike to author and editor. Mr. Wilde has brains, and art, and style; but if he can write for none but outlawed noblemen and perverted telegraph boys, the sooner he takes to tailoring (or some other decent trade) the better for his own reputation and the public morals. (Beckson 1970, 75)

What the reviewer was identifying in the novel, made evident in his reference to 'outlawed noblemen and perverted telegraph boys' is a version of masculinity which radically unsettled all the sacred Victorian beliefs about what it meant to be a man. The reference is to the Cleveland Street Scandal of 1889, when a number of prominent figures (including Queen Victoria's second son, Prince Albert Victor) were implicated in illegal homosexual practices following a police raid on a male brothel in Cleveland Street. The telegraph boys were laid on, as it were, as part of the entertainment. In its aftermath, several aristocratic men had fled to the Continent to avoid prosecution and scandal. The reviewer was picking up on hints in Basil's moralising speech to Dorian that the 'nature' of his crimes was that of 'unnatural vice' – of homosexuality.[6] If this is indeed the issue (but see note 4), no wonder women are so spectacularly excluded from the text.

The source of *Dorian Gray*'s ability to unsettle its readers derives perhaps from its rewriting of the categories of masculine and feminine, a rewriting that takes place in the figure of Dorian himself, but which also implicates his upper-class circle of friends. Basil Hallward, the artist, Henry Wotton, the dandy, and Dorian himself are all men who refuse the masculinity inscribed by writers like H. Rider Haggard, G. A. Henty, Robert Louis Stevenson (in his guise as a writer of adventure stories), Rudyard Kipling or Andrew Lang.[7] In *Dorian Gray*, the men belong to the leisure class. They have no work outside the home. Even Basil, who works as an artist, has his studio 'at home'. There is no necessity for them to work; and they do not choose to work as an assertion of their manhood. Instead, they do nothing; conversation and parties, drink and good food, music and theatre are their occupations: as Lady Brandon says when she introduces Dorian to Basil: 'Charming boy ... Quite forget what he does – afraid he – doesn't do anything – oh yes, plays the piano – or is it the violin, dear Mr Gray' (Wilde 1985, 30). Whether it is piano or violin, neither would count as a proper occupation for a man; indeed, both might be thought of as the feminine accomplishments of upper-class women. As such, then, the three men are scandalous to a hegemonic bourgeois version of masculinity which is supposed to be active, hard-working, independent. Indeed, in the novel as a whole, precisely those men who conform to the bourgeois standard are those who are ridiculed by Lord Henry's languid cynicism. To a greater or lesser extent, Basil, Henry and Dorian are feminised men. They are passive, idle and often bored. Basil, is marginally uncomfortable with all this, since he has retained his conscience; but Henry enjoys his position and he teaches Dorian to enjoy it too.

The single most significant thing about Dorian is his appearance. He is a beautiful young man and his face is both his fortune and his downfall. It endows him with an effeminacy that makes him an object to others, and which thus renders his own subjectivity and self-consciousness painful. We first meet him in the object of the portrait of which he is also the subject. He has been painted as the fulfilment of Basil's artistic dreams, and the portrait is so successful that all three men begin to confuse the object with the subject – the picture with the man. As Dorian tells Basil, 'I am in love with it ... It is part of myself', to which Basil replies: 'Well, as soon as you are dry, you shall be varnished, and framed, and sent home. Then you can do what you like with yourself' (51). The effect of the picture – or rather, of the series of pictures that Basil has painted of him – is that Dorian is commodified, in much the same way as a woman of his class and beauty might also have been commodified in the art of the period. The first appearance of the picture emphasises its status as an object with monetary as well as aesthetic value. When Lord Henry first sees it, he advises Basil to send it to the Grosvenor Gallery which specialised in avant-garde art, as opposed to the Royal Academy, the exhibition that was the contemporary index of mass taste (24). The painting is thus registered as a commodity with a specialised market, which would have value only for the *cognoscenti* (amongst whom Lord Henry, of course, includes himself). The buyers are male, and the objects they buy or exchange amongst themselves, most usually pictures of women, function in the feminine mode. When Dorian is confused with his painted image, this is also a sign of the confusion of normative gender roles.

The other pictures that Basil has painted of Dorian idealise his image, displacing it in the safe space of mythology. Basil has represented Dorian as Paris, as Adonis, as Adrian and as Narcissus:[8] 'And it had all been what art should be, unconscious, ideal and remote' (144–5). In idealising the image, Basil had displaced the desire that his representations articulated. The danger of the image arises when it is placed in contemporary clothes and in a contemporary setting. Without the clothing of 'long ago and far away', the explicitness of the male beauty in the painting becomes 'idolatry' (145) – a profane and perverse worship of the male image by the male viewer. And the profanity of Basil's worship of Dorian's image is replicated in Lord Henry's, when we discover from his wife that he has seventeen or eighteen photographs of him in his rooms (69–70). In this concentration on the image, image is placed way above substance in a reversal of contemporary values, in which depth was supposed to matter more than surface, sincerity more than style.[9]

Moreover, it is not only in the fact of Dorian's multiplying image that he is feminised. It is also in the substance of the image, in the ways in which the other two men, and the narrative as a whole, see him. The effect that Basil seeks in his painting is that of a feminine arousal. What he wants to capture is: 'the half-parted lips, and the bright look in the eyes' (43), precisely the image of the sexually receptive female in the commodity representations of both cosmetic advertising and pornography, in which parted lips and shining eyes are the essence of feminine appeal.[10] At the beginning of the novel, furthermore, Dorian acts and is treated like a virginal young girl. For example, when he first sees Henry, he blushes; and Henry warns Dorian not to sit out in the sun for too long: 'You must not allow yourself to become sunburnt. It would be unbecoming', he says (45). The painting itself, like the mirror in *The Strange Case*, is a sign of Dorian's self-consciousness of his own beauty, and the temporality of his existence. Basil and Henry are not alone as idolators in the text. Dorian learns to worship his own image, to be conscious of the effects he has on people through the combination of seeing the picture and of listening to Henry's tempting words. His fascination with his face, his concentration on external appearance, replicates the concerns of upper-class femininity.

In these circumstances, it is no wonder that the woman he falls in love with is an actress, a woman whose commodity status is obvious for all to see, and whose implication in appearances and surfaces is the hallmark of her trade. Indeed, Sibyl is so much a commodity that the old Jew who owns the East End theatre where she performs has effectively bought her for fifty pounds. The word 'theatre', like the word 'theory' derives from the Greek for seeing. What Dorian sees in Sibyl Vane is a multiplication of performed images taken from the 'long ago and far away' world of Shakespeare, and he falls in love with the proliferation of images that she represents, as well as with her ability to transcend the sordid reality of the surroundings in which her performances take place:

> 'One night she is Rosalind, and the next evening she is Imogen. I have seen her die in the gloom of an Italian tomb. I have watched her wandering through the forest of Arden, disguised as a pretty boy in hose and doublet and dainty cap. She has been mad, and come into the presence of a guilty king, and given him rue to wear, and bitter herbs to taste of. She has been innocent, and the black hands of jealousy have crushed her reed-like throat. I have seen her in every age and in every costume. Ordinary women never appeal to one's imagination. They are limited to their century. No glamour ever transfigures them. One knows their minds as easily as one knows their bonnets ... They have their stereotyped smile and their fashionable manner. They are quite obvious. But an actress! How different an actress is!' (76)

Dorian's description here dramatises his infatuation with Sibyl as a series of images which require nothing from him but seeing and admiration. His paratactic rapture, which makes no logical connection between the images, articulates a fascination that words are scarcely adequate to represent. His words disguise the cheap theatre which is 'like a third-rate wedding cake' (74), maintaining the illusion of Sibyl's transcendence. She acts in the dramas, and he observes her in a mirror image of Henry and Basil's appropriation of his figure and face in their various representations of it. But although his relationship with Sibyl might potentially reinscribe him in the usual position of the powerful gazing male subject who gazes at the passive female subject, in fact, their relationship is all about image – his as well as hers. When Sibyl sees Dorian, she sees him as a theatrical figure – as Prince Charming, the rescuing hero of stage fairy-tale, not as he is. 'She regarded me merely as a person in a play,' Dorian tells Henry. 'She knows nothing of life' (79). Just as Basil and Henry interpret Dorian's face, so too does Sibyl; and the fact that Dorian and Sibyl's fantasmatic interpretations of each other are mutual does not make them any the less fatal.

Sibyl and Dorian are both works of art. Sibyl, as Rosalind, dressed as a boy, has the 'delicate grace' of a 'Tanagara figurine' (103); Dorian dreams of placing her on 'a pedestal of gold' and seeing 'the world worship the woman who is mine' (105). But the works of art from which they derive their form are tragedies. Whilst Dorian admires Sibyl in Shakespeare's comedies, he is more fascinated by the roles in which she dies, when she plays Ophelia, Desdemona and, most importantly, Juliet. Juliet is the first role in which he sees her, and it is the last role she plays before her death; indeed, one might even say that she plays Juliet to the death, since, like the Shakespearean heroine, she poisons herself once Dorian has announced to her that his love for her is dead. Dorian, schooled by Henry, insists on seeing her death as a passage 'into the sphere of art' (139), as a 'strange lurid fragment from some Jacobean tragedy' (133), which fixes her meaning in a remote aesthetic sphere. This attitude enables him to discern beauty in her death without having to examine its morality. Dorian's tragedy is that his own work of art, the painting that he hides in the attic, the space given over to mistakes and madness, is not similarly fixed. With his moral degradation, the image ceases to be ideal. It is an object over which he can exercise no masculine control, except to keep it hidden in his closet, as Henry Jekyll hides his mirror.

The text intends no moral message, no feminist content. But in following up the hint of 'sexual anarchy' implied by the effeminacy of the three male characters who are the centre of the plot, the reader is permitted to see more in Dorian's image than Wilde meant to put there. Wilde himself licenses us to excavate his texts for our own meanings: in the Preface he writes, 'It is the spectator, and not life, that art really mirrors' (22). And at *this* time, *this* spectator sees unease with contemporary (1890s) sexual relations. The novel, that is, charts how men as well as women were trapped by gendered and classed codes of sexuality and behaviour. If it is fatal for Dorian to be treated as if he were a woman, as if he were both subject and object in culture, then it shouldn't surprise us that it is fatal for Sibyl too. The only difference is that Dorian – a powerful, rich, upper-class man – in terms of contemporary codes of behaviour, has more power and ought to exercise it for moral good. His story, however, shows that making the human subject – whether male or female – into an object, exposes him/her to a dangerous split. For Dorian and for Sibyl, who inhabit the slash line between the binary opposition of subject/object, this split is entirely destructive. The feminist reader, then, can extrapolate from this particular example to a general point: a femininity which means objectification is dangerous.

Civilisation and its discontents: *Heart of Darkness*

In its technique and plot, Conrad's *Heart of Darkness* dramatises the spirit of the masculine romance – it is a novel told by and to men, and it is a narrative about the limitations of 'the highest rank whereto we can attain – the state and dignity of English gentlemen.' The setting establishes an internal audience which represents the flower of English middle-class manhood. Marlow, the veteran sailor of imperial voyages tells his tale to a Director of Companies, a Lawyer ('the best of old fellows' [Conrad 1983, 28–9]), and an Accountant, as well as to the unnamed narrator of the frame story. It is a tale about men, for men, told to men by a man whose own status as a proper man is not in question. It radically excludes women from its setting in the all-male space of the ship on the Thames, a space which is continuous with the Clubland of Stevenson's novella and the quasi-bachelor world of Wilde's *Dorian Gray*. But instead of shoring up the meaning of masculinity as its apparent genre of masculine romance would tend to do, *Heart of Darkness* questions it on its own grounds, in a critique of manliness that is perhaps even more radical than Wilde's homo-erotic fantasy. Henry Jekyll is a man apart; similarly, Dorian, Henry and Basil live on the margins of hegemonic manliness. Marlow and his audience, however, are the very source and exemplars of defini-tions of proper masculinity. Marlow's narrative is by far the greatest threat to such definitions, since it is a narrative which has bought into the dream of the English gentleman and yet which nonetheless exposes the dream as a nightmare of horror.

What Marlow articulates is the fear that the project of active, adven-turing masculinity has no basis in reality. The world of the empire which Dorian and Jekyll's domestic lives eschew is the world in which Marlow has come to self-consciousness – and it is a very different self-consciousness from that which haunts the other men. He has discov-ered, from grim experience as an explorer and professional sailor, that:

> The conquest of the earth, which mostly means the taking it away
> from those who have a different complexion, or slightly flatter noses
> than ourselves, is not a pretty thing when you look into it too much.
> What redeems it is the idea only. An idea at the back of it; not a senti-
> mental pretence, but an idea; and an unselfish belief in the idea –
> something you can set up, and bow down before, and offer a sacrifice
> to ... (31–2, ellipsis in original)

Precisely what the 'idea' is, however, Marlow is unable to say, signalled by his failure to define it, and his trailing off into a silence marked textually by an ellipsis. Indeed, the idea looks very much like a pagan god, worshipped, as Dorian's image is worshipped, perhaps, out of a blind faith without reason. The nature of the 'idea' has to be reconstructed out of Marlow's disconnected story. When it is recon-structed, it is not a pretty thing.

Presumably, the basis of the idea is that of civilisation. The rhetoric of empire was a rhetoric which spoke of civilising the savage, of bring-ing the benefits of progress to the poor benighted native. It was based on the assumption that so-called civilisation was actually a good thing, and that the indigenous peoples of colonised countries had nothing equivalent to the profound values of Western European culture. The rhetoric disguised 'the robbery with violence, [the] aggra-vated murder on a grand scale' (31) which was the method used to achieve the economic goals which were the 'real' idea behind imperialism. What Marlow discovers is the absolute disjunction between cash and ideals, between the facts on the ground and the idealistic justification of them. It forces him to call into question not only what actually happened in late nineteenth-century Africa, but also the basis of the society in Western Europe which licensed such excess. In a world supposedly structured by binary oppositions – primitive/civilised; Africa/Europe; nature/technology; darkness/enlightenment; black/white; female/male; economic necessity/ideals; ignorance/knowledge – Marlow is forced to confront the fact that the binaries structure only thinking, not the reality thought is supposed to represent. There is a leakage across the slash lines that supposedly divide the oppositions which confuses and destabilises the neat taxonomies by which Western philosophy has structured the world and its meanings.

The metaphor for this is the metaphor of the river which flows into the sea – just as all rivers flow into the sea. Geography – the maps over which the young boy Marlow once was used to pore with such excitement – represents, as an order of knowledge, an ordering of knowledge. A map is a document which organises the natural world into boundaries, naming places as a mode of controlling them. Africa is no longer a blank space, says Marlow, but has 'got filled ... with rivers and lakes and names' (33). But geography on the ground, as it were, is a very different thing. It is far more confusing, less ordered than the maps would have us believe. Borders on the ground are not clear. Water borders are even less discernible, a fact signalled by the novel's setting, with Marlow speaking in a ship at anchor in the Thames, a river that connects geographically and economically with all the other waterways of the world. As Marlow says of the Thames, 'this also ... has been one of the dark places of the earth' (29), just as Africa was described by contemporary commentators as the Dark Continent. The novel's last sentence, with its connection of the dark Thames to the dark Congo River shows us what is at stake in the novel: 'The offing was barred by a black bank of clouds, and the tranquil waterway leading to the uttermost ends of the earth flowed sombre under an overcast sky – seemed to lead into the heart of an immense darkness' (121). If the Thames flows into the Congo, and vice versa, what principle of structure guarantees a Western, European, civilised, masculine identity against contamination or invasion by the Oriental or African, primitive and savage identities that are 'out there – somewhere'.[11]

It is not, however, merely the confrontation with an alternative culture which produces Marlow's disquiet. In this economy of opposition and otherness, there is one site of otherness within the same, which also destabilises the cosy space of self and other. That site is the space of femininity, of women in culture. The paradox of the novel is that women are contradictions; they inhabit both sides of any binary opposition, and they thereby dramatise the instability of the order which depends on those binaries. At the outset of the novel, we are introduced briefly to Marlow's aunt, who he sets to service in getting him a job on a boat. Her influence in this matter is indirect: she gets the desired result through her acquaintance amongst the wives of powerful men. Marlow is rather disturbed to discover that he has been 'represented to the wife of the high dignitary, and goodness knows to how many more people besides, as an exceptional and gifted creature ... Something like an emissary of light, something like a lower sort of apostle' (38–9). But the small facts of feminine influence, and of female (mis)representation, at least signal the economic importance of women even when they are apparently most excluded from the realms of the cash nexus.

Despite her influence, though, the unnamed aunt has no sense of the reality of the company's work, and especially the fact that it is run for profit and with tremendous brutality. She has bought into the rhetoric of empire, but the words are divorced from the reality that Marlow suspects, and then comes to know in his journey to the centre of Africa. In his musing about his aunt, he comments to his listeners:

> It's queer how out of touch with truth women are. They live in a world of their own, and there had never been anything like it, and never can be. It is too beautiful altogether, and if they were to set it up it would go to pieces before the first sunset. Some confounded fact we men have been living contentedly with since the day of creation would start up and knock the whole thing over. (39)

Later, speaking of Kurtz's Intended in an amplification of this point, Marlow says: 'They – the women I mean – are out of it – should be out of it. We must help them to stay in that beautiful world of their own lest ours gets worse' (84). Women,[12] that is, live with the ideal, not the real. And the edifice of their ideal is very fragile indeed – signalled by the fragility of the Intended, a china doll of a woman who would be shattered by the truth. But the fact is that men are equally out of touch with the real and with the truth. It is only an 'idea', another kind of ideal, that has redeemed the 'conquest of the earth' from mere brute savagery. As Marlow learns, the idea is not enough to save individual imperial workers from the true implications of their work: hence Kurtz is moved to the savage sentiment, 'Exterminate all the brutes', scrawled on his writings about enlightenment and civilisation and to the savage decor of severed human heads with which he defaces his African dwelling and through which he inscribes his own degeneration. Women, in their safe domesticity, hold true to the idea; men, faced with reality, discover that the idea they worship is a graven image, a false god.

The narrative of Marlow's meeting with Kurtz's Intended shows the extent to which the ideal is rotten to the core. Marlow is a conspicuously manly, and perhaps even gentle-manly figure. He subscribes to the hegemonic ideal of masculinity – the ideal of playing the game, of giving one's word, of speaking the truth, of being chivalrous. He believes in 'truth' as a positive moral value, and speaks of his disgust at lies: 'You know I hate, detest, and can't bear a lie, not because I am straighter than the rest of us, but simply because it appals me. There is a taint of death, a flavour of mortality in lies ... It makes me miserable and sick, like biting something rotten would do' (57). Yet, for all that, he lies to the Intended, rewriting Kurtz's last words as her name, not 'the horror, the horror'. He cannot tell what Kurtz had really said for fear that it would actually destroy civilisation – the fragile facade behind which china-doll, middle-class women live with their ideals ridiculously intact. Marlow's lie is born of chivalry. But it demonstrates the internal contradictions in his version of proper masculinity: lies are bad, taste of mortality; but lies are necessary to protect enfeebled femininity. One of the sources of the darkness, then, is that civilisation is based on lies, not the ideals that are claimed for it; civilisation is therefore tainted by mortality and immorality.

If the Intended is the ideal – the attenuated womanhood that civilisation licenses – then Kurtz's African mistress is ... what, precisely? In one sense, she is, of course, the absolute Other: the racial, gendered, geographic and savage Other to Marlow's white, male, European civilised self, the self that represents the norm to himself and the novel's internal audience. As Marlow's descriptions of her imply, her otherness makes him fear her. He describes her as 'the wild and gorgeous apparition of a woman', a phrase which speaks both of her attractiveness and her otherness, as an almost ghostly spectacle:

> She walked with measured steps, draped in striped and fringed cloths, treading the earth proudly, with a slight jingle and flash of barbarous ornaments. She carried her head high: her hair was done in the shape of a helmet; she had brass leggings to the knees, brass wire gauntlets to the elbow, a crimson spot on her tawny cheek, innumerable necklaces of glass beads on her neck; bizarre things, charms, gifts of witch-men, that hung about her, glittered and trembled at every step. She must have had the value of several elephant tusks upon her. She was savage and superb, wild-eyed and magnificent; there was something ominous and stately in her deliberate progress. And in the hush that had fallen suddenly upon the whole sorrowful land, the immense wilderness, the colossal body of the fecund and mysterious life seemed to look at her, pensive, as thought it had been looking at the image of its own tenebrous and passionate soul. (100–1)

At the very end of her approach, she makes a startling gesture, raising her arms above her head, 'as though in an uncontrollable desire to touch the sky' (101). She never speaks, but her gesture is somehow eloquent and frightening. It has meaning, but the Western observers are not equipped to interpret it.

Everything about her is radically other to what Marlow expects of femininity. The Mistress has an air of dignity and command – there's no feminine cringing, no lowering of the eyes in the gestures expected of Western womanly modesty. Her adornments emphasise power – hair like a helmet, jewellery like armour, ostentatious wealth. For the Western observers the whole picture is threatening, to the extent that Marlow reports the response of the Russian sailor who '"would have tried to shoot her"' had she come any closer. Had he done so, his response would have been an 'un-manning' since proper men, within their codes of masculinity, never offer violence to women. The facade of civilisation is undermined by her presence and her silent – but somehow articulate – gesture.

The native woman never speaks except in this single gesture. Kurtz's Intended, however, speaks all the time. The *mise-en-scène* of Marlow's meeting with the Intended could not be more different from the African landscape of his encounter with the Mistress. Where the latter takes her setting from wild nature, the former is staged in a house that articulates all the values of civilisation. Marlow waits for the Intended in a 'lofty drawing-room with three long windows from floor to ceiling that were like three luminous and be-draped columns. The bent gilt legs and back of the furniture shone in indistinct curves. The tall marble fireplace had a cold and monumental whiteness. A grand piano stood massively in a corner; with dark gleams on the flat surfaces like a sombre and polished sarcophagus' (117). This staging speaks the language of civilisation and of the domestic space of femininity within that civilisation – windows like Greek columns, the tekhne of complex furniture, the monumental whiteness of marble, the piano which signals culture. But as Marlow has already observed of the Belgian city, it is like a whited sepulchre (35); the civilised Western world is a tomb with the mere veneer of civilisation which disguises but does not dispel the corruption underneath. Thus the piano, whilst it is a marker of culture, is also a tomb – it has the 'flavour of mortality' about it, as Marlow says that lies always do. The Intended, then, lives in a lie, and is presented with a lie 'to live with' (121). The failure of civilised language to represent reality is mirrored in this setting, as well as in the words that Marlow and the Intended exchange. Her language has no substance; that is what the context of Marlow's narrative as a whole demonstrates: as her sorrow bursts out, she says to Marlow:

> 'Forgive me. I – I – have mourned so long in silence – in silence ... You were with him – to the last? I think of his loneliness. Nobody to understand him as I would have understood. Perhaps no one to hear ...' (120–1, ellipses in original)

She speaks hesitantly, with many gaps and ellipses, many unfinished thoughts. This is supposed to be the language of articulate western civilisation. It is, in fact, a language that disguises rather than expresses, much as the Kristevan semiotic is supposed to do (see above, Chapter 5). There is meaning in the gaps, but it is not easy to read.

There is a sense, then, in which the encounter with proper femininity is more radically disturbing to Marlow's sense of civilised masculinity than the meeting with the so-called primitive woman of Africa. Both the Intended and the Mistress demonstrate the contamination of categorical certainties. But the Intended brings that contamination home – literally as well as figuratively. The Symbolic order of the West is shown as a mere fiction, dependent on the semiotic murmurings of one bereaved woman and on 'the holy terror of scandal and gallows and lunatic asylums' (85). The novel shows that it is only fear and lies that make order; what price the great idea of civilisation then?

About these readings

There are lots of other things that could be said about these texts; any approach represents a limitation on the text as well as an elucidation of it. The value of such readings, of taking 'the boys' own stories' and reading them against the grain, is that they are texts brimming with contradictions. So that whilst they may appear to present and perpetuate very attenuated and partial versions of women (and, indeed, of men), a certain kind of reading allows us to interrogate the fissures, the logical gaps, the holes, the inconsistencies, in the structures which are based on women's marginalisation in male-dominated cultures. It is certainly my view that feminist literary theories *cannot* ignore texts such as these. Whilst we may prefer the gynocritical route, any theory of literature has to be prepared to approach any mode of writing. These readings are about looking for the holes. A text (a word that derives from the Latin *texere*, meaning to weave) has holes as well as threads in its structure. Without them, it is nothing. Traditional modes of reading often insist on reading the threads to the exclusion of all else. Feminist readers just adopt different places to stand in relation to texts, and different points of focus within them.

Notes

1. Freud's essay, 'The Uncanny' establishes that unsettling effects are caused when something that is familiar or known becomes momentarily unknowable; he argues that it is especially when the homely space of home becomes unknowable that the uncanny is most powerful. This is in part a linguistic argument, derived from the etymology of the German word '*unheimlich*' which literally means unhomely, and is usually translated as 'uncanny'. See Sigmund Freud, 'The "Uncanny"' [1919], in *The Penguin Freud Library*, Volume 14, *Art and Literature* (Harmondsworth: Penguin, 1990), pp. 335–76.
2. Of course, these ideals of femininity and masculinity were heavily influenced by social class. Working-class women were almost always also

workers outside the domestic sphere as well as within it, and had been from time immemorial. The Woman Question ('What shall we do with our old maids?' as Frances Power Cobbe put it in 1861) was felt very acutely because it brought middle-class women into the equation of paid work. The articulate middle classes who wrote in and read the newspapers of the mid and late century were writing about their own sisters and daughters, and feared for their futures in a way that they had never bothered with when the women concerned came from the lower orders.

3. As Sally Ledger has noted, this 'poem' appeared in *Punch* just as Wilde's second trial for gross indecency – the legal term for homosexual offences – was beginning at the Old Bailey. There was a tendency to read masculine women as a cause of effeminacy in men (and vice versa), and *Punch* was particularly vitriolic in its attacks on New Women (who demanded various forms of equality with men) and what it saw as effeminate and decadent men. See Sally Ledger, 'The New Woman and the Crisis of Victorianism' in Sally Ledger and Scott McCracken (eds) *Cultural Politics at the Fin de Siècle*, Cambridge: Cambridge University Press, 1995, 25–6. For a more sustained discussion of the New Woman, see Sally Ledger, *The New Woman: Fiction and Feminism at the Fin de Siècle*, Manchester: Manchester University Press, 1997.

4. Indeed, Showalter argues that Stevenson's *Strange Case* can be 'most persuasively read as a fable of *fin-de-siècle* homosexual panic, the discovery and resistance of the homosexual self' (Showalter *Sexual Anarchy*, London: Bloomsbury, 1991, 107). The term homosocial was coined by Eve Sedgwick in her book *Between Men: English Literature and Male Homosocial Desire* (New York: Columbia University Press, 1985). She argues that even heterosexual relationships in literature are signs of attraction between men, and that the guy who wins the gal most usually does so in order to become closer to the gal's male relations or protectors. Homosociality (male–male friendship) exists on a continuum with homosexuality (male–male sexual relationships). The heterosexuality of marriage often exists as a cloak for homosocial/sexual desire.

5. For further information on the 'cult' of the English gentleman, see Mark Girouard, *The Return to Camelot: Chivalry and the English Gentleman* (New Haven and London: Yale University Press, 1981); James Eli Adams, *Dandies and Desert Saints: Styles of Victorian Manhood* (Ithaca and London: Cornell University Press, 1995); Richard Dellamora, *Masculine Desire: The Sexual Politics of Victorian Aestheticism* (Chapel Hill and London: University of North Carolina Press, 1990).

6. Dorian's 'crimes' are actually wider than the label 'homosexuality' implies. He has also corrupted women, including Lord Henry's own sister, Gwendolen, who is now beyond the social pale to the extent that no respectable woman would receive her, and even her children are no longer allowed to live with her (Wilde 1985, 185). Basil also accuses him of financial irregularities, and of sensual debauchery in brothels and opium dens. To reduce his 'crimes' to homosexuality is to reduce the impact of his corruption. Alan Sinfield's *The Wilde Century* argues this case very fully, insisting that pinning Dorian down as a homosexual is a misreading of a text that carefully evades such easy identification of Dorian's 'vice'. For Sinfield, Dorian's effeminacy is not a simple equivalent for his sexuality. Our identification of the effeminate male with the decadent homosexual is a 'reading back', a retrospective position which arises from our knowledge of Wilde's eventual fate, when he was prosecuted and imprisoned for homosexual offences in 1895. See Sinfield, *The Wilde Century*, London and New York: Casell, 1994, 98–105.

7. These were all late nineteenth-century writers of adventure stories that were specifically addressed to male audiences. Elaine Showalter identifies their chosen genre as 'masculine romance'. See Showalter, *Sexual Anarchy* (London: Bloomsbury, 1991) for more information.

8. All these figures, Paris, Adonis, Adrian and Narcissus, are tropes of same-sex (male-male) desire, which perhaps belies Sinfield's insistence that the reader cannot identify a specifically homo-erotic theme in the novel.

9. For a development of this argument about masculinity and values, see Jonathan Dollimore's *Sexual Dissidence: Augustine to Wilde, Freud to Foucault* (Oxford: The Clarendon Press, 1991, 3–18).

10. For a graphic demonstration of this, see Griselda Pollock's photo-essay, 'Signs of Femininity' in *Vision and Difference: Femininity, Feminism and the Histories of Art* (London: Routledge, 1988), 115–19.

11. The reference is to the opening titles of the popular television series *The X Files*. My point is simply that Western cultures still seek to shore up their own identities by reference to a dangerous and insidious 'Other'. It's just that today, we call our 'others' aliens, technologies, or conspiracy theories. The point is that by making them look 'bad', we guarantee our own sense of ourselves as 'good'.

12. Again, we are speaking of middle- and upper-class white women here: the women who 'count' in the narratives of middle- and upper-class white men.

10 Reading the Writing on the Wall: Charlotte Perkins Gilman's 'The Yellow Wall-paper'

> A few years ago, Mr. Howells asked leave to include this story in a collection he was arranging ... I was more than willing, but assured him that it was no more 'literature' than my other stuff, being definitely written 'with a purpose.' In my judgement it is a pretty poor thing to write, to talk without a purpose.
>
> Charlotte Perkins Gilman, *The Living of Charlotte Perkins Gilman*

Much – perhaps too much – has been written about Charlotte Perkins Gilman's 1892 story, 'The Yellow Wall-paper'. Since it resurfaced as a feminist text in the feminist context of a single volume edition published by the Feminist Press of New York in 1973, it has become a paradigmatic text of feminist criticism and for feminist theory. There are many reasons for its importance. Its republication in 1973 exemplified the feminist scholarship, the recuperation and rereading of a female literary tradition, that Elaine Showalter had described in her 1979 essay, 'Towards a Feminist Poetics', when she suggested that 'the manuscript and archival sources' for a gynocritical tradition were 'both abundant and untouched' (in Showalter 1986, 132), and that it was the task of feminist criticism to uncover them. It has attracted feminist critics because it draws on the autobiographical experiences of the author, because those experiences speak to our stereotyped ideas of Victorian femininity and because it has an easily recovered historicist basis. It has therefore been a 'useful' text for historical and contextual literary studies of the material conditions of women's lives. It enabled critics to establish literary-historical methodologies which went against the grain of practical criticism's insistence on the text itself, and made contexts (a woman's experience, a woman writer's experience, the discourses of medicine and proper femininity) a legitimate part of the reading experience in the academy. Moreover, it is a very short, short story, its brevity being one of its virtues for the purposes of student readings where length is a notorious inhibitor of commentary.

The earliest readers of the story, however, had not read it this way at all. As Gilman herself narrates in her autobiography, *The Living of Charlotte Perkins Gilman* (1935), she at first struggled to find a publisher for it, despite the recommendations of William Dean Howells (1837–1920, American journalist, critic, editor and novelist). The first editor to whom she sent it rejected it with the comment that it had disturbed him so much that he 'could not forgive myself if I made others as miserable as I have made myself' by publishing it (Gilman 1990, 119). And when it was published, a letter appeared in a rival magazine that deplored it as 'Perilous Stuff', written in a 'somewhat sensational style', holding the reader in 'morbid fascination'. The letter-writer wondered if such texts were really fit to be printed (121). As Annette Kolodny suggests, 1890s' readers, though well-versed in the American Gothic tradition inaugurated by Edgar Allan Poe, could not connect Gilman's story to the Gothic because its narrator/protagonist is a white middle-class wife and mother who belongs in the tame space of domestic fiction, not the monstrous domain of the horror story. Their disgust arose from the story's transgression of the limits of proper femininity, and it was dismissed as an unreadable story that should not have been written (Kolodny in Golden 1992, 153–5).

The story arose from Gilman's experience of what we would probably now describe as post-natal depression, following the birth of her daughter in the late 1880s. Her mental suffering was devastating, particularly as it became clear that her mental health improved as soon as she was away from her husband and child, and that it immediately deteriorated on her return. Her depression, that is, was a function of the conditions of proper femininity, the domesticity of wifedom and motherhood. Her madness was caused by the very aspects of her life that were supposed to codify her as a proper woman. Following a break away in California with friends, Gilman returned to her husband and daughter feeling much better, but 'within a month I was as low as before leaving ... This was a worse horror than before, for now I saw the stark fact – that I was well while away and sick while at home' (Gilman 1990, 95, ellipsis in original). In order to try to recover from her mental discomfort, she submitted herself to the treatment of Silas Weir Mitchell, the leading 'nerve' specialist. Mitchell's treatment was that of the 'rest cure', and is described in his medical treatise, *Fat and Blood: And How to Make Them* (1877).

Mitchell differentiated between mental disorders in male and female patients. He suggested that male patients (always white, always middle class and wealthy in his expensive practice), had come to sickness through overwork, and needed rest. His middle-class female patients, on the other hand, had generally become ill from the pursuit of too active a social life, too many visits and parties. There were alternative cases where female patients were suffering from the stress of the long-term nursing of a sick relative, but mostly the women were sick from too much frivolous pleasure. This did not, however, mean that Mitchell believed in 'work' as a cure for women as 'rest' was a cure for men. Rest was the answer to nervous conditions in both sexes, despite their different pathologies. His treatment consisted of isolating his patients from their families in his sanatorium. He then insisted that they go to bed for periods between six weeks and two months. During this time they were fed a bland diet of fattening food (sickness was indicated by pallor and thinness – hence the need to manufacture 'fat and blood'), and they were allowed to do nothing for themselves:

> At first ... I do not permit the patient to sit up or to sew or write or read. The only action allowed is that needed to clean the teeth. In some instances, I have not permitted the patient to turn over without aid ... because sometimes the moral influence of absolute repose is of use. In such cases I arrange to have the bowels and water passed while lying down, and the patient is lifted onto a lounge at bedtime and sponged, and then lifted back again into the newly-made bed. In all cases of weakness, treated by rest, I insist on the patient being fed by the nurse, and, when well enough to sit up in bed, I insist that the meats shall be cut up, so as to make it easier for the patient to feed herself. (Weir Mitchell in Golden 1992, 49)

In other words, the patient was returned to a state of infantile dependency, with the result, according to the doctor, that, having been obliged to lie still for a month or more, 'rest becomes ... a rather bitter medicine, and they are glad enough to accept the order to rise and go about' when the doctor so orders (48). The infantilisation of the female patient (notice Mitchell's use of the feminine pronoun) is retold in the story, in which the narrator is isolated from her family and friends in an ancestral mansion, confined there to a room like a nursery, allowed no company, no stimulus, no reading, no writing and not even the supremely feminine activity of sewing. Every aspect of her existence is controlled, just as the existence of the helpless infant is controlled by the adults around it.[1]

This is precisely the treatment that Gilman received. 'I was put to bed and kept there. I was fed, bathed, rubbed, and responded with the vigorous body of twenty-six,' she wrote in her autobiography. After a month she felt better, and was sent home with Mitchell's advice ringing in her ears:

> 'Live as domestic a life as possible. Have your child with you all the time. ... Lie down an hour after each meal. Have but two hours' intellectual life a day. And never touch pen, brush or pencil as long as you live.' I went home, followed those directions, and came perilously near to losing my mind. (Gilman 1990, 96)

Mitchell's prescription, that is, is a medicalised version of the cultural judgement that 'women can't paint, women can't write' that so hurts Lily Briscoe in Woolf's *To the Lighthouse* (Woolf 1992, 94). It gives the authority of science to the cultural judgements about women's intellectual capacities. Intellectual activity is diagnosed by patriarchal discourses as harmful to the female mind and body. Gilman's story presents a continuum of medical discourse that shades into literary writing. It is also a continuation of the infantilisation of the treatment proper in which every aspect associated with adulthood from physical autonomy to self-expression was denied to the patient, which might also be read as a metaphor for the infantilised position of women in general.

Gilman insists that her breakdown and its treatment left her permanently incapacitated, especially for systematic intellectual work. After a month or two at home, her distress returned, and eventually she and her husband agreed to divorce, and she took up a career as a public speaker and writer on feminist issues. The breakthrough to mental health came only when she decided to disobey doctor's orders, having recognised that it was precisely her domestic life that was making her sick in the first place. The story of 'The Yellow Wall-paper' is a response to insanity and its treatment, written, says Gilman with a purpose (Gilman 1990, 119). When she had completed the story, she sent it to Mitchell, and though he never acknowledged it, she later heard that he had modified his treatment of nervous ailments in his female patients (20). For her this was success. Her purpose had been fulfilled. Her refusal of the category of 'literariness' for her writing, however, is one of the things that contemporary feminist criticism challenges in its insistence that the aesthetic is also a political category. Politics and poetics are not so easily separated.

The quasi-autobiographical content and the historical context have laid the story open most obviously to materialist feminist criticism. The story and the autobiography, the individual's fiction and her history, alongside the evidence of Mitchell's own writings on the treatment of neurasthenia, are read as a metaphor for the collective experience of women in general, and of women writers in particular. For Gilbert and Gubar, for example, with their interest in the material and cultural obstacles placed in the way of the nineteenth-century woman writer, and their insistence on seeing women's writing as multiple instances of covert and overt protest against these conditions, Gilman's story 'seems to tell *the* story that all literary women would tell if they could speak their "speechless woe"' (Gilbert and Gubar 1979, 89). Like *Jane Eyre*, it is the story of a madwoman in the attic, a tale of the dis-ease as well as the disease at the heart of the family home. It is a disease that renders that home unhomely – Freud's word is uncanny – and the story of this disease is told through the conventions of Gothic fiction, with an unreliable narrator, incipient insanity and the reader's uncertainty about the status of what she reads. Under patriarchy, madwomen is what all women are, or risk becoming since their being is so radically 'other' to the dominant discourses that organise social and psychological life. In this context, the period of the 'sexual anarchy' (Showalter 1991) of the late nineteenth century, the social dissatisfaction of women with their limited horizons was read as a pathological disease; the smallest claims of feminism for female autonomy became the feminine condition of hysteria.

There are, however, problems with this view, not least the class and race blindness that sees Gilman's narrator's plight as the plight of *all* women, and *her* story as *the* story. There is a contextual specificity to this woman's distress which depends on her class position; it is absolutely a privileged white woman's problem. And this is one of the dangers of the insistent reading and rereading of 'The Yellow Wall-paper', and its establishment as the paradigmatic feminist text. Whilst materialist privilege clearly does not do away with psychic pain, we should be very wary of any assumption that lack of material privilege and the existence of physical pain does away with psychological difficulties. Hunger, torture and exhaustion all take a mental toll as well as having physical effects. Gilman herself wrote that she would prefer any kind of physical pain, including childbirth, to the mental distress she suffered during her breakdown (Gilman 1990, 91), and it's difficult to doubt her sincerity, but it is a metaphysical comparison. The articulacy of the story's protest should not blind the reader to those other women whose woe is rather more 'speechless', since they have neither the materials to write it down (education, pen and paper), nor an audience prepared to listen.

Materialist contexts and the content of the text, however, are not the only aspects of 'The Yellow Wall-paper' that have been considered during its insistent reappearance as *the* text about which to write. Just as feminist criticism in general has moved away from purely materialist concerns, and towards psychoanalytic and post-structuralist concerns with language, the criticism of the story has changed as well. For it is, of course, primarily a story about a woman who writes – a woman writer – a woman who is also going mad. That fact, along with its insistent references to and rewritings of the conventions of gothic fiction placed alongside the theme of writing in its content, has tended to make it a fruitful text for readings through the various lenses of psychoanalytic feminisms. In her autobiography, Gilman comments: 'In those days a new disease had dawned on the medical horizon. It was called "nervous prostration". No one knew much about it, and there were many who openly scoffed, saying it was only a new name for laziness. To be recognisably ill, one must be confined to one's bed, and preferably in pain' (90). She is writing of the late 1880s, and nervous prostration or neurasthenia can quite legitimately be seen as the forerunners of the Freudian diseases of neurosis and hysteria in which physical symptoms were traced to unconscious mental causes, as opposed to having an organic pathology rooted in the body.

As Barbara Ehrenreich and Deirdre English argued as early as 1973, the psychoanalytic intervention in medical discourse is also a historical moment. Psychoanalysis is often criticised for ahistoricity, but that does not mean that it has no history of its own. Whilst, on the one hand, Freud's separation of mental disease from physical causes represented a break with the past and the insistence that hysteria arose from the anatomy of the womb, on the other, his theories still made biological anatomy into social destiny: 'the female personality was still inherently defective, this time due to the absence of a penis, rather than the presence of the domineering uterus' (Ehrenreich and English in Golden 1992, 109). They read hysteria as a protest against confining social roles; but they also see it as a kind of dead end, firstly because it was an individualised protest which brought about no political changes, since hysterics do not unite to fight their common enemies, and second, because it confirmed patriarchal prejudices that judged women as 'irrational, unpredictable and diseased' (107). And, moreover, as Paula Treichler has suggested, laying the (female) body open to the discourses of medical diagnosis which are associated with masculinity permits the male doctor immense power over the existential rights of the female patient: once a diagnosis is pronounced, it 'not only names reality, but also has considerable power over what that reality is now to be' (Treichler in Golden 1992, 196). Thus, whilst the story expresses an absolute social dissatisfaction and articulates the mental pain that is its result, it also emphasises the trap of femininity from which there is no escape. The narrator is either repressed out of existence, or she expresses an insane self, which is in turn 'read back' onto her body and its symptoms: whatever choice she makes, she will eventually be silenced.

Psychoanalysis can be a materialist discourse, connecting social oppression and repression with mental aberration, which is, I think, its ideal position. In addition, one of the sources of the importance of psychoanalysis for feminist *literary* theory is that it pays close attention to the textuality of the text. A reading that recovers what Gilman saw as the story's purpose – a political protest against medical discourse – without recuperating its poetics, its literary qualities (which Gilman suggested it did not have), is missing something that even the author missed. Psychoanalysis looks at manner as well as content, how as well as what, poetics as well as politics.

The story tells of the steady mental decline of a unnamed female narrator. It opens with the narrator's feeling that there is something 'queer' (uncanny, unfamiliar, unhomely) about the colonial mansion that she and her husband, along with her sister-in-law and narrator's small baby, have rented for the summer. The house has been taken for her benefit, though there are several logical inconsistencies here. On the one hand, husband John, 'does not believe that I am sick' (Gilman, 1990, 3). Yet despite his disbelief, he has 'diagnosed' her 'condition' as 'temporary nervous depression – a slight hysterical tendency' (4) and prescribed 'phospates or phosphites ... and tonics, and air, and exercise, and journeys' and has forbidden his wife to work (which appears to mean, 'to write') until she is well again. John is clearly a supreme realist, an absolute believer in rationality. He will not stomach his wife's feeling that there is something 'queer' about the house, and laughs at her when she talks of anything 'not to be felt and seen and put down in figures' (3). He refuses to see her as sick, and yet his every action proclaims that he does not see her as well. What space can his wife have for an identity between these binary oppositions of health and disease?

The space the story offers her is a room at the top of the house – a room of her own since she is often alone in it, but also a kind of prison. The room was once used as a nursery, with bars at the windows, presumably to stop the children from falling out, though other readings of the bars, apart from this 'common-sense' realistic reading, are also possible. The furniture doesn't match. The bed is nailed to the floor. Except for one thing, it is a pleasant room, big and airy and filled with sunshine. Unfortunately, the walls are covered with a disgusting yellow wallpaper, torn off in patches; it is a sulphurous colour, and has an unfathomable pattern. As the tenancy of the colonial mansion continues, the narrator becomes increasingly obsessed by the paper; at first angered and repulsed by its ugliness, she eventually begins to see a female figure trapped behind the bars of the paper. With no other stimulus, it takes over her entire existence and she becomes determined to make sense of the pattern, and then to 'free' the woman she has 'seen' (or perhaps hallucinated) trapped behind its bars. She studies the wallpaper, and then begins to tear it from the walls. The story ends with her creeping around the walls, having removed all the paper. When her husband observes her state, he faints; but the narrator continues to creep, and creeps over his prostrated form at every rotation.

Plot summaries never tell enough of a text's effects which is why the manner of the telling is as important as the story itself. How we read the story depends on how we read the wallpaper. Jeffrey Berman, for example, sees the wallpaper as 'projection screen or Rorschach test of the narrator's growing fright'. Its inconsistent pattern represents the inconsistencies of her own life, her need for security and love opposing her will towards independence, her contradictory impulses towards conventional feminine duty and unconventional feminist protest (Berman in Golden 1992, 232). This is an interesting insight, but it is more complicated than Berman's content-based psychoanalysis presents it as being, since the inconsistencies of the narrator's life are not symptoms of an idiosyncratic pathology: it's not just *her* problem, but goes wider than that. One can see also the gaps and fissures, the holes in the argument, as it were, of the discourses that oppress her. Hence my emphasis above on John's insistence that she is not sick, but that she nonetheless needs treatment. When the voice of reason is so illogical, no wonder the narrator has problems. The concentration on the female figure of the text and on her pathology and problems displaces the need to read the male other of the text, and authorises his version of reality as a seamless whole that is not open to criticism. Children are told not to 'answer back' meaning that they must resist being impertinent and insolent to the adult version of the world. But telling a child not to answer back is usually the response of an adult whose arguments or reasoning are a bit shaky. The story shows a woman being treated like a child. One way of reading the story, then, is to see it as a 'reading back' and a 'writing back', an insolent, improper version, which shakes up a particular version of the real, just as, eventually, the narrator's imaginary double shakes the pattern of the wallpaper (Gilman 1990, 11). Part of its subversive effect comes from the manner of the writing, which should not be simply ignored in favour of the story's content.

When one sees 'The Yellow Wall-paper' on the page, one becomes immediately aware of the staccato effect of the prose. The paragraphs are very short, often consisting of no more than one short sentence. The style is paratactic – that is, connection is made by juxtaposition (placing of ideas in space) rather than by the logic of grammatical subordination. Disconnected ideas are placed side by side as if they have a connection: the connection is spatial, rather than logical, as in the sentence: 'John laughs at me, of course, but one expects that' (3). This sentence is written in the context of two pieces of information, first the narrator's feeling that the house might be haunted, and second, the 'practical' nature of her husband. That simple sentence is, however, very loaded. Its three parts, John's laughter, the narrator's 'of course', and her generalised expectation that John will continue to laugh at her, beg a lot of questions. Why is it 'of course' that a husband laughs at his wife? Why is it expected? It seems stylistically very simple, like a child's narrative, but appearances are deceptive. If there is a power relationship implicit in the way that John reads his wife, there's an answering back insolence in her writing of him in which the tone is very uncertain. Do all husbands laugh at their wives, or just this one? What are we being asked to accept as 'of course'?

The parataxis of the style is an act of political, personal and aesthetic resistance to the totalising narratives of cause and effect (narrated in long sentences, long paragraphs, and, indeed, long novels as well as in the discourses of science and medicine) that usually go by the name of Realism. This is the discourse through which John, who believes in fact, the narrator's brother, who agrees with him, and Silas Weir Mitchell define the world. Medical diagnosis is precisely a realist discourse: a cause produces a symptom (effect); a diagnosis is a reading of that effect; a prescription (which is a kind of writing that comes from the reading) supposedly effects a cure. The story is over, and there are no loose ends. Or, at least, that is the way that the story is supposed to go, as Weir Mitchell's *Fat and Blood* suggests.

Only this isn't really the whole story no matter how totalising Realism attempts to be. Like the pattern in the paper, this story is multiple rather than singular. It does not simply say that the narrator's version of the world is right, and that John's is wrong. The paratactic style, engagingly and disarmingly simple as it is, undoes the distance of perspective required by Realist discourses to make their allegedly objective judgements. It undoes the pretence of objective interpretation. Its performance of naivety and innocence is also therefore a performance of cunning – its textual gestures collapse the structures by which we are used to judge. The style draws the reader into complicity with the narrator, requesting our sympathy and identification with the poor, put-upon writer whose story we are reading. We get too close and suspend our judgement. The reader's conventional position of dispassionate interpretation is interfered with. Mary Jacobus argues that we must never forget the creepiness of the story, the way it makes skins crawl (Jacobus 1986, 234–5): the uncanny effect is played out on the reader – the reader of either sex. If we identify with the narrator, we identify with madness. If we identify with John's realist perspective, we identify with the forces of a highly unattractive oppression. There is no solid ground here. The inconsistencies of the text undermine any reading position.

So, for example, the voices of authority (the brother and husband who are both doctors) are represented in the narrator's text. The brother and the husband say 'the same thing' (Gilman 1990, 4), tell the same story, read the same symptoms and come up with the same diagnosis and treatment. But because their narratives are displaced from the centre of the narrative, retold from a different perspective, their certainties are undermined. The narrator comments:

> Personally, I disagree with their ideas.
>
> Personally, I believe that congenial work, with excitement and change, would do me good.
>
> But what is one to do?
>
> I did write for a while in spite of them; but it *does* exhaust me a good deal – having to be so sly about it, or else meet with heavy opposition.
>
> I sometimes fancy that in my condition, if I had less opposition and more society and stimulus – but John says the very worst thing I can do is think about my condition, and I confess it always makes me feel bad.
>
> So I will let it alone and talk about the house. (4)

The structures and juxtapositions of sentences here are very tightly put together. Seemingly random ideas do, in fact, have a very close logic. The assertions the narrator makes of her disagreements, for example, do double service. They are at once insistently self-expressive: this is what *I* think; and they are also idiosyncratic – personal opinion is set in opposition to the expert voices of the doctors. Who is to say which discourse is right? Moreover, she expresses what she thinks only to the 'dead paper' on which she writes, not to the men whose pronouncements her writings at once challenge ('I disagree') and endorse ('it *does* exhaust me'). Her writing about her 'condition' is unfinished. She has no language to imagine an alternative because John's reported authoritative voice interrupts her sentence, and sets her off on another track – she will 'talk about the house' instead. Since the house is the only thing that she has to talk about, the house becomes the site of her 'condition', as well as its emblem. It is a beautiful place, with a '*delicious* garden'; but it is also uncared for, derelict and damaged. Which might just be a description of the narrator herself – trapped by a domesticity she does not desire, which, indeed, repulses her, she too becomes derelict and damaged, uncared for despite all the care that is being taken, because it is the wrong kind of care.

Increasingly, therefore, because the text unsettles the totalising and naturalising narratives of Realism, it has been read with a post-structuralist bent; the wallpaper becomes the projection of a female/ feminine writing effect. Treichler sees the wallpaper as 'women's discourse' (Treichler in Golden 1992, 195). More recently, Julian Wolfreys has read it as exemplifying the Cixousian notion of *écriture féminine*, a writing of excess and defiance, which resists the closures of definition and telos (Wolfreys 1997, 83). It destabilises any sense that meaning might be 'there' just to be grasped, which in turn destabilises the reading positions that we 'outside' the text might adopt.

I placed the word 'outside' in inverted commas to signal the provisionality of the reading positions that 'The Yellow Wall-paper' dramatises. Jacques Derrida has written that there is nothing outside the text, no outside text – there is no position outside textuality, no metalanguage in which interpretation is concretised and authorised, nothing outside the languages which we inscribe and by which we are inscribed. Although she uses language differently from the linguistic structures of her husband, for example, the narrator of the story remains implicated in the same language, unable to escape from its hold on her – the ways in which it inscribes her, describes her, prescribes for her and proscribes her: these are all words to do with writing, deriving from the Latin verb *scripere*, to write. In Lacanian terms, one might say, language speaks her even as she speaks language. Treichler's insight that the wallpaper is 'women's discourse', or Wolfreys's sense that it is a mode of *écriture féminine*, both speak of an entrapment in a language that the narrator has not made or chosen, yet to which she must appeal in order to express anything at all.

The wallpaper, then, is an emblem of many things. Attached to the walls of the house, it is a marker of the kind of domestic space the house is: this is a house that is not quite a home, a domestic space that has been neglected and untenanted, not a home-from-home, rather an unhomely or uncanny space, though we have only the narrator's word for it. It has been rented for three months, so that there is no point in John undertaking repairs or redecoration, for they will not be there long enough. Before their tenancy, 'the place has been empty for years' (Gilman 1990, 4), following legal troubles amongst the heirs. The logical explanation of its emptiness does not, however, quite exorcise its ghostliness: the narrator remains determined to express her feeling that 'there is something strange about the house', something 'queer', a ghostliness and a haunted quality that seems to her the 'height of romantic felicity' despite her husband's insistence on draughts as the sole explanation of its strangeness, and his exhortations to self-control and away from fancy. The Gothic and the realist narrative compete.

The wallpaper signifies the neglect of the house. Even before the narrator arrives, someone – she surmises that it was the children, the previous tenants of the attic – has already started to pull the paper from the walls. The narrator is not surprised because the paper is so very bad:

> One of those sprawling, flamboyant patterns committing every artistic sin. It is dull enough to confuse the eye in following, pronounced enough constantly to irritate and provoke study, and when you follow the lame uncertain curves for a little distance they suddenly commit suicide – plunge off at outrageous angles, destroy themselves in unheard-of contradictions. (5)

The point about patterns is their regularity. A pattern is supposed to be a repeating structure which has its own coherence, and which might even be thought of as restful so long as it retains its equilibrium. But this wallpaper, although the different lengths repeat, has no other source of repetition. If it is a pattern, it is idiosyncratic. The paper has no balance. And in the absence of other stimuli, the narrator begins to study it, and to see things in it. She feels the pattern has a vicious influence, and that there is a suppressed violence in it that disturbs her, as she sees 'a broken neck and two bulbous eyes' staring at her hundreds of times in the room, an image of strangulation or stifling which invites us to read it as the metaphor of the narrator's own condition. Even the regularity which, at first, she sought in the pattern has become a source of potential horror, since the reiteration of the pattern, reproduced throughout the room becomes, with constant study, endless and uncanny:

> I get positively angry with the impertinence of it and the everlastingness. Up and down and sideways they crawl, and those absurd

unblinking eyes are everywhere. ... I never saw so much expression in an inanimate thing before, and we all know how much expression they have! I used to lie awake as a child and get more entertainment and terror out of blank walls and plain furniture than most children could find in a toy-store. (7)

The reference to childhood here is important because the room is a nursery, and the patient has been deprived of her position as an adult in charge of her own destiny. The childlike games of imagination that she plays hark back to an age of innocence, but also speak of regression and loss of adult identity. Moreover, where for a child endowing inanimate objects with human powers is a harmless game, for an adult it is a less innocent pursuit. It is a dangerous lapse into fancy, a refusal of the real. Thus, eventually, the wallpaper obtrudes itself into every thought. The narrator might be thinking about the countryside and the wallpaper enters her mind. She sees different things in different lights so that the idea of seeing and knowing (or seeing and believing) is belied by her narrative. The meaning of the wallpaper is not just a single meaning, and it is not just 'there' to be grasped. It is full of spectral traces – but there's nothing you can put your finger on, even in language – nothing you see and feel and put down in figures (3). In daylight, for example, a second sub-pattern become discernible, a subtext for the main pattern. This subtext is only visible at certain times of day, when 'the sun is just so': seeing is no guarantor of knowledge here. Then the narrator can see 'a strange, provoking, formless sort of figure that seems to skulk about behind that silly and conspicuous front design' (8). As Wolfreys suggests, a formless figure is an oxymoron, a contradiction in terms (Wolfreys 1997, 79–80), much like the Kristevan *chora*. Furthermore, none of the adjectives, none of the description as a whole gives a concrete depiction of what the narrator sees. If the wallpaper is dangerously suggestive to her, her descriptions are suggestive too, rather than obvious.

Suggestive of what? Excess, perhaps. It breaks artistic laws (Gilman 1990, 9) and commits every artistic sin. It operates by no design principle of which the narrator has ever heard. Rather it is monstrous, because it is overflowing and excessive: it has 'bloated curves and flourishes' and it 'waddles' rather than progressing regularly (according to the rules of design – regularity is a term derived from the Latin word for 'rules'). The diagonal patter is an 'optic horror, like a lot of wallowing seaweeds in full chase' (9). Suggestive images indeed, but still no obvious answer as to what they suggest. A vulgar Freudian answer might suggest the terror of the female body, and in particular what Cixous sees as the last taboo, the *pregnant* female body. Those bloated curves, that waddling movement, the entrapping motion of the wallowing seaweed which is at once like entrails (the obscenity of the body when it transgresses its own limits) and the head of the Medusa. Conventionally, according to the *laws* of design, the paper is highly improper. According to the laws of representation, there are some things that should never be represented. And after all, the narrator has just given birth to a baby that she cannot bear to be with, so parturition and the limits (of the body, of representation, the limits imposed by motherhood on ambition and independence) are probably on her mind. The wallpaper speaks of a physical body it represents as grotesque, of artistic representation and its laws, and of sociological context: female nature, feminine culture, sociological observation of a mind going mad. For Gilman and her readers, it is indeed an ugly story.

Reading the wallpaper is a question of multiplying perspectives, and none of the perspectives is valorised over the others. Like the paper, the text proliferates possible meanings, rather than settling on one version. The hidden activity of the paper – its subtexts – come to mirror the subterfuges and evasions of the narrator, who increasingly withdraws even from the limited human contact of her husband and sister-in-law, refusing to discuss the paper with them as the story goes on. This leaves her free to see all its possibilities, 'the things in that wallpaper that nobody knows about but me, or ever will' (11). What she sees is a 'dim shape' that gets clearer with passing time: the clarity is presumably illusory, since what she sees is 'like a woman stooping down and creeping about behind that pattern' – the image gives the narrator the creeps, makes her feel 'creepy' in a terrifying verbal prefiguring of the story's final actions, but there is no escape from it since her husband will not take her away. What the narrator seeks is mastery over the paper (12), since she has mastery nowhere else in her life. But the attempt to take control of the paper, to comprehend it, results in violence: 'You think you have mastered it, but just as you get well under way in following, it turns a back-somersault and there you are. It slaps you in the face, knocks you down, and tramples upon you. It is like a bad dream' (12). The organic images of seaweed and toadstools in florid arabesques (12) are seen by daylight: by night, they solidify into bars, and the sub-pattern resolves itself into a woman behind the bars. The creeping figure of the woman (or sometimes, many women) is trying to escape the paper, but cannot because of the florid bars of the top pattern, which 'strangles them off and turns them upside down, and makes their eyes white!' (15). This horrifying image is placed in the context of John's increasing concern for his wife, as if her madness is becoming more discernible. But by now it is clear that the narrator associates his solicitude with the entrapment of the woman in the paper – his fear of madness traps her – and she has become overtly afraid of him, wishing he would leave her alone, and that she could spend the night alone. With the loss of realist perspective the narrator *becomes* the creeping woman she has 'seen'.

When the opportunity arises, she locks herself into the room – an act of assertion that implies that she is choosing her own status as prisoner – and peels the paper off the walls. By now, she is quite mad: she believes herself to be the figure in the wallpaper, fears being put back behind the bars, and tears the paper down to prevent herself from being trapped again. Like Bertha Mason before her, she considers burning the house to effect her escape from the wallpaper's pervasive influence; and she thinks for a moment of jumping through the window, both of which are Bertha's actions. Her behaviour is that of the caged animal, a relentless, repeated, pathological motion of creeping around the room. The claim she has made for autonomous selfhood has finally robbed her of any semblance of a sane identity; she is no longer a wife and mother: indeed, she has even lost her humanity. When John comes home and sees her state, as well as the state of the room which is a sign of her state, he faints. She crawls over him, in an endless repetition.

The story resists the closure of defining what will happen next. The final image of the creeping woman is creepy precisely because it refuses us a resolution of the problems the text has raised – social, economic, biological, cultural, psychic problems: none is resolved. All that has happened is that the self-styled voice of reason has collapsed in a dead faint in the face of creeping unreason. One system has toppled. But nothing has been erected in its place. There is a blank space for new writing, new patterns on the wall, a space that Gilman has left empty.

Critics have read the narrator's last moments as a scene of temporary triumph over patriarchy. I'm not sure that the story invites any kind of even qualified optimism for our particular protagonist. The problems it enacts are presented as the diagnosis of a disease: the lack of closure implies that there is no prescription, no cure, as yet. There are hints as to what a cure might be: a more varied life, more stimulus, more work for the narrator, and for women like her – though not necessarily for all women. But this is not finally a therapeutic text. D. H. Lawrence spoke of shedding sickness in books, of writing away pain and distress. A feminist text, however, is not necessarily one that makes its readers feel better. For Gilman, the feminism of this text was bound up with its purpose: for her, it was meant to be a transitive text, a story that acted on the world, that made a difference. Inasmuch as Mitchell hinted that reading it had modified his clinical practice – changed his discourse, altered the stories he told – it was a success in Gilman's terms. For contemporary readers, that fact remains important. But the story itself leaves us with an image of pain, not of recovery. And if this is *the* paradigmatic story of feminist literary theory, the story that all women might tell, the theory, like the narrator, remains trapped in a very grim world. Perhaps it is time to imagine, to write, and to read, some of the other possible stories in the blank space of the bare wall. ... That is, after all, what Gilman's text itself invites us to do in its radical refusals of monolithic points of view, and its proliferation of alternative meanings and possible interpretations. We've had the diagnosis that women are sick because they are oppressed and repressed, and because they lack the means of self-expression. But that is not the end, the sole aim, of feminist theories. There are more spaces to conquer than attic rooms.

Notes

1. A version of Weir Mitchell's rest cure was the treatment received by Virginia Woolf during her periodic bouts of mental distress. She hated the treatment, and satirised the doctors who provided it in her 1924 novel *Mrs Dalloway*. As Elaine Showalter has noted (in *The Female Malady*, London: Virago, 1987), the effects of the treatment were to infantilise the patient into a state of complete dependency; infantilisation and feminisation go together, which is what helps to constitute insanity as the 'the female malady'.

Afterword: The Mark on the Wall – Marking Differences, Marking Time

> ... it is impossible to say 'this is comic', or 'that is tragic', nor are we certain, since short stories, we have been taught, should be brief and conclusive, whether this, which is vague and inconclusive, should be called a short story at all.
>
> Virginia Woolf, 'Modern Fiction'

Virginia Woolf's short story 'The Mark on the Wall' (1917) is perhaps not really a short story at all, or rather, it is a story that rethinks the meaning of the short-story form, and meditates on the question of genre, amongst other things. It is not a traditional short story in that it has no external incidents to speak of – no 'story'. As E. M. Forster puts it in *Aspects of the Novel* (1927), a story is 'a narrative of events arranged in their time sequence'; the story is the 'something' that happens. In contrast, plot refers to the narrative of events where the emphasis 'falls on causality', on the relations between the events; plot need not be chronologically organised. When story elements are paramount, the reader asks, 'what next?' When plot is more significant, she asks, 'why?' (Forster 1993, 55). For the early theorists of what a short story is, writers such as Edgar Allen Poe and Randall Stevenson, the obligation of the short story is that it tell about incidents, and that the shape of the incidents must lead to an inexorable conclusion: the question 'what next?' leads to an identifiable conclusion. As Poe puts it:

> Nothing is more clear than that every plot, worth the name, must be elaborated to its *dénouement* before anything be attempted with the pen. It is only with the *dénouement* constantly in view that we can give a plot its indispensable air of consequence, or causation, by

making the incidents, and especially the tone at all points, tend to the
development of the intention. (Poe in May 1994, 67)

And further, the conventions of the short story imply that the denoue-
ment must also be a twist in the tale, an unexpected conclusion to the
events that have been elaborated.

In these terms Woolf's story does not behave itself properly. It is all
plot, one might say, and no story; its force is in the manner of the
telling rather than in the substance of the narrative. The narrator,
some time ago – probably in January, she's not quite sure – had
noticed a mark on the wall in her sitting room. She did not know what
the mark was, where it had come from, what it might mean; but it did
provoke a chain of associative thinking about the nature of consciousness, and a whole range of random memories and images, all of which
are indicative of the narrator's own attitudes to various things. The
story meanders for three or four pages, revisiting those associations
until the chain of thought is interrupted by the other occupant of the
room who tells the narrator that he is going to buy a paper. Before he
goes, he announces that the mark on the wall is, in fact, a snail. And
the stream of consciousness comes to an abrupt but inconclusive end.
That the male figure is going to buy a paper, and that he fixes and
defines the marks on the wall into the realm of fact, thereby causing
the story to break off is important: the incursion of facts on the meditation (the newspaper which will report facts, the fact that the mark is
a snail) stems the flow. The fact that the mark on the wall that has
provoked this whole narrative sequence is a snail might of course be a
kind of twist in the tale, aligning the story with the traditions of short-
story writing – it is an unexpected explanation; but the real kink
comes from the fact that the whole 'story' takes place in the narrator's
mind. Its events are mental not physical. Moreover, these mental
events take place at several removes. The narrator does not recount
what she is thinking 'now'; she is recalling what she was thinking
'then', in January, when she first saw the mark on the wall. The tense
of the narrative, the apparent immediacy of the thoughts that appear
in the narrator's mind, however, conspire to disguise that distance
from the reader. We have no perspective that permits us to make reliable, objective judgements.

When Forster 'read' this tale in *Aspects of the Novel*, he quoted a
long passage from it in the immediate context of a passage from
Laurence Sterne's eighteenth-century novel, *Tristram Shandy*

(1759–67), a novel remarkable for its inconsequentiality, its refusal of narrative lines of cause and effect. The passage from 'The Mark on the Wall' that Forster chose suggests that Woolf's story has similar features:

> But for that mark, I'm not sure about it; I don't believe it was made by a nail after all; its too big, too round, for that. I might get up, but if I got up and looked at it, ten to one I shouldn't be able to say for certain; because once a thing's done, no one ever knows how it happened. Oh! dear me, the mystery of life; the inaccuracy of thought! The ignorance of humanity! To show how very little control of our possessions we have – what an accidental affair this living is after all our civilization – let me just count over a few of the things lost in one lifetime, beginning, for that seems always the most mysterious of losses – what cat would gnaw, what rat would nibble – three pale blue canisters of book-binding tools? Then there were the bird-cages, the iron hoops, the steel skates, the Queen Anne coal scuttle, the bagatelle board, the hand organ – all gone, and jewels, too. Opals and emeralds, they lie about the roots of turnips. What a scraping paring affair it is to be sure! The wonder is that I've any clothes on my back, that I sit surrounded by solid furniture at this moment. Why, if one wants to compare life to anything, one must liken it to be being blown through the Tube at fifty miles an hour – landing at the other end without a single hairpin in one's hair. (Woolf 1993b, 54)

In fact, Forster omitted the references to the Tube and the hairpins with ellipses, perhaps feeling that the quotation was quite long enough already, perhaps deliberately stopping before the specifically intimate feminine reference to lady's coiffure – mind and millinery, as George Eliot has already shown us, are not supposed to go together. What he concludes from this passage is that Woolf, like Sterne, was a fantasist, by which he appears to mean that Woolf took a very small object as the basis of her meditation. She fluttered from it, and then settled on it again. She combined 'a humorous appreciation of the muddle of life with a keen sense of its beauty'; and her tone is 'a rather deliberate bewilderment, an announcement to all and sundry that [she does] not know where [she is] going' (Forster 1993, 35). The fantasist, in other words, writes not in order to make sense of things, but in order to register their confusion. The very word 'fantasist' tends to imply a vaguely negative judgement: the fantasist plays fast and loose with the rules of representation, and unsettles the reader's expectations. As Forster comments at the end of his brief remarks on Woolf's story: 'life is such a muddle, oh dear, the will is so weak, the sensations fidgety ... philosophy ... God ... oh dear, look at the mark ... listen to the door – existence ... is really too ... what were we saying?' (35–6, ellipses in original). He does not say what he thinks, but his mimicry in his own criticism (criticism, after all, being a discourse which is supposed to 'make sense of things') demonstrates that he finds these strange juxtapositions unsatisfactory.

Now this is not only not what a short story is supposed to be, or to be about, but it is also not what artistic production has traditionally been supposed to be. The organisation of Woolf's fiction here is in fact more like a creative dis-organisation. Unlikely things are more or less randomly juxtaposed. The mark on the wall – in itself a very small thing whatever its cause, and also a random thing, apparently uncontrolled by the narrator's conscious intention – is made the spur to meditations on everything from the impossibility of human knowledge to the loss of three canisters of book-binding tools. There is no order to the list of things one can think about. Indeed, lists, as Patricia Waugh has noted, extol the 'principle of substitution instead of contextuality' (Waugh 1984, 144). They are thus dis-ordering, unstructured structures because they imply that any one thing in the list is as important or insignificant as any other: in this case, the ignorance of humanity, a Queen Anne coal scuttle and a bunch of hairpins have a kind of equality in their randomised invocation. And this dis-ordering can be seen as a feminist intervention in the taxonomies of masculine knowledge. As Laura Marcus puts it: '"The Mark on the Wall" explores the difference between the "masculine" point of view – fact-bound, hierarchical, constraining – and a free-associative thinking which revels in the multiple imaginings opened up by freedom from the desire to find out what things "really" are' (Marcus 1997, 19). This is a writing with no sense of proportion or precedence.

The narrator's juxtapositions of trivial and important things are explicitly a critique of another kind of listing, that claims the importance of order: 'the masculine point of view which governs our lives, which sets the standard, which establishes Whitaker's Table of Precedency' (Woolf 1993b, 57). *Whitaker's Almanack*, an annual publication, contains a table that establishes social precedence: which members of the Royal Family are more important than others, which Archbishops take precedence over the others, which kinds of peer come first. Woolf's story implies that this is a false ordering that has no real meaning. Disorder in fiction may, in fact, make more sense because life itself is disordered and disproportionate. As she put it in one of her most famous essays, 'Modern Fiction' (1919):

> Examine for a moment an ordinary mind on an ordinary day. The mind receives a myriad impressions – trivial, fantastic, evanescent, or engraved with the sharpness of steel. From all sides they come, an incessant shower of innumerable atoms; and as they fall, as they shape themselves into the life of Monday or Tuesday, the accent falls differently from of old; the moment of importance came here, not there; so that, if a writer were a free man and not a slave, if he could write what he chose, not what he must, if he could work upon his own feeling and not upon convention, there would be no plot, no comedy, no tragedy, no love interest or catastrophe, and perhaps not a single button sewn on as the Bond Street tailors would have it. (Woolf 1993d, 8)

Life, says Woolf, is not symmetrical and enlightening. Life is hazy; it does not make sense. The task of the writer is therefore to express life's peculiarities, not to express the mere conventions of Realism which are not, in the end, at all real, and which make sense only at the expense of falsification and exclusion. Where the proliferation of meanings in the writing on the wall was terrifying evidence of incipient insanity for the narrator of Gilman's 'The Yellow Wall-paper', for Woolf it is the condition of human life. It is terrifying only when one is hemmed in by discourses that insist that there is only one meaning, one way of seeing. In *A Room of One's Own*, Woolf suggested that the woman writer's problem was that she had 'altered her values in deference to the opinions of others' (Woolf 1993a, 67). Gilman's narrator tells her story of resistance to the professional opinions of others as painful and difficult because of her deference to their opinions. The 'others' are men who wield real power, and they do have the power to drive you mad. But Woolf tries to rewrite that monolithic version of reality. Her writer in this case is a man – the generic figure of the writer in Woolf's writing almost always is. But he is a man who is a slave to convention, to the necessity imposed on writing that it must tell a particular kind of story, that it must be packed with incident (love interest and catastrophe), and with detail (a button sewn on, or not).

What Woolf's works dramatise is a rewriting of the patriarchal plots which trap male writers as well as women – though her concern is more for women. She refuses the categorisation that says 'this is an important book ... because it deals with war. This is an insignificant book because it deals with the feelings of women in a drawing-room' (67). Literary value – human value – is not to be found in either 'this' or 'that', male *or* female. There is not one version, there are many. As a whole, Woolf's works constitute an important example for all kinds of feminist theories. For all that Woolf herself was a privileged upper-class white woman, living at a very specific historical period, who often articulated uncomfortably prejudiced views, she continues to have much to say to all of us. Her own life, for all its privilege, ended with a suicide by drowning – a dramatic yet also clichéd gesture (the fallen woman in nineteenth-century literature always drowned herself) that remains as a painful reminder that even privileged femininity, even the femininity that has a private income and a room of its own, can be a frighteningly narrow space. *A Room of One's Own* is a foundational text for feminist literary theories. It discusses the material difficulties of the woman writer and the psychic and literary consequences of social subordination; it begins a process of uncovering a female tradition of writing; it challenges the assumption that 'women can't paint, women can't write' (Woolf 1992, 94), and creates an imaginative, fictional, personal criticism in which questions of value can be re-evaluated, a criticism that undoes the alleged neutrality of the objective voice. Her focus on multiplicity and dis-ordering has much in common with the insights of French feminisms into language and its power: the pulse of the semiotic on the Symbolic order; the *parler-femme* of speaking as a woman to other women; the resistance to the logic of the same; her will to make an *écriture féminine* out of her own resources. The mark on the wall is impoverished when it is revealed to be only a snail. While it is an unknown quantity, while its meaning is unfixed, it has much more to offer, and is a figure that reveals the necessity of differences which both feed the imagination and validate real lives.

Where now? How now?

'I'll be a post-feminist in post-patriarchy'.

T-shirt slogan

Rachel Bowlby begins her book *Feminist Destinations and Further Essays on Virginia Woolf* (1997) by wondering about 'the possible ends or destinations implied in speaking of "feminist" writing and criticism.' 'Where is feminism, or feminist theory going, and what would constitute its "arrival"?, the end of the "movement"?' (Bowlby 1997, 3). It is, of course, an unanswerable question, not least because, as I hope I have shown, feminist theory doesn't always begin from the same departure-gate, and takes very different routes for its multiple destinations. One kind of answer might be that there is a sense in which 'feminist *literary* theory' at least, has already 'made it', inasmuch as it is already an indispensable part of the study of literature in universities in Britain and the United States. Courses on women's writing proliferate; and alongside specifically gynocritical approaches, it is increasingly unacceptable to teach a literary canon that contains only two and half women writers. Where women writers can't be included, on Shakespeare courses for example, there's lots of feminist material out there that reads Shakespeare differently, 're-visions' his oeuvre from a woman's point of view. So, the battle's won. We can all go home.

Only ... every year in my teaching career to date, I have spoken to groups of female students about women's writing and feminist theory, and I've asked my students a version of the 'McCarthy question': are you now, or have you ever been, a feminist? I say 'McCarthy question' because the answers I have usually received have generally been negative – often vehemently so. My students all believe in the rights that liberal feminism achieved for them. The very fact that they are in university classes at all is testament to that. They believe in equal rights, equal pay for equal work, in universal suffrage, in racial equality, in the equality of the lesbian woman, in equality of opportunity regardless of gender, race, sexuality or disability. And they enrol on women's writing courses, and enthusiastically learn the lessons that feminist literary theories seek to teach them – at least in the relatively safe space of academic life. But they aren't feminists.

They aren't feminists for two reasons. The first is that they are optimistic, and believe that the world is already a better place, and that they will be able to do anything within it. The second reason however undercuts that optimism. They are afraid to be labelled as 'feminists' since they perceive it as a term hurled with hostile purposes, a term that makes them ugly and angry, that rewrites them into those old stereotypes of the shrew and the witch. They conform to new definitions of what nice girls are, and do not see that they are conforming. Femininity might be a wider space than once it was for First-World women – but it's nowhere near 'as wide as the sky' (Atkinson 1996, 374). Even for Western women, there is still work to be done in consciousness-raising and techniques of resistance.

And in the rest of the world, the problems are often more acute and more urgent. We cannot stop being feminists in the West just because we've got equal rights legislation when the women of so many other countries lack even basic rights. I cannot claim that feminist literary theories will directly change the real conditions of women's lives. But I can claim that that ought to be the aim; and if feminism has a 'destination', an end-point, it is a destination that will be reached by making the links between our historical oppressions and the current oppressions of those other women. The battle isn't over, and won't be over until my students don't even need to call themselves feminists because all women are freed from terror and pain, and liberated into the selves that they want to be. Utopian? Yes, because future Utopias should be better places for all people to live in than the dystopias of the here and now, and of the there and then, and of the there and now.

For now, then, Woolf's indeterminate mark on the wall, the unknown mark, not the mark resolved into a snail, is a figure that holds out the possibility of seeing things differently. Feminist literary theory is not one body of knowledge that speaks only to or about a particular set of female bodies. It is a creative multiplicity that has many other sides. Some of the things that it sees are highly improper; many are disturbing; a few are funny and happy. As the snail moves on, it presumably leaves a trail, the physical evidence of its journey. But where the snail ends up is not predetermined, already foreclosed by forceful logic. The theories, like the snail, do not need a fixed destination to have meaning; and both can make a difference if we are prepared to see things differently.

Annotated Bibliography

The texts selected here are largely texts that get only the briefest of mentions in the rest of the book, or that are not mentioned at all. They are, nonetheless, important contributions to the fields of feminist literary theories and are helpful places to begin you own adventures in theoretical thinking. I have chosen examples from many different approaches, from the post-structuralist to the liberal humanist/womanist. Many of these texts are 'difficult' to read. Don't let that put you off. Read slowly and use what you can. Feminisms are not totalisng – none of the texts here gives the whole answer. That being the case, you can try to make the most of them, an activity which will not be the same as making everything of them.

Armstrong, Isobel ed. *New Feminist Discourses: Critical Essays on Theories and Texts*. London and New York: Routledge, 1992.

A collection of essays by a number of important theorists, including Rachel Bowlby, Laura Marcus, Jane Moore and Lynda Nead. The usefulness of this collection resides in the fact that most of the essays are 'readings' of texts, readings inflected through well-argued theoretical positions. It provides helpful examples of 'how to do' feminist readings.

Armstrong, Nancy. *Desire and Domestic Fiction: A Political History of the Novel*. New York and Oxford: Oxford University Press, 1987.

Armstrong's concern is to historicise the reading of literary history. She argues that previous histories of the novel, such as those by Ian Watt, and by Gilbert and Gubar, have failed to take proper account of gender and sexuality as formative in the construction of the novel. Using the insights of Michel Foucault, she suggests that gender and sexuality are not fixed qualities, but qualities that take place in and through language and which are subject to historical variation. The history of the novel is a writing and a creation of female desires. The book contains interesting, approachable and historically contextualised readings in the works of Jane Austen and the Brontës, readings that are a very useful supplement and corrective to the assumptions of Elaine Showalter (1978) and Gilbert and Gubar (1979).

Braidotti, Rosi. *Nomadic Subjects: Embodiment and Sexual Difference in Contemporary Feminist Theory.* New York: Columbia University Press, 1994.

A philosophical rather than a literary-theoretical text, *Nomadic Subjects* emphasises the relationships between bodies, their material conditions and the psychic effects of those conditions, which is a relatively traditional formula forward in feminist theory. Instead of merely anlaysing current structures of oppression and repression for women, however, Braidotti is anxious to try to create and imagine alternative futures. The figure of the nomad – precisely a figure who is not fixed – is for her a way of imagining the journey towards a female subjectivity that is fully embodied, fully subjective and which can therefore become free.

Cixous, Hélène and Mireille Calle-Gruber. *Rootprints: Memory and Life-Writing.* London and New York: Routledge, 1997.

A very accessible introduction to Cixous's more recent thought. *Rootprints* contains interviews and meditations as well as autobiographical writing, all of which reflect on sexual differences and writing. The book's very form demonstrates a commitment to multiple points of view, and it eschews the terms of so-called academic writing to make the personal voice and experience central to any theoretical project. It is theory as creative writing.

Felski, Rita. *Beyond Feminist Aesthetics: Feminist Literature and Social Change.* London: Hutchinson Radius, 1989.

Felski's book provides one of the very best recent examples of an attempt to read literary texts closely within the frameworks of theoretical models. She takes very seriously the implications of French feminism, yet also mounts a critique of its assumptions that language might change the world. Through readings in a wide range of contemporary women's writing, she argues that realist forms are still an essential part of feminism's project to see the world anew; *écriture feminine* is only one possible strategy for women's writing, and it is not the chosen mode of the majority of women writers who have activist purposes. All in all, a very important book, a model of fully theorised argument.

Friedman, Susan Stanford. *Mappings: Feminism and the Cultural Geographies of Encounter.* Princeton: Princeton University Press, 1998.

This important recent book examines literature and feminism in a global context. Friedman argues that narrative, the process of story-telling, requires a new kind of reading, a 'feminist geopolitical literacy'. The ways in which stories are made in different cultures can act as a primary resource for the feminist critic who wants both to explore difference and to see commonalities of experience. Friedman suggests that systemic oppression has to be analysed in the contexts of its individualised expressions. She reads a number of modemist novels by Joyce, Forster, Woolf and Hurston, as well as examining film, in order articulate the acute differences between groups, caused by the barriers of race, nationality, ethnicity, sexuality and gender. But, she suggests, those differences should not cripple analyses that make common cause against structures of oppression.

Gallop, Jane. *Feminism and Psychoanalysis: The Daughter's Seduction.* London: Macmillan, 1982.

A very witty book that examines the relationships between feminist thought and psychoanalysis through a variety of different analyses. For example, Gallop reads not only the texts of Jacques Lacan, but also reads the performance situation of the seminars that generated the texts to demonstrate his 'mastery' of the situation. There are also useful commentaries and introductions to the work of the British pyschoanalytic critic, Juliet Mitchell, and the works of Irigaray and other French critics. Gallop is irreverent and funny, but also helpful and academically serious.

Greene, Gayle and Coppélia Kahn, eds. *Making a Difference: Feminist Literary Criticism.* London and New York: Methuen, 1985.

A really useful anthology, demonstrating a range of different approaches. There are essays on language, society, class, race, gender and sexuality, all related to feminist thinking. This was one of the early anthologies of feminist criticism, but it remains a helpful introduction to the main issues. The essays are all readable and approachable.

Hennessy, Rosemary. *Materialist Feminism and the Politics of Discourse.* London and New York: Routledge, 1993.

A major rethinking of the meaning of materialism for feminist theory. Hennessy argues that the definition of materialism has to be broadened to include not only the conditions of individual women, the materiality of their bodies and their economic circumstances; materialism must, she suggests, be understood as more than local conditions. In a world where capitalism effectively rules, materialist analysis has to take into account global conditions, and in particular, it must focus on the very real deprivations of the Third World. Hennessy, in other words, offers a real rebuke to feminist discourses that hide in universities in the West, and pay no attention to the world beyond their own immediate context. A challenging book in every way.

Jacobus, Mary. *Reading Woman: Essays in Feminist Criticism.* London: Methuen, 1986.

Reading Woman is a collection of quite disparate essays written over a number of years. It provides dazzling readings of a number of literary texts, including Gilman's 'Yellow Wall-paper', Brontë's *Villette* and Eliot's *The Mill on the Floss.* It also reads psychoanalytical texts by Freud through the lens of literature. It was one of the first books by an Anglo-American critic to take the idea of theory as centrally important. The readings are difficult to approach at first, since their range of allusion is so wide; but perseverance is definitely recommended.

Lydon, Mary. *Skirting the Issue: Essays in Literary Theory.* Madison: University of Wisconsin Press, 1995.

This is a particular favourite of mine. Lydon's book is a collection of essays written over a number of years, so that there are cases where she revisits the same texts and reads them differently. Her work is feminist in approach, but it is a feminism profoundly influenced by post-structuralist thought. The essays are funny and interesting, covering a range of (mostly French-authored) literary and artistic texts. The book exemplifies the usefulness of post-structuralism's unsettling of assumptions for a feminist approach to literature.

Minh-ha, Trin T. *Woman, Native, Other: Writing Post-Coloniality and Feminism.* Bloomington and Indianapolis: Indiana University Press, 1989.

A remarkable book, written lyrically and passionately as an examination of the particular problems faced by the Third-World/post-colonial woman writer. Minh-ha discusses the various ways in which sex and race discourses conspire to erase the subjective identity of the woman writer as both woman and writer, by labelling her to suit the purposes of the labeller. The book presents its case through both traditional academic argument, and through dramatic examples of personal experience. The text is interspersed with stills from Min-ha's own films, reclaiming and celebrating her own gendered, classed, racialised identities through her own choice of how she is represented. Very persuasive, and well worth reading.

Moi, Toril. *Sexual/Textual Politics: Feminist Literary Theory.* London and New: Methuen, 1985.

One of the founding feminist introductions to feminist thinking in literature. In this book, Moi introduced a generation of readers to Kristeva, Irigaray and Cixous, and gave lucid account of the necessity for a properly theorised feminist theory. *Sexual/Textual Politics* has been criticized for assuming an absolute divide between Anglo-American traditions of thought and French feminisms; this is really a function of the book's aim to introduce a less-well-known tradition to English-speaking readers. It remains a very useful book, lucid, readable and approachable.

Pykett, Lyn. *The Improper Feminine: The Women's Sensation Novel and the New Woman Writing.* London: Routledge, 1992.

Charts a literary history which is not found in the so-called Great Tradition. Pykett concentrates on the 'women's' forms of fiction in the nineteenth century – the forms written by and for women in the 1860s (the sensation novel) and the 1890s (the New Woman writing). She reads these texts as articulations of protest against the constrictions of proper femininity, and argues that their exclusion from the canon is at least partly due to 'improper' femininity. This is a book which uncovers female traditions of writing that have been hidden from literary history. In presenting less-well-known texts and authors in this academic context, Pykett argues for a broadening of the terms of literary value.

Rich, Adrienne. *Blood, Bread and Poetry: Selected Prose, 1979–1985*. London: Virago, 1987.

Since the early 1970s, Rich has been a major feminist thinker, introducing new terms and new ways of approaching texts and society. *Blood, Bread and Poetry* contains her important essay 'Lesbian Existence and Compulsory Heterosexuality' as well as a range of other shorter essays on poetry, autobiography and education. Her writing is very approachable, warm, one might almost say; well worth reading for insights into lesbian existence and the place of woman as writer and teacher.

Robbins, Ruth. '"Snowed Up: A Mistletoe Story": Feminist Approaches' in Julian Wolfreys and William Baker, eds. *Literary Theories: A Case Study in Critical Performance*. London: Macmillan, 1996, 103–26.

A gentle and very short introduction to feminist theories in literature. The main merit of this essay, though, is that it does provide an exemplary reading of a text from a variety of feminist perspectives. It's brief, but it is to the point, even if I say so myself.

Sedgwick, Eve Kosofsky. *Between Men: English Literature and Male Homosocial Desire*. New York: Columbia University Press, 1985.

Strictly speaking, this is perhaps not quite a feminist text since its emphasis is on male–male bonding in literature and culture. In the analysis of these bonds, however, Sedgwick's readings of texts such as Dickens's *Our Mutual Friend*, George Eliot's *Adam Bede* and James Hogg's *Confessions of a Justfied Sinner*, provide a useful point of leverage on the issue of female exclusions and subordinations. Sedgwick establishes both that woman is an object who mediates between men, and that her object-status is required to maintain the status quo. But because women are not only objects, but also subjects, that status quo is always potentially threatened by women's autonomy. Interesting to read, and not too difficult once you get started.

Showalter, Elaine. *The Female Malady: Women, Madness and English Culture 1830–1980.* London: Virago, [1985] 1987.

A cultural and historical approach to literary texts, which sees texts as evidence of the social mores out of which they were produced. Showalter demonstrates how ideas about proper femininity have shaped the ways in which women have been defined as psychiatric patients. She argues that madness is the female malady not because women are madder than men, but because masculine forces in the medical professions have the power of definition. She discusses a wide range of sources in support of this argument, including works by Virginia Woolf, Mary Wollstonecraft and Doris Lessing.

Spencer, Jane. *The Rise of the Woman Novelist: From Aphra Behn to Jane Austen.* Oxford: Blackwell, 1986.

Establishes a literary history of different phases in women's writing for the eighteenth century, as Showalter's *Literature of their Own* had done for the nineteenth century. Spencer demonstrates the relative freedom of subject and genre that women writers early in the century enjoyed; but as writing became more professionalised, and as proper femininity became increasingly narrowly defined, the woman writer was hemmed in by social expectations. Novels of protest and of didacticism were the two main results, though the Gothic novel and the romance offered compensatory escape routes. Scholarly and easy to read; indispensable for those setting out to study the eighteenth-century woman writer.

Spender, Dale. *Mothers of the Novel: One Hundred Good Women Writers Before Jane Austen.* London and New York: Pandora, 1986.

As its title suggests, *Mothers of the Novel* is a rewriting of the terms of literary history and its implicit values. Spender's text is furious with the exclusionary literary history provided by writers like Ian Watt and F. R. Leavis. In a massive act of feminist recuperation of women's literary texts, she elucidates a new theory of value that allows women writers access to their own cultural capital. Spender's indignation makes for a very easy read.

Bibliography

Adams, James Eli. *Dandies and Desert Saints: Styles of Victorian Manhood.* Ithaca and London: Cornell University Press, 1995.

Anzaldúa, Gloria, ed. *Making Face, Making Soul: Haciendas Caras.* San Francisco: Aunt Lute Books, 1990.

Armstrong, Isobel, ed. *New Feminist Discourses: Critical Essays on Theories and Texts.* London and New York: Routledge, 1992.

Armstrong, Nancy. *Desire and Domestic Fiction: A Political History of the Novel.* New York and Oxford: Oxford University Press, 1987.

Atkinson, Kate. *Behind the Scenes at the Museum.* London: Black Swan, 1996.

Atwood, Margaret. 'Running with the Tigers'. *Flesh and the Mirror: Essays on the Art of Angela Carter.* Ed. Lorna Sage. London: Virago, 1994, 117–35.

Austen, Jane. *Pride and Prejudice.* Harmondsworth: Penguin, [1813] 1972.

Beauvoir, Simone de. *The Second Sex.* Trans H. M Parshley. London: Vintage, [1949] 1997.

Beckson, Karl ed. *Oscar Wilde: The Critical Heritage.* London and New York: Routledge and Kegan Paul, 1970.

Belsey, Catherine. *Critical Practice.* London and New York: Routledge, 1980.

Berman, Jeffrey. 'The Unrestful Cure: Charlotte Perkins Gilman and "The Yellow Wall-paper"'. *The Captive Imagination: A Casebook on the The Yellow Wall-paper.* Ed. Catherine Golden. New York: The Feminist Press at CUNY, 1992, 211–41.

Bowlby, Rachel. *Feminist Destinations and Further Essays on Virginia Woolf.* Edinburgh: Edinburgh University Press, 1997.

—. 'Still crazy after all these years'. *Between Feminism and Psychoanalysis.* Ed. Teresa Brennan. New York and London: Routledge, 1990, 40–59.

Braddon, Mary Elizabeth. *Lady Audley's Secret.* Oxford: Oxford University Press [1862], 1987.

Braidotti, Rosi. *Nomadic Subjects: Embodiment and Sexual Difference in Contemporary Feminist Theory.* New York: Columbia University Press, 1994.

Brennan, Teresa, ed. *Between Feminism and Psychoanalysis.* London and New York: Routledge, 1990.

Bristow, Joseph. *Sexuality.* London: Routledge, 1997.

Brody, Miriam. Introduction to Mary Wollstonecraft. *A Vindication of the Rights of Woman.* Harmondsworth: Penguin [1792], 1992.

Brontë, Charlotte. *Jane Eyre.* Harmondsworth: Penguin, [1847], 1996.

—. *Villette.* Harmondsworth: Penguin [1853], 1979.

Butler, Judith. *Gender Trouble: Feminism and the Subversion of Identity.* London: Routledge, 1990.

—. *Bodies that Matter: On the Discursive Limits of 'Sex'.* New York and London: Routledge, 1993.

Carter, Angela. *Nights at the Circus.* London: Picador, 1985.

Castle, Terry. *The Apparitional Lesbian: Female Homosexuality and Modern Culture.* New York: Columbia University Press, 1993.

—. *The Female Thermometer: Eighteenth-Century Culture and the Intervention of the Uncanny.* Oxford: Oxford University Press, 1995.

Chodorow, Nancy. *The Reproduction of Mothering.* Los Angeles: University of California Press, 1978.

Cixous, Hélène. 'The Laugh of the Medusa' *New French Feminisms: An Anthology.* Eds Elaine Marks and Isabelle de Courtivron. Hemel Hempstead: Harvester Wheatsheaf, 1981, 245–64.

—. *The Hélène Cixous Reader.* Ed. Susan Sellers. London: Routledge, 1994.

— and Catherine Clément. *The Newly-Born Woman.* Trans. Betsy Wing. Manchester: Manchester University Press [1974], 1986.

— and Mireille Calle-Gruber. *Rootprints: Memory and Life-Writing.* London: Routledge [1994], 1997.

Conrad, Joseph. *Heart of Darkness.* Harmondsworth: Penguin [1900], 1983.

Cornillon, Susan Koppelman ed. *Images of Women in Fiction: Feminist Perspectives.* Bowling Green, Ohio: Bowling Green University Popular Press, 1972.

Coward, Rosalind. *Female Desire: Women's Sexuality Today.* London: Grafton Books, 1984.

Derrida, Jacques. *A Derrida Reader: Between the Blinds*. Ed. Peggy Kamuf. New York: Columbia University Press, 1991.

—. 'Khora'. *The Derrida Reader: Writing Performances*. Ed Julian Wolfreys. Edinburgh: Edinburgh University Press, 1998, 231–62.

—. 'Preface' to Hélène Cixous, *The Hélène Cixous Reader*. Ed. Susan Sellers. London and New York: Routledge, 1994, vii–xiii.

Dollimore, Jonathan. *Sexual Dissidence: Augustine to Wilde, Freud to Focault*. Oxford: The Clarendon Press, 1991.

Eagleton, Terry. *Marxism and Literary Criticism*. London: Routledge, 1976.

—. *Literary Theory: An Introduction*. 2nd edition. Oxford: Basil Blackwell, 1996.

Ehrenreich, Barbara and Deirdre English. 'The "Sick" Woman of the Upper Classes'. *The Captive Imagination: A Casebook on the The Yellow Wallpaper*. Ed. Catherine Golden. New York: The Feminist Press at CUNY, 1992, 90–109.

Eliot, George. 'Silly Novels by Lady Novelists' [1856]. *Selected Essays, Poems and Other Writings*. Ed. A. S. Byatt. Harmondsworth: Penguin, 1990.

—. *Adam Bede*. Harmondsworth: Penguin, [1859] 1985.

—. *Middlemarch*. Harmondsworth: Penguin, [1871–2] 1965.

Ellmann, Mary. *Thinking About Women*. New York: Harcourt, Brace, Jovanovich, Inc., 1968.

Emecheta, Buchi. *Second-Class Citizen*. Oxford: Heinemann, [1974] 1994.

Faderman, Lillian. *Surpassing the Love of Men: Romantic Friendship and Love Between Women from the Renaissance to the Present*. London: The Women's Press, [1981] 1985.

Felski, Rita. *Beyond Feminist Aesthetics: Feminist Literature and Social Change*. London: Hutchinson Radius, 1989.

Firestone, Shulamith. *The Dialectic of Sex*. New York: Bantam Press, 1972.

Forster, E. M. *Aspects of the Novel*. Harmondsworth: Penguin, [1927] 1993.

Freud, Sigmund. *The Essentials of Psychoanalysis*. ed. Anna Freud. Harmondsworth: Pelican, 1986.

Freud, Sigmund. 'The Uncanny' in *The Penguin Freud Library*. Volume 14. *Art and Literature*. Harmondsworth: Penguin, 1990, 335–76.

Friedman, Susan Stanford. *Mappings: Feminism and the Cultural*

Geographies of Encounter. Princeton: Princeton University Press, 1998.

Fuss, Diana. *Essentially Speaking: Feminism, Nature and Difference*. London and New York: Routledge, 1989.

— ed. *Inside/Out; Lesbian Theories, Gay Theories*. London and New York: Routledge, 1991.

Gallop, Jane. *Feminism and Psychoanalysis: The Daughter's Seduction*. London: Macmillan, 1982.

Garber, Marjorie. *Vested Interests: Cross Dressing and Cultural Anxiety*. Harmondsworth: Penguin [1992], 1993.

—. *Vice Versa: Bisexuality and the Erotics of Everyday Life*. Harmondsworth: Penguin, [1995] 1997.

Gaskell, Elizabeth. *Mary Barton, A Tale of Manchester Life*. Harmondsworth: Penguin [1948] 1982.

Gates, Henry Louis (ed). *'Race', Writing and Difference*. Chicago and London: Chicago University Press. 1986.

Gilbert, Sandra M. and Susan Gubar. *The Madwoman in the Attic: The Woman Writer and the Nineteenth-Century Literary Imagination*. New Haven and London: Yale University Press, 1979.

—. *No Man's Land: The Place of the Woman Writer in the Twentieth Century*. 3 volumes. *The War of the Words* (1988). *Sexchanges* (1989). *Letters from the Front* (1994). New Haven and London: Yale University Press, 1988–94.

Gilman, Charlotte Perkins. *The Yellow Wall-paper* in *The Charlotte Perkins Gilman Reader*. London: The Women's Press, 1980.

—. *The Living of Charlotte Perkins Gilman*. Madison: University of Wisconsin Press, [1935] 1990.

Golden, Catherine, ed. *The Captive Imagination: A Casebook on the The Yellow Wall-paper*. New York: The Feminist Press at CUNY, 1992.

Greene, Gayle and Coppélia Kahn eds. *Making a Difference: Feminist Literary Criticism*. London and New York: Methuen, 1985.

Halberstram, Judith. 'Technologies of Monstrosity: Bram Stoker's *Dracula*'. *Cultural Politics at the Fin de Siècle*. Eds Sally Ledger and Scott McCracken. Cambridge: Cambridge University Press, 1995 248–66.

Hardwick, Elizabeth. *Seduction and Betrayal: Women and Literature*. New York: Random House, 1974.

Hawkes, Terence. *Stucturalism and Semiotics*. London: Routledge, 1977.

Heath, Stephen. 'Psychopathia Sexualis: Stevenson's *Strange Case*' [1986]. *Reading Fin-de-Siècle Fictions*. Ed. Lyn Pykett. Harlow: Addison, Wesley, Longman, 1996, 64–79.

Hobsbawm, E. J. *The Age of Empire, 1875–1914*. London: Sphere Books, 1989.

hooks, bell. *Ain't I a Woman? Black Women and Feminism*. London: Pluto Press, 1982.

—. *Black Looks: Race and Representation*. Boston MA: South End Press, 1992.

Hull, Gloria T. 'Researching Alice Dunbar-Nelson: A Personal and Literary Perspective' *All the Women are White, All the Blacks are Men, But Some of Us are Brave: Black Women's Studies*. Eds Gloria T. Hull, Patricia Bell Scott and Barbara Smith. New York: The Feminist Press, 1982. 189–95.

Hull, Gloria T., Patricia Bell Scott and Barbara Smith, eds. *All the Women are White, All the Blacks are Men, But Some of Us are Brave: Black Women's Studies*. New York: The Feminist Press, 1982.

Humm, Maggie. *A Reader's Guide to Contemporary Feminist Literary Criticism*. Hemel Hempstead: Harvester Wheatsheaf, 1994.

Irigaray, Luce. *This Sex Which is not One*. Trans. Catherine Porter with Carolyn Burke. Ithaca, New York: Cornell University Press, [1977] 1985a.

—. *Speculum of the Other Woman*. Trans. Gillian C. Gill. Ithaca, New York: Cornell University Press, [1974] 1985b.

—. *The Irigaray Reader*. Ed. Margaret Whitford. Oxford: Basil Blackwell, 1991.

—. *Sexes and Genealogies*. Trans. Gillian C. Gill. New York: Columbia University Press, [1987] 1993.

Jacobus, Mary. *Reading Woman: Essays in Feminist Criticism*. New York: Columbia University Press, 1986.

Kaplan, Cora. *Seachanges: Culture and Feminism*. London and New York: Verso, 1986.

Karpinski, Joanne B., ed. *Critical Essays on Charlotte Perkins Gilman*. New York: G.K. Hall and Co., 1992.

Kolodny, Annette. 'A Map for Re-reading: Or, gender and the interpretation of literary texts', *The Captive Imagination: A Casebook on the Yellow Wall-paper*. Ed. Catherine Golden. New York: The Feminist Press at CUNY, 1992, 149–67.

Kristeva, Julia. *Desire in Language: A Semiotic Approach to Literature and Art.* Ed. Leon S. Roudiez. Trans Thomas Gora, Alice Jardine and Leon S. Roudiez. Oxford: Basil Blackwell, [1977] 1980.

—. *Revolution in Poetic Language.* Trans. Margaret Waller. New York: Columbia University Press, [1974] 1984.

—. *Polylogue.* Paris: Seuil, 1977.

—. *The Kristeva Reader.* Ed. Toril Moi, Oxford: Blackwell, 1986.

—. *Tales of Love.* Trans. Leon S. Roudiez. New York Columbia University Press, [1983] 1987.

—. 'Talking about *Polylogue'. French Feminist Thought: A Reader.* Ed. Toril Moi. Oxford: Blackwell, 1987, 110–17.

Lauter, Paul ed. *The Heath Anthology of American Literature.* 3rd edition. Boston and New York: Houghton Mifflin, 1998.

Lawrence, D. H. *Women in Love.* Harmondsworth: Penguin, [1920] 1982.

—. *The Complete Poems.* Eds Vivian de Sola Pinto and Warren Roberts. Harmondsworth: Penguin, 1977.

Leavis, F. R. *The Great Tradition: George Eliot, Henry James, Joseph Conrad* [1948]. Harmondsworth: Penguin, 1962.

Ledger, Sally. 'The New Woman and the Crisis of Victorianism' *Cultural Politics at the Fin de Siècle.* Eds Sally Ledger and Scott McCracken. Cambridge: Cambridge University Press, 1995, 22–44.

— and Scott McCracken eds. *Cultural Poltics at the Fin de Siècle.* Cambridge: Cambridge University Press, 1995.

—. *The New Woman: Fiction and Feminism at the Fin de Siècle.* Manchester and New York: Manchester University Press, 1997.

Lovell, Terry. *Consuming Fiction.* London: Verso, 1987.

Marcus, Laura. *Virginia Woolf.* Plymouth: Northcote House, 1997.

May, Charles E., ed. *The New Short Story Theories.* Athens, Ohio: Ohio University Press, 1994.

McDowell, Deborah E. 'New Directions for Black Feminist Criticism' *The New Feminist Criticism: Essays on Women, Literature and Theory.* Ed. Elaine Showalter. London: Virago, 1986. 186–99.

Millett, Kate. *Sexual Politics.* London: Virago, [1969] 1977.

Mitchell, Juliet. *Psychoanalysis and Feminism.* Harmondsworth: Penguin, 1974.

Mitchell, Silas Weir. 'From *Fat and Blood: And How to Make Them'* [1877]. *The Captive Imagination: A Casebook on the Yellow Wallpaper.* Ed. Cathering Golden. New York: The Feminist Press, 1992, pp 45–50.

Moers, Ellen. *Literary Women: The Great Writers.* New York: Oxford University Press, [1976] 1985.

Mohanty, Chandra Talpade. 'Under Western Eyes: Feminist Scholarship and Colonial Discourses', *Third World Women and the Politics of Feminism.* Eds Chandra Talpade Mohanty, Ann Russo and Lourdes Torres. Bloomington: Indiana University Press, 1991, pp. 51–80.

Moi, Toril. *Sexual/Textual Politics: Feminist Literary Theory.* London and New York: Methuen, 1985.

—. 'Feminist Literary Criticism'. *Modern Literary Theory: A Comparative Introduction.* Eds Ann Jefferson and David Robey. 2nd London: B. T. Batsford, 1986. 204–21.

— ed. *French Feminist Thought: A Reader.* Oxford: Basil Blackwell, 1987.

Moraga, Cherríe and Gloria Anzaldúa, eds. *This Bridge Called My Back: Writings by Radical Women of Color* [1981]. New York: Kitchen Table: Women of Color Press, 1983.

Morris, Pam. *Literature and Feminism: An Introduction.* Oxford: Blackwell, 1993.

Morrison, Toni. *Sula.* New York: Alfred Knopf, 1974.

Mulvey, Laura. *Visual and Other Pleasures.* London: Macmillan 1989.

Nead, Lynda. *Myths of Sexuality: Representations of Women in Victorian Britain.* Oxford: Blackwell, 1988.

—. *The Female Nude: Art, Obscenity and Sexuality.* London: Routledge, 1992.

Newton, Judith Lowder. *Women, Power and Subversion: Social Strategies in British Fiction, 1778–1860.* New York and London: Methuen, [1981] 1985.

Payne, Michael. *Reading Theory: An Introduction to Lacan, Derrida and Kristeva.* Oxford: Blackwell, 1993.

Plath, Sylvia. *Collected Poems.* London: Faber, 1981.

Poe, Edgar Allan. 'Poe on Short Fiction'. *The New Short Story Theories.* Ed. Charles E. May. Ohio: Athens University Press, 1994, 59–72.

Pollock, Griselda. *Vision and Difference: Femininity, Feminism and the Histories of Art.* London: Routledge, 1988.

Poovey, Mary. *Uneven Developments: The Ideological Work of Gender in Mid-Victorian England.* London: Virago, 1989.

Punter, David. *The Literature of Terror: A History of Gothic Fiction from 1765 to the Present Day.* London: Longman, 1980.

Pykett, Lyn. *The Improper Feminine: The Women's Sensation Novel and the New Woman Writing*. London: Routledge, 1992.

—. ed. *Reading Fin-de-Siècle Fictions*. Harlow: Addison Wesley Longman, 1996.

Rhys, Jean. *Wide Sargasso Sea* [1966]. Harmondsworth: Penguin, 1985.

Rich, Adrienne. *Of Woman Born: Motherhood as Experience and Institution*. London: Virago, 1977.

—. 'Compulsory Heterosexuality and Lesbian Existence' in *Blood, Bread and Poetry: Selected Prose 1979–1985*. London: Virago, 1987 23–75.

—. *Adrienne Rich's Poetry and Prose*. Eds Barbara Charlesworth and Albert Gelpi. New York and London: W. W. Norton and Company, 1993.

Rivière, Joan. 'Womanliness as Masquerade' [1929]. *Formations of Fantasy*. Eds Victor Burgin, James Donald, and Cora Kaplan. London and New York: Methuen, 1986.

Robbins, Ruth. '"Snowed Up: A Mistletoe Story": Feminist Approaches'. *Literary Theories: A Case Study in Critical Performance*. Eds Julian Wolfreys and William Baker. London: Macmillan, 1996, 103–26.

Roberts, Michèle. *The Visitation*. London: The Women's Press, 1983.

Roudiez, Leon S. Introduction to Julia Kristeva. *Desire in Language: A Semiotic Approach to Literature and Art*. Oxford: Basil Blackwell, 1981.

—. Introduction to Julia Kristeva. *Revolution in Poetic Language*. Trans. Margaret Waller. New York: Columbia University Press, 1984.

Rule, Jane. *Lesbian Images*. Trumansberg, New York: Crossings Press, 1975.

Ruthven, K. K. *Feminist Literary Studies: An Introduction*. Cambridge: Cambridge University Press, 1984.

Sage, Lorna. ed. *Flesh and the Mirror: Essays on the Art of Angela Carter*. London: Virago, 1994.

Sayers, Janet. *Mothering Psychoanalysis: Helene Deutsch, Karen Horney, Anna Freud, Melanie Klein*. London: Hamish Hamilton, 1991.

Sedgwick, Eve Kosofsky. *Between Men: English Literature and Male Homosocial Desire*. New York: Columbia University Press, 1985.

Shaw, Marion ed. *An Introduction to Women's Writing, From the Middle Ages to the Present Day*. London and New York: Prentice Hall, 1998.

Showalter, Elaine. *A Literature of their Own: British Women Novelists from Brontë to Lessing.* London: Virago [1977], 1978.

— ed. *The New Feminist Criticism: Essays on Women, Literature and Theory.* London: Virago, 1986.

—. 'Towards a Feminist Poetics' [1979]. *The New Feminist Criticism: Essays on Women, Literature and Theory.* Ed. Elaine Showalter. London: Virago, 1986. 125–43.

—. 'Feminist Criticism in the Wilderness' [1981]. *The New Feminist Criticism: Essays on Women, Literature and Theory.* Ed. Elaine Showalter. London: Virago, 1986. 243–70.

—. *The Female Malady: Women, Madness and Female Culture, 1830–1980.* London Virago, [1985] 1987.

—. *Sexual Anarchy: Gender and Culture at the Fin de Siècle.* London: Bloomsbury, 1991.

Sinfield, Alan. *The Wilde Century: Effeminacy, Oscar Wilde and the Queer Moment.* London and New York: Cassell, 1994.

Smith, Barbara. 'Racism and Women's Studies'. *All the Women are White, All the Blacks are Men, But Some of Us are Brave: Black Women's Studies.* Eds Gloria T. Hull, Patricia Bell Scott and Barbara Smith. New York: The Feminist Press, 1982, 48–51.

—. 'Toward a Black Feminist Criticism' [1977]. *The New Feminist Criticism: Essays on Women, Literature and Theory.* Ed. Elaine Showalter. London: Virago, 1986, 168–85.

Spacks, Patricia Mayer. *The Female Imagination: A Literary and Psychological Investigation of Women's Writng.* London: George Allen and Unwin, [1972], 1976.

Spelman, Elizabeth V. *Inessential Woman: Problems of Exclusion in Feminist Thought.* London: The Women's Press, 1990.

Spencer, Jane. *The Rise of the Woman Novelist: From Aphra Behn to Jane Austen.* Oxford: Blackwell, 1986.

Spivak, Gayatri Chakravorty. 'Three Women's Texts and a Critique of Imperialism'. *Race, Writing and Difference.* Ed. Henry Louis Gates Jr. Chicago: University of Chicago Press, 1986, 262–80.

—. *In Other Worlds: Essays in Cultural Politics.* London: Routledge, 1988.

Stetson, Erlene. 'Studying Slavery: Some Literary and Pedagogical Considerations on the Black Female Slave'. *All the Women are White, All the Blacks are Men, But Some of Us are Brave: Black Women's Studies.* Eds Gloria T. Hull, Patricia Bell Scott and Barbara Smith. New York: The Feminist Press, 1982, 61–84.

Stevenson, Robert Louis. *Dr Jekyll and Mr Hyde, and Other Stories*. Harmondsworth: Penguin, [1886] 1979.

Stoker, Bram. *Dracula*. Harmondsworth: Penguin, [1897] 1984.

Todd, Janet. *Feminist Literary History: A Defence*. Cambridge: Polity Press, 1988.

—. *The Sign of Angellica: Women, Writing and Fiction, 1600–1800*. London: Virago, 1989.

—. *Gender, Art and Death*. Cambridge: Polity Press, 1993.

Treichler, Paula. 'Escaping the Sentence: Diagnosis and Discourse in "The Yellow Wall-paper"'. *The Captive Imagination: A Casebook on the The Yellow Wall-paper*. Ed. Catherine Golden. New York: The Feminist Press at CUNY, 1992, 191–210.

Walker, Alice. *In Search of Our Mothers' Gardens*. London: The Women's Press [1983] 1984.

—. 'One Child of One's Own: A Meaningful Digression within the Work(s) – An Excerpt'. *All the Women are White, All the Blacks are Men, But Some of Us are Brave: Black Women's Studies*. Eds. Gloria T. Hull, Patricia Bell Scott and Barbara Smith, New York: Feminist Press, 1982, pp. 27–44.

Ward Jouve, Nicole. *Female Genesis: Creativity, Self and Gender*. Cambridge: Polity Press, 1998.

Warner, Marina. *Alone of All her Sex: The Myth and Cult of the Virgin Mary*. London: Picador, [1976] 1990.

—. *Monuments and Maidens: The Allegory of the Female Form*. London: Vintage, [1985] 1996.

Washington, Mary Helen. *Invented Lives: Narratives of Black Women (1860–1960)*. New York: Anchor, Doubleday, 1987.

Watt, Ian. *The Rise of the Novel: Studies in Defoe, Richardson and Fielding* [1957]. London: The Hogarth Press, 1987.

Waugh, Patricia. *Metafiction: The Theory and Practice of Self-Conscious Fiction*. London and New York: Routledge, 1984.

Whitford, Margaret, ed. *The Irigaray Reader*. Oxford: Basil Blackwell, 1991.

Wilde, Oscar. *The Picture of Dorian Gray*. Harmondsworth: Penguin, [1891] 1985.

—. *The Complete Works of Oscar Wilde*. Ed. Merlin Holland. Glasgow: HarperCollins, 1994.

Williams, Raymond. *Keywords: A Vocabulary of Culture and Society*. London: Fontana, 1988.

Wolf, Naomi. *The Beauty Myth: How Images of Beauty are Used Against Women.* London: Vintage, 1991.

Wolfreys, Julian. *The Rhetoric of Affirmative Resistance: Dissonant Identities from Carroll to Derrida.* London: Macmillan, 1997.

—. *Deconstruction • Derrida.* London: Macmillan, 1998a.

—, ed. *The Derrida Reader: Writing Performances.* Edinburgh: Edinburgh University Press, 1998b.

Wolfreys, Julian and William Baker, eds. *Literary Theories: A Case Study in Critical Performance.* London: Macmillan, 1996.

Wollstonecraft, Mary. *A Vindication of the Rights of Woman.* Harmondsworth: Penguin, [1792] 1992.

—. *Mary and The Wrongs of Woman.* Oxford: Oxford University Press, [1788 and 1798] 1980.

Woolf, Virginia. *A Room of One's Own and Three Guineas.* Harmondsworth: Penguin, [1929, 1938] 1993a.

—. *Selected Short Stories.* Harmondsworth: Penguin, 1993b.

—. *Mrs Dalloway.* Harmondsworth: Penguin, 1993c.

—. *The Crowded Dance of Modern Life.* Harmondsworth: Penguin, 1993d.

—. *To the Lighthouse.* Harmondsworth: Penguin, [1927] 1992.

Wright, Elizabeth. *Psychoanalytic Criticism: A Reappraisal* (2nd edition). Cambridge: Polity Press, 1998.

Wynne-Davies, Marion. 'Abandoned Women: Female Authorship in the Middle Ages', *Writing, From the Middle Ages to the Present Day.* Ed. Marion Shaw. London and New York: Prentice Hall, 1998, 9–36.

Zimmerman, Bonnie. 'What Has Never Been: An Overview of Lesbian Feminist Criticism'. *The New Feminist Criticism: Essays on Women, Literature and Theory.* Ed. Elaine Showalter. London: Virago, 1986. 200–24.

Index